THE FRANKSTON MURDERS

By the same author:

The Phillip Island Murder (with Paul Daley)
Kerr Publishing, 1993

Victims, Crimes and Investigators
Victoria Press, 1994

THE FRANKSTON MURDERS

The true story of serial killer Paul Denyer

Vikki Petraitis

NIVAR PRESS

A Nivar Press Publication

Published by Nivar Press
P.O. Box 2392
Carrum Downs, Victoria 3201

First published in 1995

National Library of Australia
Cataloguing-in-publication data:

Petraitis, Vikki, 1965 -
    The Frankston Murders:
    (the true story of serial killer, Paul Denyer.)

    ISBN 0 646 22828 5.

    1. Denyer, Paul.
    2. Serial murders - Victoria - Frankston.
    I. Title.

364.1523099451

Edited and designed by Janet Blagg.
Cover design by Vikki Petraitis and John Thompson.

Cover map copyright Melway Publishing Pty. Ltd.
reproduced from Melway Street Directory,
Edition 21, with permission.

Cover photo of Paul Denyer courtesy *Herald Sun*.
Typeset by Design Plus.
Printed in Australia by Australian Print Group.

This book is dedicated
to the memory of:

Elizabeth Ann-Marie Stevens

Deborah Ann Fream

Natalie Jayne Russell

Contents

Foreword

WHILE all murders are tragic, the worst nightmare for the homicide investigator is the active serial killer: knowing from experience that he will strike again but not knowing where or when. A feeling of helplessness can affect both the investigator and the community at large.

A classic example of this is the case popularly known as the Frankston Murders. This investigation included the traditional pressures of racing against the clock to identify the offender before he could strike again; the anguish and soul searching when your worst fears become a reality and another victim is found. The old adage that time is on the side of the investigator is irrelevant when investigating serial killings. The pressures demanding a quick solution can be awesome.

Community concern rises with the passage of time. Fear of the unknown and a feeling of powerlessness emerge. The investigators know all too well that any mistakes can prove to be fatal — literally.

All the while the investigator is facing the dilemma of just how much information should be made available to the public to satisfy their legitimate concern. They know the most interested person listening is usually the offender himself. Release of certain information to the media may delay the apprehension of the offender and cost more lives.

Investigators are spurred on by desperation, searching for answers, frustrated by false leads deliberately provided by a few miscreants in the community. Sixteen hour days, seven day weeks looking for the vital clue — the lucky breakthrough — become the norm.

Above all else, the homicide investigator knows that patience, persistence and a meticulous application of proven procedures will produce results in the majority of cases. The serial killer adds a new dimension as attempts are made to anticipate his next move or encourage him to make a mistake.

It is difficult for the seasoned homicide investigator to come to terms with such senseless, brutal murders of innocent young people.

Vikki Petraitis's book is a detailed examination of the investigation and the personal trauma experienced by those involved. Hopefully a detailed knowledge of Paul Charles Denyer and people of his ilk will contribute to future homicide prevention.

I am confident The Frankston Murders will provide interesting reading for many — who will at the same time be left with a sense of abhorrence.

Peter Halloran
Detective Chief Inspector
Officer in Charge, Homicide Squad

Acknowledgements

THE following story is the result of extensive interviews both with the families of the victims and members of the Victoria Police Force. Without exception, people offered their accounts with candour in order to help the public gain an insight into the case and its effects on those it touched.

Because so many people have helped with this book it is impossible to pay individual thanks to all of them. However, there are some who deserve special mention. My sincere thanks go to the families of the victims, who spent many hours giving me valuable insights into the women about whom I was writing: the Russell family, Bernadette Naughton, Rita and Paul Webster and Sara Smith.

I extend my gratitude to Steve and Melissa Denyer who spent many, often painful, hours with me tracing Paul Denyer's life, his crimes and their effect on the Denyer family.

My sincere appreciation is extended to all members of the Victoria Police who generously gave their time to share their accounts of the investigation. While many police officers took a special interest in this book, special acknowledgement must go to Chief Inspector Peter Halloran, Chief Superintendent John Balloch, Inspector Danny Tuck, Inspector John Noonan, Inspector Ron Cooke, Senior Sergeant Rod Wilson, Senior Sergeant Peter Bull, Senior Sergeant Chris Jones, Sergeant Mick Hughes, Sergeant Charlie Bezzina, Senior Constable Mark Woolfe, Sergeant Steve Lewis, Sergeant Fred Barton, Sergeant Michael Barry, Sergeant Brian Gamble, Senior Constable Tony Kealy, Senior Constable Darren O'Loughlin, Sergeant Andy King, Senior Constable Colin Clark, Senior Constable Michael Glowaski, Constable Angela Butts, Sergeant Alan Dew, Senior Constable Danny Hower, Constable Michael Lynch, Sergeant Paul Dacey, Sergeant Tony Jay, Sergeant Phil Atkins, Sergeant Richard Brown, Sergeant Colin McKinney, Sergeant Chris McCann, Senior Constable Mick West and Senior Sergeant Geoff Perret.

Others who gave generously of their time include: Claude Minisini, Dyson Hore-Lacy, John Allin, Professor Stephen Cordner, Neil Mitchell, Andrew Rule, John Silvester, Fred Michelmore, Maria Pantling and Lorna Stark. My sincere thanks to my tireless proof-readers Danny Tuck, Peter Halloran, Steve Petraitis and Helen Burke.

Preface

I began writing the story of the Frankston murders in July 1994 and two and a half months later I had over 50,000 words. By then, I knew that the book would run to at least 90,000 words. Poring over the homicide brief and newspaper clippings, I painstakingly put the story together. From an initial outline of around twenty chapters, the total soon grew to nearly forty as more information came to light. Once the story began to take shape, I started the long process of interviewing. Sitting at the computer with mountains of pages, it is easy to forget the impact of such a spate of vicious crimes on the community and on the people who were directly hurt by Paul Denyer. Speaking to the people involved soon made me remember.

The more I researched the series of events surrounding the murders of Elizabeth Stevens, Debbie Fream and Natalie Russell, the more I felt that the public had a right to know the full story. Denyer's guilty plea, while saving the financial and not to mention human cost of a lengthy trial, deprived the community of hearing what really happened. It was all over so quickly.

I interviewed over thirty police officers and without exception, the case had made a huge impact on each one of them. Many were still agonising over whether they could have done more to catch Denyer sooner. It was a case none of them will ever forget.

Then it was time to contact the families involved. Never comfortable with this aspect and concerned that I was intruding on their grief, I wrote to members of each family and waited. Would they be angry at me for writing the book? I hoped not. I wanted to tell the story. I didn't want to sensationalise the events. The day she received my letter, Carmel Russell rang me. We spoke for an hour on the telephone. She made me cry with her strength and the almost tangible sense of loss. When I got off the phone, I went and gave my own small daughter a hug. Carmel welcomed me into her home and I spent many hours discussing Natalie and her life. In a small way, I felt that I got to know her. I also spent many hours with Paul and Rita Webster and Sara Smith.

I approached the Denyer family. Speaking with them I felt an awful sadness. They too were victims and lived daily with the fact that Paul was a killer.

I wrote to Paul Denyer in Pentridge Prison asking if he would agree to an interview. He flushed my letter down the toilet.

All the reconstructions in this book are based on extensive interviews, and police and Coronial statements taken from witnesses. Some witnesses are identified by a first name alone to protect their privacy.

What follows is a true and accurate account of the police investigation into the Frankston murders committed by Paul Denyer in 1993 and the effect on the community and the families of the victims.

Vikki Petraitis
March 1995

1
Pro Marine

IN late February 1993, Jason Bartczak had been working for a month at the Seaford boat building firm Pro Marine when another young man joined the company, doing general clean up duties as part of a government employment scheme. His name was Paul. Being a big man, over six feet tall and around sixteen stone, Paul quickly earned the nickname 'John Candy' after the overweight Canadian actor. Paul had worked at Pro Marine for a couple of weeks when Jason noticed something odd about him.

One morning, he walked into the store room and saw Paul standing in the corner near the paint shelves. His back was towards Jason, but the young man could see that Paul was fiddling with something. When he turned around, Jason quickly went to another shelf and stood there pretending to be looking for something. Without a word, Paul abruptly walked out of the store room.

After Paul left, Jason went over to where he had been standing. Wondering what his co-worker had been doing, he pushed aside a couple of large tins and found hidden there a dagger-shaped piece of metal around half a centimetre wide and twenty centimetres long. It looked like it had been cut out of scrap aluminium with one of the band saws. He took the knife out into the factory and showed it to another worker, Peter McKeown.

'Look what I've found that John Candy has been trying to hide in the store,' he said, not quite knowing what to make of the knife.

Between them, they decided it would be best to cut the aluminium into smaller pieces and throw it out.

A few weeks later, Peter McKeown also saw something peculiar. Paul borrowed a heat gun from one of the electricians and disappeared with it into the store room. Minutes later McKeown entered and saw Paul bending over with his foot up on a cable roll, torching the end of his running shoe. As McKeown was trying to figure out what on earth Paul was doing, the manager, Leon Balatli walked in and asked sharply what was going on. Paul explained that his runners were too small and he was trying to stretch them. Balatli told him to do it in his own time.

After two months at Pro Marine, it was clear that Paul could not be relied upon to carry out even the most simple task and the manager decided not to continue his employment past the three month trial period.

While he was unpopular with other workers, and he certainly did some strange things, nobody thought to connect him with the holes cut in the cyclone wire fence bordering Pro Marine, nor was his name mentioned in connection with the slaughter one night of two goats in a nearby paddock.

2

The Cats

DONNA Vanes was uneasy. With her tiny baby nestled in a bassinet, she asked her boyfriend Les to take them on his pizza delivery run. She just didn't feel like being alone at the flat in Claude Street. It was a pleasant flat and they had only lived there for three weeks, but an anonymous telephone call a couple of days earlier had spooked her. The caller had telephoned, said nothing and then hung up.

Les packed them both in the pizza delivery car and they drove around the streets of Seaford delivering pizzas to customers with late night appetites. They were only gone an hour.

Walking into the darkened hallway of the flat around 11 pm, Donna was hit by a foul odour; it was like nothing she had smelt before. She and Les were making their way through the lounge room towards the kitchen when Donna saw the blood. Smeared on the wall just before the kitchen doorway were swirls of blood about shoulder height and splatters of something else near the skirting boards. In a scared voice, Donna suggested that they all get out of the flat as quickly as possible. Les agreed.

Shaking and scared, Donna remained outside while Les summoned a neighbour to go in to the flat with him to see just what on earth was going on. Where was Donna's cat and its two kittens? Entering the flat again, he saw a sight he didn't understand and would never forget.

Awakened early the following morning, Detective Sergeant Chris McCann of the special response squad took a call from Frankston CIB detective Peter Stirling. 'We've got some dead cats,' Stirling told him. 'Not sure whether it's your job, but you might want to come down and have a look.' McCann scribbled down the address in Claude Street, Frankston North. The special response squad handled mostly aggravated burglaries and he wasn't sure whether this was within their charter but it was best to take a look anyway.

After a quick briefing out the front of the flat, McCann and two other detectives from his squad entered through the front door and the odour that Donna had smelt the night before immediately assaulted them. The smell of death reminded McCann of a body find he had attended where a woman had died in her flat and hadn't been found for a week. In the forty-six cases McCann had investigated since the squad had begun operations six months earlier, he had never seen anything like the flat in Claude Street.

In the lounge room was an orange baby bouncer sitting in the middle of the floor on a pink and blue checkered rug. Also on the rug lay a baby's rattle and a disposable nappy. McCann muttered to the others, 'Lucky they weren't here.'

On the white wall of the lounge room, next to the television, the intruder had written what looked like 'Dead Don' in a red substance that the detectives suspected was blood. Entering the kitchen, Chris McCann looked down at the body of Donna Vanes's dead cat. It had been horribly slaughtered.

McCann shuddered involuntarily. He loved animals and the one before him brought to mind his own cat Daisy. Daisy however was alive, this one was not. Trailed across the floor about half a metre away from the dead cat lay a string of intestines that had been ripped out after the attacker had cut it open. One of the cat's eyeballs was bulging out of its socket while the other was missing. But what made the whole scene even more bizarre was the picture of a naked woman placed on top of the cat's body, covering its abdominal wounds. To McCann, with fourteen years in the police force under his belt, the attack seemed particularly brutal. Small animals were so defenceless; people could fight back, animals couldn't.

Written in blood above the stove were the words 'Donna You're Dead' and next to that was the name 'Robyn', all printed in block letters. As McCann took in the scene, he echoed the thoughts of the other detectives, 'This bloke's sick!'

In the bathroom, the detectives found the two kittens. Floating one at each end of a half-filled bath, the water had turned rust coloured with their blood. Their throats had been cut.

The attack had obviously occurred in the laundry over a plastic laundry basket of baby clothes. Blood had splashed everywhere, spraying high up the walls and around a packet of kitty litter that Donna Vanes would no longer need. In the cats' blood was a distinct shoe impression.

Walking into the main bedroom, McCann saw that the attacker had ransacked cupboards and drawers, and he had sprayed a can of shaving cream all over Donna's mirror and through the creamy swirls, the detectives could make out the words 'Donna and Robyn.' One of the cupboard doors had been covered in pictures of scantily clad models. These had been slashed and only a few jagged corners of the pictures remained. The intruder had also slashed the cupboard door, leaving deep gouges in the wood. Oddly, the door had swirls of dirty, dried water marks as if the attacker had wanted to clean the surface for some reason. Had he written another message on it then changed his mind?

In the baby's room, the intruder had put a picture of a naked model into the baby's crib and stabbed through the picture into the bedding. Some of the baby's clothes had been slashed.

Looking around outside, the point of entry was clear; the intruder had climbed onto a nappy bucket around the back, forced a window open and climbed through. Left behind on the blind was a gloved hand impression in blood.

So brutal and bizarre was the attack on the cats and the threat to Donna Vanes, that detectives called in crime scene examiners, photographics and fingerprint experts to examine the flat in Claude Street. They also arranged for officers from the Australian Animal Protection Society to perform post-mortem examinations on the cats to try and come up with anything that could help in the investigation. The examinations came up with nothing of any value but it was confirmed that the messages scrawled in the kitchen and the lounge room had been written in cat's blood.

Obviously the attacker knew Donna Vanes and hated her. Chris McCann drove to where she was staying at a relative's house and questioned her about any enemies she might have. Donna was at a loss to explain the vicious attack. She could think of no enemies except perhaps the father of her child with whom she had ended the relationship before the baby was born. But she doubted that he would have had anything to do with such a violent attack. The break up had certainly been acrimonious, but never violent. She could think of no-one else who could do such a thing. Referring to the second name mentioned in the written threats, McCann asked her who Robyn was. Donna had no idea. Her father's name was Robert but some people called him Robyn. Otherwise, she was at a loss.

Chris McCann located the ex-boyfriend and questioned him at the

Dandenong police station. He had an alibi for the previous evening and welcomed the detectives into his home to have a look around. The detectives found nothing incriminating at his house, and after speaking at length to the young man, Chris McCann doubted that he would have been responsible.

The detective also contacted Donna's father to see if he could think of anyone who hated him and his daughter. He couldn't. After spending all day checking the few leads, McCann headed home to a couple of hours sleep before being called out to a house in Bulleen where an elderly couple and their son had been burgled and attacked by a gang armed with machetes.

Donna Vanes moved out of the flat, staying temporarily with her sister Tricia. One of Tricia's neighbours, Paul, had known Donna for a while. He told her that she was safe now and that if they ever caught the person responsible, he would take care of him.

3

Elizabeth

AS eighteen-year-old Elizabeth Stevens jumped off the bus that had brought her from Frankston to Cranbourne Road, Langwarrin, she was unaware that she was being watched.

It was 7.15 on the evening of Friday 11 June 1993, and heavy rain had soaked Elizabeth's curly short hair so that it clung damply to her neck. She didn't usually come home this late, but she had been working at the Frankston Library for a bothersome English assignment that she had already completed — her teacher had asked her to conduct more research on the topic.

A couple of weeks earlier, Elizabeth had dropped a history course that she had been taking at the TAFE. She enjoyed her English course, but history wasn't a subject that she was good at. Her real dream was to join the army and the TAFE course was a means to that end.

Elizabeth shivered in the cold June rain and hurried quickly down Paterson Avenue towards the home she shared with her aunt and uncle, Paul and Rita Webster. Her own parents were separated and Elizabeth had lived in a children's home in Tasmania from the time she was fourteen until her eighteenth birthday last October. She had lived for a while with her mother and then another aunt before the Websters had offered her a home in Langwarrin. Being a short bus ride to the TAFE college, the arrangement suited Elizabeth perfectly and she finally felt settled.

She was unaware that a man had followed her along Cranbourne Road and was drawing closer as she turned into Paterson Avenue.

The rain grew heavier and it was hard to see.

Out of the darkness, the man in the green army jacket and navy baseball cap lunged at her from behind, clasped a hand roughly around her mouth and pushed what felt like the barrel of a gun to her head. She screamed in fright but the sound was drowned out by the wind and the rain. He dragged her onto the front lawn of somebody's house. She struggled against him, thinking she could protect herself: she had taken karate lessons for four years, but he was a big man, strong, and he had a gun. There was nothing she could do.

The sexual urges that had overcome him when he first saw Elizabeth step off the bus were now replaced by urges of a much more deadly nature.

'Shut up or I'll blow your head off,' he shouted at her, his voice rising above the heavy rain, chilling her into submission.

'Kiss the end of the gun!' he ordered but Elizabeth was too afraid to move.

'We're going to take a walk,' he told the young woman, pushing her to her feet and leading her on down the road. She was terrified. What did he want with her? Was he a rapist? Or worse? A couple of cars drove past and the man grabbed her hand trying to make their walk down Paterson Avenue look innocent.

As they walked past one house, a man and a woman ran from the driveway towards a car parked in the street. They barely noticed the man and his captive hurrying past them. If it hadn't been raining so hard, the couple would have recognised the large man whom they had both known at school.

He forced Elizabeth Stevens down another street towards Lloyd Park. He knew exactly where he was going. Passing bushland and the park's tennis courts, the man dragged Elizabeth into a clump of bushes, holding his home-made gun to her head. He stopped her when they had passed a dirt track near some sand hills.

'Can I go to the toilet?' asked the panic-stricken girl, trying desperately to think of some way to get away from the man. He agreed and led her to a mound of dirt and grass, gesturing that she crouch behind it. It was dark.

The man watched Elizabeth open her school bag and remove two pieces of folder paper to use as toilet paper. She went behind the mound and he turned away, not wanting to watch.

'What's your name?' he asked when she had finished.

'Elizabeth, but everyone calls me Liz,' she told him, not believing what was happening to her.

'How old are you?'

'Seventeen,' lied the eighteen-year-old. Perhaps she thought seventeen sounded younger and he wouldn't hurt her. She was wrong.

'Do you want a fuck?' he asked bluntly.

The terrified young woman stalled. She told him she didn't know how and her abductor asked if she was a virgin. She nodded.

'Well, I won't rape you or anything,' he assured her.

Elizabeth Stevens's relief was very short-lived.

The man began walking her over towards the football oval goal posts and the urge to kill overcame him. He grabbed her around the throat and started choking her. Elizabeth had enough oxygen in her body to struggle feebly for a couple of minutes before darkness overcame her and she collapsed onto the wet grass.

He pulled a red-handled knife from his pocket and lunged at her throat, slashing in a frenzy until the blade bent. Elizabeth momentarily regained consciousness, struggled against her killer and tried to stand. He grabbed her and she slowly stumbled around him in circles, bleeding heavily. Her track suit top was up around her head. The man grabbed it, pulled it off and flung it in a puddle. He slashed at her as her arms flailed wildly, cutting her arms, her hands and her face.

When he finally let her go, she fell heavily to the ground where he stamped his foot viciously on her neck. The frenzy was over. He took a couple of steps backwards to calmly survey his work. He could hear the blood and air gurgling from her neck and watched her for a full five minutes as the life blood drained from her body. Impatient for her death, the man lifted his foot above her head and brought it crashing down on her face, shattering her nose and cutting her cheek and eyebrow with the sheer force. Elizabeth Stevens died.

The man dragged her by the legs the short distance to a creek bed flowing with shallow dirty brown drain water. Blackberry bushes clawed viciously at her skin but she was dead now. Her bra top ended up around her neck as she was dragged, exposing her chest.

Then the man took the blade of the broken knife and slowly and methodically made long cuts from her breasts right down to her stomach. He didn't slash, he wasn't in a frenzy now. He was enjoying himself. The rain fell heavily all around him but he hardly noticed it. When he had finished carving the vertical lines, he carved four lines across at right angles. After the criss-cross pattern was complete, the man slowly plunged the knife into her chest six times.

When he was finished with his handiwork, he put the broken pieces of the knife back into his pocket. Water lapped around the young woman's body, washing away her blood. Grabbing a branch from a tree above the drain, he wrenched it free and partly covered the young woman's body. The rain and the water from the drain would wash away clues of footprints and blood.

The man threw Elizabeth Stevens's bag ten metres from where her body lay and began the long walk to his girlfriend's mother's house for dinner. When he passed the golf course on Cranbourne Road, he tossed the pieces of knife into bushes and continued on through the night.

He just wanted to kill. He had wanted to kill since he was fourteen. Now he had fulfilled the ambition that had been gnawing inside him for seven years. Elizabeth Stevens died because she had been the only person to get off the bus on this cold June night. She had simply been in the wrong place at the wrong time.

Less than an hour after the brutal murder, the man tucked into a hearty meal of soup and a roast and waited for his girlfriend to come home from work.

4

Missing Person

PAUL Webster arrived home on Friday 11 June at 4 pm. He had picked up his motorcycle from a bike shop in Bentleigh after working an early shift at the Ventura Bus Company. When he left for work at 4.35 that morning, his wife Rita and his niece Elizabeth had been still asleep.

He pulled the Yamaha into the driveway of his Langwarrin home and saw the family dog, Blaze, in the back yard. He realised that Elizabeth must be out because she always put Blaze outside and turned on the alarm when she left the house. Paul Webster flicked his remote switch to de-activate the alarm, entered the house and put the kettle on to make a cup of coffee. He glanced at the bench and saw a note from Elizabeth.

Uncle Paul or Aunty Rita,

I will be at the Frankston TAFE Library or the Frankston City Library. Home about 8 pm. Frankston TAFE Library 784-8241. Frankston City Library 783-9033.

Liz.

He thought to himself that Lizzie must have left late to go to the library because she was normally home well before eight o'clock in the evening. It meant she would have to catch the last bus to Langwarrin. If she missed the bus, she would be stranded. He could imagine her voice over the telephone. 'Uncle Paul, I've missed the bus, can you come and get me please?' Not that he'd mind. He and Rita had become very fond of their niece since she had come to live with them. She had been looking for a family and found one with them. Now it seemed like she had always been there.

When he took his coffee into the lounge room, the alarm's siren sounded. He was sure he had turned the alarm off outside, but this was the first time the switch had failed to work. Puzzled, he turned it off again.

Rita Webster arrived home around 6.30 pm after doing some shopping at Chadstone. Driving home from the mall, she'd been caught in the atrocious storm that had swept the city. She hadn't seen her niece that morning either, having left for work at 6.30 am.

'Where's Liz?' she asked her husband in a voice showing faint traces of her childhood in England.

'She's at the library and she won't be home until eight. She left a note with the phone numbers on it.'

Paul and Rita ate dinner in front of the television and waited for Liz to come home. 'Sale of the Century' had just finished and the couple had watched Glen Ridge offer a lucky contestant the opportunity to consider over the weekend whether she would play for the cash jackpot and risk all the prizes she had just won. As the contestant waved goodbye and the credits rolled, Paul told his wife that he needed cigarettes and, after checking that the rain had temporarily stopped, the two decided to walk the dog up to the local shops, wrapped snuggly in thick coats. They would probably meet Liz as she got off the bus.

Arriving at the shops, Paul and Rita Webster watched as the eight o'clock bus pulled into the nearby bus stop. Only one person got off, but it wasn't Lizzie.

Rita wasn't overly concerned. She thought she may have mistaken the time that Liz said she would be coming home. At any rate, her niece had just been paid her Austudy allowance and if worst came to worst, she could always ring them for a lift or catch a taxi home.

After buying Paul's cigarettes, the Websters walked back home and settled in front of the television to watch a movie. When nine o'clock came around, Rita began to get a little anxious. It wasn't like Liz to be late. She always telephoned to let them know where she was and when she was coming home. It was one of the rules they had decided when Liz had moved in six months ago. Rita remembered the three of them sitting around the kitchen table discussing what they expected of each other. When Rita had told her niece that she always wanted to know what time she would be home, it had been mostly for the practical reason of planning meals but Liz had taken it to the extreme and always let them know exact times and left notes for them. Rita knew that Liz was in many ways much younger than her eighteen years. The two women had had great fun since Elizabeth joined the family, cooking and painting; things that Liz hadn't done much of. For Rita, it was the daughter she never had. Rita smiled to herself remembering one of the other rules they had decided upon. Since Rita and Paul both worked, Liz took responsibility for cooking one meal each week. Liz would go through cook books and had so far produced rubber chicken fillets and a cake half an inch high and as solid as a rock. Her roasts however, were improving under Rita's guidence.

Trying not to overreact, Rita reasoned that the library didn't close until nine; Liz had probably got caught up in her studies. She didn't mention her concerns to her husband.

The movie finished at ten thirty and by then both the Websters were worried. They figured that Liz must have missed the bus and decided to walk home so Paul suggested that he drive around and try to find her while Rita waited at home in case she arrived or telephoned. He drove up Paterson Avenue and along Cranbourne Road and then all the way to Frankston TAFE, his eyes scanning the footpaths for his niece.

He stopped the car and went to the front door of the college but the place was in darkness; there were two security cards pushed into the locked door. Worried, he drove around to the Frankston Library but that too was deserted. Pulling out of the carpark, Paul had a quick look in McDonalds, but the place looked like it was about to close. He knew his niece didn't have any friends in Melbourne. She wasn't interested in boys and her closest friends lived in Tasmania. She was a bit of a loner and he was at a complete loss to explain her disappearance.

He couldn't see her at the Frankston railway station nor at the bus stop, so he drove once again around the main streets of Frankston before heading for home. Perhaps he would find her at home and she would have some reasonable explanation for her lateness and he could breathe easy once again. But it was not to be.

Rita wanted to ring the police as soon as her husband arrived home alone, but torn between his fears and over reacting, Paul Webster headed off once again in his car to shine a torch in the darker areas all the way to the TAFE college and then to the railway station. Driving past Ballam Park, he stopped the car and illuminated the barbecue area and the children's play ground with his torch beam. He saw no sign of the missing teenager so he came home and finally called the Frankston police.

He told the officer who answered the phone that his niece Elizabeth was missing and that she was a very reliable girl. After taking a description, the police officer said that he would pass on the information to Cranbourne as the Webster's house was in the Cranbourne police sub-district.

Around 1.10 am, the Websters were visited by Sergeant Steve Lewis and Senior Constable Alan Robinson who had received the missing person call through D-24 about twenty minutes earlier. The two officers had been making a routine patrol of their district in a marked police car. The weather was shocking and the night had been quiet.

Sergeant Steve Lewis, with seventeen years experience in the police force, usually knew what to expect with a missing persons call. In the first couple of questions, the person making the report usually admitted to some sort of domestic fight or family trouble and the missing person invariably returned home. Hurrying through the heavy rain to the shelter of the Webster's carport, Lewis stepped up to the front door and knocked. Paul Webster answered the door and invited the two officers inside, leading them through the kitchen to a dining area where they all sat down at a wooden dining table. Rita Webster offered them coffee but the officers refused — these reports usually didn't take very long.

Paul and Rita Webster began by explaining that Elizabeth had gone to the library to study and had been expected home at 8 pm. Lewis sensed that they were worried yet trying to keep their fears in check. Her disappearance was totally out of character. Paul Webster told the sergeant that he had driven around Frankston but he couldn't find Liz.

Lewis asked the customary question, 'Could she have gone off with a friend or boyfriend?'

The Websters explained that while Liz was free to do as she chose, she was a home-body with no friends that they knew of since she had only moved from Tasmania at the beginning of the year. She had been living with them since mid-January. It wasn't long before Steve Lewis got the impression that Elizabeth Stevens was a nice young woman who loved her school work and while being friendly to everyone, had yet to find close friends in Melbourne.

Lewis asked if there had been any domestic difficulties but the Websters couldn't think of anything that could have upset their niece. The only fight they'd had was when Liz had ridden a pushbike home from Frankston after dark without lights a couple of weeks earlier. Rita had been angry at the risk her niece had taken. 'But I could see all the cars,' Liz had said. 'Well, you might have been able to see them but they couldn't see you!' Rita had cried, exasperated. Liz didn't always show common sense but she always saw reason and wouldn't repeat her mistakes.

When Lewis asked if Elizabeth had any money on her, Rita Webster told him that she had just received her Austudy cheque. A possibility that occurred to the sergeant, although he didn't share it with the concerned couple, was that Elizabeth Stevens had been 'rolled' or robbed for her meagre student allowance.

There was something about the Websters and their story that gave the sergeant a strong gut feeling that something was terribly wrong. Elizabeth didn't drink or take drugs and she always let them know where she was and what time she would be home. To illustrate the point, Paul Webster got up from the table and walked over to the kitchen bench. He picked up the note that Liz had written and showed it to the officers. As soon as Steve Lewis read it, he became really concerned about the safety of Elizabeth Stevens. He thought that any kid who left such a detailed note for her uncle and aunt wasn't the sort of kid not to ring and let them know where she was.

According to the Websters, they didn't exercise strict control over their niece. She had chosen from the outset to leave notes regarding her plans and she had always let them know where she was. It sounded to the officers as if it were more for Elizabeth's own security rather than her uncle and aunt's peace of mind.

The sergeant asked to see her room on the chance that it could contain clues to her whereabouts, perhaps a diary or an address book. The Websters showed the officers into a neat bedroom with a double bed which made the room look smaller. Next to the bed was a free-standing wardrobe and chest of drawers. The room was sparse and confirmed the Webster's description of their niece. It seemed to be the bedroom of a neat, conscientious young adult. Lewis had a quick look around but he couldn't find a diary or address book or anything else that might suggest what had become of the missing teenager.

Obtaining a full description of the young woman, Lewis filled out a missing persons report form. Neither Paul nor Rita knew what Liz had been wearing when she left that morning, in fact neither had seen her since the night before when she had gone to bed after watching a movie. They guessed that she would be carrying her navy and white sports bag with her school books. Rita checked Liz's wardrobe and found her white runners were missing as well as a new grey top that Liz had recently bought. She also guessed that Liz could have been wearing her favourite grey tracksuit pants. The Websters found her passport and showed the officers her photo.

As they left, Steve Lewis gave the Websters his card, telling them to call the police station immediately if Elizabeth turned up. Offering a parting gesture of reassurance, he told the couple that she may have met up with a friend they didn't know and simply forgotten to telephone. There were many possibilities — not all of them bad. Despite his concerns in this case, Steve Lewis had never taken a missing persons report where the person hadn't eventually turned up again. Paul Webster asked if it was all right that he drive around Frankston again to see if he could find his niece and, when Steve Lewis encouraged it, the worried man headed straight for his car. He gave the officers a parting look which did little to quell their own concerns.

Driving away from the home in Langwarrin, Steve Lewis hoped that Elizabeth Stevens had done something totally out of character and gone to visit a friend, or gone down the pub — anything as long as she came home.

Back at Cranbourne, the officers treated the matter seriously. People went missing all the time but this was different. Lewis's gut feeling grew stronger. He telephoned through a description of Elizabeth Stevens to be broadcast via D-24 for all units in the Cranbourne and Frankston areas to keep a lookout for her. He then telephoned the shift supervisor to inform him of the missing teenager and faxed a copy of the report to the Hallam community policing squad.

Out on patrol again at 3.30 am, Sergeant Lewis duplicated the route taken earlier by Paul Webster, checking the TAFE college and the railway station. He also kept an eye out for her school bag in case she had dropped it in a struggle or left it somewhere. The most frustrating aspect for the two officers was the early hour of the morning. There was no-one they could call; the library was shut and so was the bus company. There was little else to do besides cruise around and hope to find the missing woman. Two of the more remote possibilities were that she had been robbed and assaulted or that she had been abducted and raped.

While Steve Lewis was aware that the Websters had only contacted police in desperation as the evening had worn on, valuable hours had elapsed before the report and Elizabeth had now been missing for eight hours. But he also knew that it was a catch twenty-two situation — if the Websters had reported their niece missing when she was only an hour late home, the police would have just told them to wait — after all, she was eighteen years old. Lewis just hoped for the phone call that would tell him that Elizabeth had arrived home safely. But the call never came.

At 7 am when his shift ended, Lewis passed on the report to the officers arriving to work the next shift.

On Saturday morning, Paul and Rita Webster played the waiting game. Elizabeth still hadn't returned and they frantically rang relatives to see if she had gone to visit one of them. When Rita Webster telephoned her boss and his wife to cancel a dinner date that evening, she explained they couldn't make it because their niece was missing. As she spoke to the boss's wife, her voice slowed as a strong feeling came over her that she would never see Liz again.

Constable Sally Davis came on duty at 2.30 pm as watch house keeper at the Cranbourne police station. She checked the missing persons notice board and made herself familiar with the events surrounding the missing eighteen-year-old. At 3.30 pm she telephoned the Websters to learn that Elizabeth still hadn't come home, but Paul Webster told her that he had found another photo of Liz and Davis asked if he could bring it to the station. Paul arrived half an hour later with the photo.

Constable Davis tried to contact the TAFE library but received an answering machine reply. She arranged for police to visit Elizabeth's younger sister in Brunswick.

Less than an hour later, Sally Davis answered a telephone call from John Cleary at the Langwarrin Football Oval.

'There's been a body found,' he told the young constable breathlessly.

'Where?' she asked grabbing a pen to take down the details.

'In the track off the Langwarrin Sports Club off the Cranbourne-Frankston Road.'

Constable Davis wrote down the address and told him she would send the police, immediately setting the investigative wheels in motion by informing a divisional van crew and the duty sergeant of the body find. Senior Constable Jeff Brennan and Constable Tamara Shauer left immediately for the scene.

Barely ten minutes after the news of the body at the Langwarrin Football Oval, Paul Webster rang the Cranbourne police station to tell officers that he had received a phone call from Liz's younger sister who had spoken to Liz around five o'clock the previous afternoon to organise a shopping trip. While he was talking to one of the officers, Paul Webster overheard the discussion in the background about a body being found and then he heard one officer say, 'I bet it is that girl.'

Paul Webster put his hand over the mouthpiece, turned to Rita and told her what he had heard. 'I think they may have just found Liz's body.'

5

Lloyd Park

ON Saturday 12 June, Rod Hill went bowling with his children and picked up some timber from Mitre 10 on the way home. Then his wife Cheryl, who was having a dinner party that evening, sent him out in the afternoon to do some shopping. The theme was a mid-year Christmas party and when her husband returned with the shopping, Cheryl asked him to get a small pine branch from Lloyd Park to decorate like a Christmas tree.

Driving around to the football oval near their house, Hill reversed his car near the netball courts and got out to look for a suitable tree. He knew the layout of Lloyd Park because he took his children there for Vic Kick sessions most Sunday mornings. Heavy rains and hail had turned much of the surface of the oval into a quagmire and Hill tried to avoid the large puddles as he wandered about. He spotted a pine tree a few metres into the scrub adjacent to the football field and while he was figuring out how to cut one of its branches, he glanced further into the bushes and saw what looked like a body.

Taking a couple of tentative steps forward, he saw that it was a woman lying in a shallow natural drain with water around her upper body. He could make out that she was wearing grey tracksuit pants and runners. Although a branch covered the woman's top half, Rod Hill could see part of her face — there was dried blood underneath her nose as if she had had a nose bleed. It was obvious to him that she was dead.

Rod Hill jumped back into his car and drove around to the sports club where he knew there would be a telephone. Hill ran in and asked the barman, John Cleary, to call the police.

'What's the problem?' Cleary asked Hill.

'I've found a body,' he told the startled barman. 'Near the bend in the dirt track. There were a couple of trees down and that's where the body is.'

The barman quickly telephoned the Cranbourne police station and spoke to Constable Sally Davis who answered the phone.

Davis asked Cleary and Hill to go back to wait near the location for the police to arrive. They made their way down the dirt track where Hill pointed to where the body lay. The two men didn't get too close but Cleary also saw the grey tracksuit pants and the runners as well as a black watch band on the dead woman's left wrist.

'How did you find it?' Cleary asked Hill as they stood waiting for the police to arrive.

'We're having a dinner party and I was looking for a tree,' Hill explained somewhat cryptically.

Senior Constable Jeff Brennan and Constable Tamara Shauer soon arrived and the two men hurried over to meet them. They pointed to where the body lay. 'It's over there in the scrub.'

The two police officers left their car near a heavy chain fence and approached the location, careful not to go too close to the body in the event of destroying any possible evidence. But they had to ascertain first of all that the person was dead and secondly whether or not the body find was suspicious. After all, it could have been someone walking through the bush who had suffered a heart attack. Senior Constable Brennan was quick to note the absence of clothing to the woman's upper body and the blood around her face. It certainly looked like she had met with foul play. They got close enough to see that the area would have to become an official crime scene.

Brennan directed Shauer to protect the area and stop anyone from getting too close, while he returned to the police car to radio D-24. Homicide, forensics and crime scene examiners would soon surround the scene to each perform their respective tasks.

Brennan also radioed his superior at Cranbourne, Sergeant Fred Barton. After twenty years in the force, Barton was used to body finds. Just as he was leaving the station, Sally Davis handed him the missing persons report and photograph of Elizabeth Stevens. 'It could be her,' she told him.

During the afternoon, Sally Davis had kept him up to date on the status of the missing person report and she had told him earlier that she had a bad feeling about the missing student. 'I don't like this one, Sarg,' she had said. Sergeant Barton also had the feeling that the missing teenager had just been found.

Driving to Lloyd Park in the pouring rain, Barton knew that any evidence such as shoe impressions and blood would literally be washed away and he also knew that he would spend most of the night standing around in the rain co-ordinating traffic, media and the officers under his command. He glanced over at the thick black plastic raincoat on the seat beside him and hoped the rain would stop.

When he arrived at the scene, Barton donned his raincoat and positioned his police hat over his collar so that the rain ran down the back of the coat and not down his neck. He walked through the long grass over to the creek bed where the body lay, careful to walk the same path that the other two officers had taken so as not to contaminate the scene more than was absolutely necessary. Coming within three metres of the body, he noticed immediately that the dead woman bore a strong resemblance to the photograph he had of Elizabeth Stevens except now her hair was plastered flat against her head so that it almost looked like a wig.

As Fred Barton studied the scene, he was puzzled. He could see that the woman's body was naked from the waist up and through the branch he made out the strange criss-cross cuts in her chest. The body was whitish-blue in colour and the death, considering the chest wounds and the dried blood around her nose, was certainly suspicious. In his considerable experience, Barton knew that if the attack was sexually motivated then the pants would have been removed as well as, or instead of, the top — that was how these things normally went. But this victim was still wearing her grey track suit pants and there didn't seem to be any suggestion of a sexual attack — but why was the top missing? If someone wanted to kill the woman out of spite or revenge, why remove the top? Somehow, this scene was odd.

Two detectives from the Dandenong criminal investigation branch, Michael West and Steven Mansell, arrived at Lloyd Park at 5.40 pm. They had been working a district response shift and, having heard the body find call over the police radio, were already on their way to Lloyd Park before they were officially called. Sergeant Barton directed them into the Langwarrin Sportsman's Club after procuring an upstairs room as a temporary command post in order to get out of the pouring rain. Barton told the two detectives that Cranbourne had received a call from John Cleary and Rod Hill regarding the body and he showed them the missing persons report on Elizabeth Stevens. The men discussed the similarities between the missing woman and the body even though there were obvious differences between the photograph of the happy, smiling woman and the bluish-white body lying in the ditch. Even so, the grey track suit pants and the runners fitted the description of clothes belonging to Elizabeth Stevens.

After Barton had passed on all the available information, he directed the detectives to the location of the body. Walking through the rain, up the narrow track towards the crime scene, Michael West didn't know what to expect. Like Fred Barton, he too had seen countless bodies in his line of work and considered himself lucky that none had been children. When the body came into view, West was immediately struck by her small size. He thought she looked young and frail — almost child-like.

Bruising and a long cut around the left eye were obvious to the officers as was the blood that had formed at the base of her nose. When Michael West saw the criss-cross cuts in the dead woman's chest, he said, 'It looks like someone's been playing noughts and crosses on her.'

Because of the water running down the creek bed, there was little blood around and the conditions were eerie. Darkness was falling, rain pelted down in the deserted park and the body of the woman lay before the detectives.

'Doesn't look like a sexual assault,' West observed, noting that the woman's track pants were still in place as were her runners, although the detectives did discuss the possibility that it was a sexual assault gone wrong. Considering the injuries to her face and the fact that her bra was pulled up around her neck, they considered the possibility that someone had grabbed her with the intention of raping her, but that she may have struggled and her attacker may have hit her and killed her. Rain had washed away any signs of the body being dragged into the creek bed and it was impossible to tell where she had been murdered.

Michael West gingerly stepped over the body and lifted the branch to get a better look at the dead woman. Shining his torch at her, the eerie feeling became stronger. He looked up at Barton and Mansell and said, 'Shit, her throat's been cut.'

In the minds of the three officers, it put a different slant on the murder. If the killing had been an attempted rape gone wrong, it would have been easy for the attacker to hit her to keep her quiet, but it took a different type of killer to cut a woman's throat. To West, it suggested that the killer was some kind of maniac. But their theories were all academic because they knew that the homicide squad would be the ones to investigate this murder.

West and Mansell immediately contacted homicide and made arrangements for a command post to be set up in Lloyd Park. It was Fred Barton's job to direct the human traffic through the scene and help maintain the log of all members coming and going.

Through the rain, Barton saw a huge red Country Fire Authority bus pull into the park's driveway. He walked over and asked the driver what it was doing there. The driver explained that a police officer from Chelsea, who was also a volunteer CFA member, had heard about the body find via the police radio and organised for the vehicle to be sent to Lloyd Park. To Barton, it was like a gift from the gods — the rain hadn't let up and there was no shelter in the immediate area. He directed the driver to park the bus near the chain link fence and it became the command post. The CFA bus was equipped with telephones, fax machines and, of immediate importance to the half-frozen officers, a hot coffee machine. A huge awning was lifted from one side of the bus to provide shelter.

As darkness fell, the whole area was illuminated by huge, bright scene lights erected by State Emergency Service workers. The body couldn't be moved until crime scene photographs were taken as well as a video-tape of the scene. Crime scene examiners began searching the area.

Sergeant Paul Dacey from the Hastings crime scene section arrived at Lloyd Park at 7.30 pm. By then it was freezing cold, raining heavily and hailing intermittently. Dacey knew that the weather conditions in this case favoured the killer because valuable forensic evidence such as blood, hair and shoe impressions would be washed away. In fact, it was the worst weather Dacey had ever struck at a crime scene; he had to balance an umbrella on his shoulder as he made his written notes. A crime scene photographer took pictures of the surrounding area, including the gravel road, the chain link fence and the nearby scrub, carefully noting the photograph number and each location.

After the dead woman had been photographed, Dacey measured and described the culvert in which she lay. Once the body had been photographed as it had been found, the branch could be removed. Detectives West and Mansell watched as further injuries became obvious. The savage throat wound could be seen properly and the detectives counted at least six knife wounds to the woman's chest, four deep cuts running from her breast to her navel and four running at right angles — forming the criss-cross pattern that they had seen earlier through the branch. There were cuts and abrasions to her face and the bridge of her nose was swollen enough to suggest it was broken. Her bra was caught up around her neck. Dacey collected the branch for evidence.

Six and a half metres from the body was a tree with similar foliage to the branch and Dacey noted that the tree had a broken limb. He arranged photographs of the damage to the tree.

Homicide detectives arrived at 8 pm and were briefed by Detective Mansell. They made their way over to view the body and speak to the other officers.

A couple of hours after he arrived, homicide detective Rob Hardie went around to Paterson Avenue to speak to the Websters. He told them that on the strength of the evidence it was probably Elizabeth they had found. He told the couple that he couldn't confirm it yet but to prepare themselves for the worst. Angry at the state of shocking limbo, Paul Webster asked why they couldn't confirm it was Liz. Hardie gently explained that the identification couldn't be made until Paul Webster identified the body. The distraught uncle fell silent. He had a fair idea that it was Liz. He had watched over his back fence which backed on to Lloyd Park and had seen the police cars, the SES lights and the police helicopter flying around. Neither he nor Rita had sat still for a minute since they had reported Liz missing. They had both been prowling like restless animals, unable to sleep, eat or rest. They just didn't want to believe it.

Another homicide detective, Sergeant Charlie Bezzina, cleared the crime scene at 11.35 pm. In the appalling weather, crime scene examination was limited — visibility was poor and the area to be searched was best left to daylight hours. Police began packing away their equipment and a number of officers were given the duty of guarding the scene until the following morning.

Once the area was officially cleared, the body was removed. The body itself was a prime piece of evidence, and to maintain the continuity of evidence, Charlie Bezzina had the task of escorting the body in a Tobin Brothers van to the carpark of the Mornington Peninsula Hospital en route to the city mortuary. Dr Helen Hewitt came outside to the van, unzipped the body bag and examined the young woman's body. She noted that the pupils were fixed and dilated, there were no heart sounds present, there was no evidence of respiration and the body showed obvious early signs of rigor mortis.

Life was pronounced extinct fourteen minutes before midnight. When Sergeant Steve Lewis came in at 11 pm to work the night shift, he had slept most of the day and hadn't seen the news. The watch house keeper said to him, 'They found your girl. She's dead.' Lewis felt like he'd been hit. He immediately thought of the Websters and their grief and, not knowing the circumstances of her murder, he wondered if he could have done something to have prevented it. Hearing the details of the body find in Lloyd Park, Lewis knew that they hadn't even checked it the night before; they had concentrated on the route between the TAFE college and the Webster's home. The inevitable 'what if...' questions came to mind. If he had driven around to Lloyd Park the night before, could he have somehow prevented the young woman's death? He couldn't know that Elizabeth Stevens was dead hours before he even took the report that she was missing.

Around 3 am, Steve Lewis took one of the marked police cars and drove by himself to Lloyd Park to relieve the other officers guarding the scene. They spoke briefly about the murder and Lewis heard that the victim's throat had been cut. By the time he arrived, the scene was almost clear of the earlier investigations and the red command post bus had returned to the CFA station. He parked near the football oval and watched as the rain ran intermittently in sheets down the windscreen. Steve Lewis could see the fences of the houses bordering the park and he reflected that most of the families living there wouldn't be touched by the death of a friendless eighteen-year-old girl.

Keeping his solitary vigil until daybreak, Lewis had hours to ponder the tragedy of the situation. He wondered who could have killed Elizabeth Stevens and why. The thought suddenly struck him that life plods along and then something like this happens that totally destroys one family's security and happiness forever. Its rippling effect would spread and affect everyone who knew the young woman. They would have to come to terms with her death and the fact that some bastard had taken her life. He remembered how Rita Webster had told him that Elizabeth had swapped History for Australian Studies. Now she would never finish her course. She would never do anything again. Her life had ended.

6
Post-mortem

LODGING the body in the homicide section of the Victorian Institute of Forensic Pathology mortuary attached to the Melbourne Coroner's Court complex around 1 am, homicide detective Charlie Bezzina had only a couple of hours to catch some sleep before he was back on duty for the post-mortem examination the following morning at 7.30 am.

Professor Stephen Cordner, the Director of the Victorian Institute of Forensic Pathology, performed the post-mortem. While other boys dreamed of driving trains or being firemen, Stephen Cordner had wanted to be a forensic pathologist since he was a child. His father was a doctor and he had grown up immersed in the world of medicine. In his career, Cordner had performed nearly 6000 post-mortem examinations in the quest to find the reasons why people had died. In his youth, he had been excited by the detective elements to forensic pathology. Now he realised that police did the detecting and he was but an aid in their work. The real challenges lay in his courtroom appearances; helping to prove or disprove the accuseds' accounts of murders with his own findings. He was well used to the sight of death.

Cordner came into the spotlessly clean, brightly lit examination room and greeted the detective through the glass separating the examination room and the viewing area. He dressed in dark blue surgical pants and top, put on a green surgical gown and covered the garments with a white plastic apron. Snapping on surgical gloves the professor turned to the young woman's body which was still sealed in the green, zipped body bag. The professor opened the bag and his two assistants helped him remove the body. Cordner began his external examination while a crime scene photographer from the state forensic science laboratory caught the proceedings on film.

The body lay on the stainless steel mortuary table, bent with rigor mortis and still clothed in the grey tracksuit pants, white runners and socks. A floral vest was rolled up to her neck exposing her chest. The black-banded wrist watch that the detectives noted the preceding day was still on the dead woman's wrist; its blackness contrasted with the pallor of her bloodless skin.

Cordner, although used to such signs of carnage, was saddened by the loss of life before him. It didn't interfere with his work but nonetheless he was fully aware of the gravity of the situation and he always found it impossible to totally divorce himself from what the victim had gone through. The black humour sometimes used by the police in situations of death had no place in the mortuary. Cordner had a strong sense of his duty. The young woman's relatives had every right to expect the best possible examination, not to mention that his findings might help police apprehend her killer. A common rhetorical question among forensic pathologists was: what can we do to help those of us who are still here and living? It helped to look beyond the face of death stretched out before them in the form of a murder victim, to a more positive approach.

After photographs were taken, assistants removed the dirty water-logged clothing which was bagged and labelled to be passed on to Charlie Bezzina as evidence.

One of the first things the professor noticed when he looked at the face of the young woman, was the tiny pin-point haemorrhages dotting the whites of her eyes, extending out to the skin around her eyes. Looking a bit like fine red pepper had been sprinkled on her skin, the haemorrhages were commonly suggestive of strangulation.

Professor Cordner weighed and measured the body and then began to describe into a hand-held tape-recorder each of the plethora of cuts, scratches and stab wounds, with their measurements and locations on the body. There were cuts and abrasions on the dead woman's face and her nose had been broken. Cordner regarded himself as a conservative pathologist and while he described the wounds, he was careful not to draw absolute conclusions as to how they came about, knowing that such absolutes were conjecture and could be misleading in the investigation. However, taking into account the abrasion above her left eyebrow, her broken nose and the abrasion under her right eye, Cordner suggested the possibility that the killer had stomped on her face with his foot or used some type of blunt instrument causing all three injuries with the one blow.

The dead woman's left cheek had fifteen scratches, some up to six centimetres in length. The right cheek had ten similar wounds. Charlie

Bezzina had described the manner and the location in which she had been found and considering the blackberry bushes growing nearby, it was likely that the woman had been dragged through them and they and other vegetation had caused the wounds.

Professor Cordner described the wounds to the dead woman's throat which had been slashed many times. Of interest was the fact that the cricoid cartilage, located just below the Adam's apple, was fractured yet the more delicate hyoid bone above the Adam's apple was intact. Often in cases of strangulation, the hyoid bone is broken. The professor concluded that the force to the neck was inflicted below the Adam's apple and reasoned that a blow by a foot, fist or knee could have been responsible for the fracture of the tough cartilage.

The professor noted the criss-cross patterns, clearly visible on the dead woman's chest, the cuts ranging in length from six centimetres to thirty-three. The chest wounds showed no obvious signs of bleeding or bruising, indicating that they had been inflicted after death. The stab wounds were neat and contained within a small area of her upper chest, indicating that they had been done deliberately and with precision rather than in a frenzied fashion which would have caused tearing around the wounds.

Examining the arms, the professor recorded each of the many cuts, bruises and abrasions covering the entire length of both.

After the external examination was complete, Professor Cordner opened the body to examine the internal damage caused by the stab wounds. Internal organs were removed and the professor sliced a tiny section of each and placed it in a microscope slide to be examined and stored as evidence. Samples of blood and urine were also taken to be sent to a toxicologist to be tested for the presence of drugs and poisons. The organs were each examined and weighed and then placed back inside the body which was sewn up again.

In his summary of the cause of death, Professor Cordner wrote:

... this woman has sustained a substantial compression of the neck. A fractured cricoid cartilage usually implies more force than can be applied by hands or a ligature alone and suggests things such as blows with a fist or foot...

A number of bruises and abrasions to the arms and hands suggest that these may have been used in attempts at self defence...

The absence of incised or stabbed defence wounds means that at the time the knife was used, the deceased was not able to defend herself for whatever reason. [Defence wounds are injuries sustained by victims of assault as the hands are used to grab the blade or fend it off.] In this case, it is quite possible this was because of the effect of the other injuries to the head and neck...

The professor found no indication that the dead woman had been sexually molested.

In his report, Professor Cordner wrote: 'In my opinion, the cause of death was: aspiration of blood and haemorrhage from stab wounds to the neck in a woman whose neck has been compressed.'

Detective Charlie Bezzina watched the entire proceeding with detached professional interest. Forensic pathology could tell him a lot about the type of crime that had been committed, whether the girl had suffered and most importantly whether injuries were made before or after death had occurred. Details like this could help lead to the killer.

Once the examination was complete, Charlie Bezzina took his evidence bags from the South Melbourne mortuary, lodged the items with the Hastings crime scene section and then made his way to the home of Paul and Rita Webster.

Watching the Channel Ten news the previous evening, the Websters had heard sketchy details of the woman's body found in Lloyd Park. They were still hoping against hope that somehow the body was not that of their niece.

However, those faint hopes were dashed when Detective Bezzina showed them two sleeper earrings and a watch with a black band. Rita Webster identified all three items as belonging to her niece while trying to comprehend that the three innocuous pieces of jewellery meant that her niece was dead. Bezzina gently questioned the couple to try and establish Elizabeth's last movements.

At Bezzina's request, Rita Webster checked the pantry in an attempt to establish if Elizabeth had eaten anything before leaving home on Friday. She noticed that a tin of baked beans was missing and Bezzina nodded. Although he didn't mention the fact to the Websters, this was consistent with the contents that Professor Cordner had examined from Elizabeth's stomach.

After giving their written statements to police, Paul and Rita Webster were asked to accompany Detective Bezzina to the mortuary to formally identify the body of their niece. On the long drive from Langwarrin to the city mortuary, Rita prayed it would not be Liz. She realised that it was hopeless, but until she saw Liz there was always a one in a million chance that there had been some kind of mistake.

At the mortuary, Paul and Rita, along with Paul's brother Peter and his wife Mary who had accompanied the couple, were led into a small glassed-in viewing room. A silent mortuary assistant added to the surreal atmosphere by pressing some unseen button and a curtain slowly drew back to reveal a body on a trolley, covered by a sheet. Another assistant on the other side of the glass window delicately pinched a corner of the sheet and drew it back to reveal a face. Mary, who had a daughter the same age as Liz, went reeling backwards but Paul and Rita Webster remained frozen in their places.

Rita Webster suddenly understood with supreme clarity why there was a glass window separating the bereaved from the dead. Her first instinct was to run forward and grab her niece to shake the life back into her. Paul Webster simply stared sadly at the scratches on her face. He heard his wife say quietly, 'Poor little girl.'

Mortuary assistants had cleaned the facial wounds; the sheet covering the body hid the rest of the wounds. The formal identification was brief. Paul Webster looked down upon the face of his dead niece and gave a short statement to the coroner's clerk:

'On the thirteenth day of June, 1993, at the Coroner's Court, I identified the body of Elizabeth Ann-Marie Stevens who formerly resided at Langwarrin and was aged eighteen years. She was by occupation a student. The deceased was my niece. I have known the deceased for eighteen years.'

The wait was over. Uncle Paul's Lizzie had now officially become 'the deceased.'

7

The Investigation Begins

JUST before 8 am on Sunday morning, Senior Constable Andrew Herdman along with five other officers from the search and rescue squad were briefed at the Frankston police station by members of the homicide squad. Experienced in conducting line searches, the officers had been called in to make a thorough examination of the crime scene at Lloyd Park and its surrounding areas. The officers consulted maps of the area and planned the course of their search before heading to the muddy grounds of Lloyd Park. Search and rescue officers briefed forty SES volunteers to assist with the line search.

Half an hour after the search began, Herdman found a small silver coloured knife blade in long grass adjacent to a footpath on the Cranbourne-Frankston Road. The blade looked like it had broken off from a pocket knife. Continuing the search in the long grass and bushes bordering the Cranbourne-Frankston road, searchers failed to find either the handle or anything else of note.

Back at Lloyd Park, Sergeant Paul Dacey joined the search. Twenty-two metres north-east of the culvert where the body was found, Dacey discovered a blue and white striped sports bag at the base of a sand hill. Opening it, he found text books and stationery items labelled 'Elizabeth Stevens'. Further away in a pool of muddy water, Dacey found a blue, hooded windcheater top with a blood-soaked grey t-shirt inside it. He had them photographed, then collected them as evidence.

At the Hastings crime scene section later in the afternoon, Dacey was still on duty when Charlie Bezzina arrived after attending the post-mortem examination. Bezzina passed on the items that Cordner had removed from the body of Elizabeth Stevens.

The media were quick to jump on the story of yet another young woman murdered in the Frankston area. They immediately linked the death of Elizabeth Stevens to those of Sarah McDiarmid and Michelle Brown. Sarah McDiarmid disappeared from the Kananook railway station on 11 July 1990. Her body had never been found although a pool of blood near her car led detectives to believe she had been murdered. On 1 March 1992, Michelle Brown had telephoned her mother from the Food Plus store on the Frankston-Dandenong Road asking to be picked up from the Frankston railway station at 8 pm. When her mother arrived, Michelle was nowhere to be seen. Her naked body was found two weeks later in a shed behind a gun shop in Playne Street, Frankston. Due to decomposition, a cause of death couldn't be established.

The moment Paul, Rita, Mary and Peter arrived home from the mortuary, a young reporter ran over to them in the driveway and asked awkwardly whether they knew the dead girl.

'She was my niece and we've just come back from the morgue,' growled Paul Webster, marvelling at the sheer lack of respect. Once inside the house, the four discussed the inevitability of the media turning up and they decided to go back outside and invite the reporter in for an interview. Foremost in their minds was to get publicity and media attention to focus on Liz's murder so that the police could catch her killer. The reporter and her crew made their way into the Webster's lounge room and the camera man immediately bumped his head on a low-hanging light fitting. It was to become a private joke to the Websters and every time another reporter or crew member would bump into the light fitting, they would add to the tally: light - six, media - none. It was the one light moment during the whole terrible time.

Setting up office at the Cranbourne police station, homicide detectives Rob Hardie and Charlie Bezzina had little to go on. Usually, detectives began at the family and worked their way outwards. Most murders are domestic in nature and detectives often need look no further than the immediate family or a disgruntled boyfriend. In the case of Elizabeth Stevens however, the normal avenues were few. She had no immediate family in Victoria except her young sister who lived in Brunswick. Aunties and uncles were investigated as were the Websters, but detectives came up with very few clues.

Could Elizabeth have been murdered by someone she knew in passing? The Websters told them that Elizabeth was friendly to many of the neighbours and that they often saw her stop as she walked up the street to chat to whoever happened to be in their front garden. Rita Webster could only imagine that her niece may have accepted a ride from someone she knew vaguely. Another avenue of investigation arose when Paul Webster told the homicide detectives about a day a couple of weeks earlier when Liz had rushed in the front door banging it violently. He had asked her what was wrong and she had told him that someone had followed her and that she had run all the way home from the bus stop.

Detectives ran the names of all the students at the TAFE college through the police computer, checking them for prior convictions, especially of a violent or sexual nature. A number of students did have priors — one was a convicted paedophile but he was investigated and cleared.

An initial objective for Hardie and Bezzina was to establish whether Elizabeth Stevens had gone into Frankston on the day she died and secondly, whether she had travelled home again.

Inquiries at both the Frankston and TAFE libraries brought no direct evidence one way or another. Librarians at neither library could remember Elizabeth but then again, they were big libraries and just because nobody remembered her, it didn't mean she wasn't there. A road block was set up near the bus stop in the days following the murder with a mannequin dressed in clothes similar to those worn by Elizabeth Stevens when she was killed. Police stopped all cars and asked if anyone had seen the murdered woman. There were few leads.

A major door-knock was initiated, with detectives visiting every house in the areas surrounding the bus stop and Lloyd Park. They spoke to every resident and asked if they had seen anything. One resident initially looked like a promising suspect. He told door knockers to 'fuck off' and when detectives returned, they found traces of blood around his house. Further investigations revealed that the man had acted suspiciously after the murder. Because rain had washed away evidence at Lloyd Park, detectives did not know if Elizabeth Stevens had actually been murdered there or murdered elsewhere and dumped at the park. When the man's house was searched, police took blood samples but the blood was found to belong to the man, who had recently cut himself. He also had an alibi for the time of the murder.

Because of the location of her body, detectives assumed that Elizabeth Stevens had probably caught the bus from Frankston to Langwarrin and was grabbed by someone as she walked home, but they weren't absolutely certain. The bus driver hadn't taken much notice of his passengers that night. It had been raining heavily and he didn't want his passengers waiting in the rain so he had hurried them on by giving only a cursory glance at their Met tickets. He couldn't recall anyone fitting Elizabeth Stevens's description but he told police that if she had caught his bus that Friday evening then he would have dropped her in Long Street between 7.45 and 7.50 pm. Appeals for passengers on the Langwarrin buses that night to come forward brought a mixture of information; some passengers said that they remembered a girl fitting Elizabeth's description while others were equally adamant that she wasn't on the bus.

Until people began coming forward with information, the only certainty was that Elizabeth Stevens had called her thirteen-year-old sister from a public telephone around five in the afternoon to organise a shopping trip for the following day. Liz told her sister that she was in Frankston at the time.

Media coverage of a murder was always helpful and in the case of Elizabeth Stevens, putting her picture on the front page of newspapers soon brought forward hundreds of people who remembered, or thought they remembered, seeing her in Frankston the afternoon she was murdered. Information reports were filled out and passed on to detectives and every lead was thoroughly investigated. There would eventually be over 1500 such reports.

One resident who owned a house that backed on to Lloyd Park telephoned police and reported seeing a suspicious car out of a side window on the night of the murder. Charlie Bezzina and his crew considered it a promising lead but though the driver was located and questioned and admitted driving aimlessly around the area on the night of the murder, there was no other evidence against him and he was released.

A number of reports detailed a woman, fitting the description of Elizabeth Stevens, seen hitch-hiking in the direction of Langwarrin. Bezzina tried his best to investigate the sightings but, taking into account the dead woman's personality and habits, he doubted that it was Elizabeth, however, it couldn't be discounted. Marko Lozina who owned a take-away food shop in Young Street, Frankston, saw Elizabeth Stevens's picture in the paper and recognised her immediately. He had seen her in his shop many times and had thought her a nice girl. He also remembered that she had been in his shop last Friday afternoon, and he contacted police at Frankston. He told detectives that he thought she had been in between three and four in the afternoon; he had left the shop at four, and he thought that it had been after the lunchtime rush. He remembered that she had ordered either chips or potato cakes. This information was also confirmed by the stomach contents found during the post-mortem examination. He was the first eye witness to definitely put Elizabeth Stevens in Frankston. It was a start.

A fellow TAFE student called Samantha also contacted D-24 after she heard about the murder on television. She told them that she had been in Frankston with her father on that Friday afternoon and they had parked in the carpark adjacent to the Frankston library. Walking towards the Cash Converters store, Samantha saw Elizabeth Stevens pass her going towards the library with her bag slung over her shoulder. Not knowing Elizabeth particularly well, Samantha didn't say hello.

The stories rolled in. Many people were sure they'd seen her. Some reports seemed totally at odds with what was known of Elizabeth Stevens. Michael Wyatt was watching television a couple of days after the murder. He looked closely at the photograph on the screen and thought he recognised her as a girl he had seen the Friday before at the Time Zone Amusement Parlour at Frankston where he was working as a security guard. He remembered the young woman because she had been on her own playing a machine near a group of children that he had just spoken to. He contacted police who visited him and showed him a photograph of Elizabeth Stevens. He identified her as the girl in the windcheater playing the machines. He told detectives that he had noticed a young man standing near the machine but he didn't know whether he had been talking to Elizabeth. Around 7 pm, the man had left by himself and ten minutes later, the girl had left – going in the same direction as the man.

Members of the McCrae division of Alcoholics Anonymous had met for a weekend convention at the Frankston TAFE college on the Friday night Elizabeth Stevens was murdered. When her photograph was published through the media, three members contacted police and told them that while they were waiting under the cover of the TAFE porch for someone to arrive with a key, a young woman fitting Elizabeth Stevens's description ran through the heavy rain to the front door. The woman was carrying a sports bag and had no umbrella; the waiting members noticed that she was soaked and shivering. She had rattled the handles and found the door to be locked. The young woman had turned to the three AA members who told her that they were waiting for the key. One of the members assumed the young woman was also an AA member who had arrived early. However the girl smiled at them, asked politely for the time and then left. It had been around 7.40 pm. When the members saw the press photos of Elizabeth Stevens, they remembered the sports bag, the grey tracksuit and her smile — or so they thought.

Elizabeth Stevens's thirteen-year-old sister Catherine was questioned in detail about her sister and the kind of girl she was. From Catherine's statement, detectives learned that six of the eight children in the family still lived in Tasmania — four in welfare homes and two with their father. Their mother Christine lived in Adelaide. Catherine explained that the day after her eighteenth birthday, Liz had left the welfare home in Tasmania to live with her mother in Adelaide but it hadn't worked out. Catherine and Liz had lived in different welfare homes in Hobart and Liz would visit her little sister a couple of times a week. Catherine described how the family used to tease Elizabeth because she wasn't interested in boys but Liz hadn't cared.

When Liz had moved to Langwarrin, and Catherine to her grandmother's house in Brunswick, visits to her little sister became monthly because of the hour and a half drive separating them. Liz telephoned regularly using either the Webster's phone or a public phone in Frankston. Catherine told the detectives that Liz was happy living with the Websters.

On her last visit to Brunswick, Liz had told Catherine that she intended taking karate lessons again and as Catherine looked through her sister's purse, she saw a card for a karate club. Catherine used to look through her sister's purse all the time and check her address book. She knew all the names listed and she also knew that Liz hadn't added any new ones since she had been in Melbourne.

On the afternoon her sister had died, Catherine had been watching *'The Flying Nun'* on television when Liz had called. Liz explained that she was in Frankston and had to go to the library because she had lots of homework to do. After a few minutes chatting, Liz said she had to go because someone else was waiting to use the phone.

The detectives asked Catherine if Liz had ever mentioned being scared of anyone or if she had ever been followed. Catherine said that Liz had never mentioned anything of the sort.

The difficulty with any investigation was the amount of information that came flooding in. The detectives had to take into account the dead woman's personality and habits in order to deduce which information was likely to be true and which was not. It was unlikely that it was Elizabeth Stevens at the Time Zone because she didn't usually frequent pin ball parlours. It was also unlikely that it was Elizabeth that ran to the door of the TAFE library because it meant that she would have missed the last bus. Another young man gave a report that Elizabeth Stevens did drink because he had seen the Websters with Elizabeth at the Berwick pub the night before she died. When detectives questioned Paul Webster he told them that he didn't even know where the Berwick pub was.

One of the more bizarre leads that Charlie Bezzina and his crew looked in to was an occult connection. A TAFE student told detectives that Liz had once taken out a book on the occult. She had seen her reading it although Liz had explained that she wasn't really interested in the subject. Considering the strange criss-cross markings on her body, it was worth looking into. But the lead went nowhere. Cults and covens don't advertise their presence and Bezzina failed to find any operating in the area.

The hours were long and the leads dwindled, but Charlie Bezzina and a number of his crew continued to travel daily from the western suburbs. They would leave at five in the morning, make the hour and a half drive and return home rarely before ten at night. They did this seven days a week for nearly seven weeks in an attempt to find the killer of Elizabeth Stevens.

8

A Lucky Escape

ON Thursday 8 July 1993, forty-one-year-old Roszsa Toth caught the 5.25 pm train from Cheltenham to Seaford. She had worked from 8.30 am until 5 pm at a Cheltenham bank and was on her way home to her family. Originally from Hungary, Mrs Toth had lived in Australia for six years. Her voice still carried strong traces of a Hungarian accent.

Ten minutes before 6 pm, the train pulled slowly into the Seaford railway station and Mrs Toth stepped down onto the platform, bracing herself against the July chill. She walked down the ramp towards Railway Parade, heading for her home.

Passing the sports reserve on Railway Parade, Roszsa Toth saw a man about twenty metres away on her right hand side, near the toilet block. She took little notice of him and kept walking. However, as she passed him, he moved away from the toilet block and began following her. Still, she took little notice. It was dark and the station was poorly lit, but there were others getting off the train and Railway Parade was reasonably busy with cars.

The man quickly decreased the distance between himself and Mrs Toth and suddenly grabbed her around the chest. Shocked, she turned to face him and he grabbed her by the hair and tried to force her off the footpath towards the toilet block in the reserve. Pushing her roughly, they both fell to the ground. Mrs Toth landed on her knees. Another violent shove sent her rolling onto her side and one of the many thoughts racing through her mind was of her expensive ring that felt loose on her finger. In a panic, she offered the man the ring if only he would let her go.

The man didn't say a word, he just grabbed her and pushed her onto her back, struggling to get on top of her. Roszsa Toth lay on the damp grass of the reserve near the busy road and couldn't believe what was happening to her.

A twelve-year-old boy riding his bike to soccer training at the field next to the reserve saw a man dragging a woman in the distance. He heard her screaming and saw her struggling violently to get away. The area was dark but as the two struggled under an overhead light, he could see pretty clearly what was going on. As the woman continued to scream, he saw the man drag her away from the light and behind some bushes. He figured, with a twelve-year-old's logic, that they were probably a boyfriend and girlfriend having a fight and continued riding past.

'I don't know what I'll do if you keep screaming,' the man yelled at Roszsa Toth, putting his large hand over her mouth to stop her from crying out. She couldn't breath because his huge hand covered both her nose and mouth. Slowly suffocating, she bit his fingers hard and gasped for air as he quickly pulled his hand away and yelled at her not to scream because he had a pistol. In the confusion, Mrs Toth heard him pronounce the word pistol as 'pistole' with some kind of accent.

The man then placed something hard at her temple. Mrs Toth thought that the object felt more like wood than the metal of a gun. It didn't feel cold enough to be metal. Although terrified and in fear of her life, she had the presence of mind to think the young man was bluffing about the gun.

Lying on the grass, Mrs Toth caught sight of oncoming lights which she thought might be a bike or a car. She managed to push the man away and got up off the ground and ran towards the road. She had barely taken three steps before the man grabbed her by the hair, pulling out a handful in the process, and dragged her down on the ground again. Struggling on her back, Mrs Toth continued to scream and bit him once more on the fingers. He again told her that he had a pistol. A train went by with a thundering roar drowning her cries for help, but it heralded the arrival of more traffic on Railway Parade as people drove out of the carpark and others were picked up by waiting cars. Mrs Toth summoned all her energy and pushed the man off her. She grabbed her handbag and one of her shoes which had fallen off in the struggle. This time, she managed to scramble to the road, running in front of some oncoming cars waving her hands desperately for them to stop. As she escaped, the man ran away into the reserve.

One of the cars pulled over and a young woman called Michaela got out and ran towards Mrs Toth.

'What happened?' she cried, alarmed when she noticed Roszsa Toth's torn stockings and trousers.

'A man attacked me,' sobbed the terrified woman. 'Can you please take me home?'

Roszsa Toth jumped into the back of the car and then said suddenly, 'I've got to get my shoe.' She pointed to where her other shoe lay near the driveway to the Seaford Reserve. When Michaela saw her reluctance to leave the safety of the car, she offered to get the shoe for Mrs Toth but the distressed woman urged her to remain in the car. She would get it herself.

As Mrs Toth raced to pick up her shoe, she begged Michaela, 'Please wait for me. Don't leave me.'

When she returned with the shoe, Michaela asked what had happened.

'The man grabbed me. I don't know what he wanted to do with me — perhaps rape me? He told me he had a gun but I didn't believe him. He tried to drag me into the building.'

Michaela thought Mrs Toth meant the toilet block, which was the closest building to where she had run from.

Even though he had thought it was a boyfriend girlfriend argument, the twelve-year-old boy was nonetheless scared by what he had seen. He had stopped his bike a little way up the road and saw Mrs Toth emerge running from the man and crying out in a language he didn't understand. He saw a white car stop and heard a woman asking if she was okay. The boy felt relieved and continued on to soccer practice. He told a couple of his mates, but they all agreed that it was probably a boyfriend and a girlfriend arguing so they didn't do anything about it.

Michaela drove Roszsa Toth to her house and at the trembling woman's urging, went inside with her and telephoned the police to report the vicious attack. Roszsa Toth's right leg was badly grazed and her head was aching where the man had pulled her hair out in the struggle.

Michaela waited for Mrs Toth's son to come home and after exchanging names with the woman she had rescued, left the family to wait for the police.

Senior Constable Danny Hower and Constable Michael Lynch were working the 6 — 2 shift out of Frankston on routine patrol when a call came over the radio:

'Report of man having assaulted a female at a toilet block, Seaford North Reserve on Railway Parade. Victim at her home address. Offender solid build wearing a beanie. Offender decamped through fields behind toilet block. Minutes old.'

Michael Lynch wrote down the details on the running sheet. It was officially a job for the Chelsea station, but their officers were tied up so Hower and Lynch took the call. They headed straight to the toilet block at the Seaford Reserve. This was a lights and siren job. The offender could still be in the area.

Further down Railway Parade, the soccer field was lit with bright overhead lights, but when the two officers pulled up at the toilet block, it was in total darkness. Hower parked the police divisional van outside the block and left the high beams on, lighting up a wide area. Getting out of the van, the officers grabbed their long batons from beside the seats and made their way over to the toilet block. Attacks in this district were frequent; usually drug addicts in search of easy money. Shining their torches around, they saw no sign of anyone and walked over towards the toilets.

Hower took the women's side and Lynch took the men's. Details about the attack were sketchy and the officers didn't know what type of offender they were looking for, but if it was a drug addict he could be spaced out inside the toilets. Lynch experienced a vague feeling of apprehension as he walked through the dark doorway, breathing out heavily against the smell common to such public conveniences. His baton hung at his side, the end of it sitting in a leather loop on his belt. He held his torch in his left hand and his right hovered next to his firearm — just in case.

The area containing the basins was empty and Lynch stepped further inside and turned towards the closed doors. Behind any one of them could be the man who had attacked the woman earlier. Rather than use his hand to push the doors, Lynch stood further away and kicked open the first. Adrenalin pumped and his heartbeat quickened slightly. It was empty. He repeated the procedure on the other cubicles but they were all empty so he hurried back outside to see if his partner had any more luck. Hower hadn't found anyone either, so both men walked around the back of the block and shone their torches around. There was no-one around.

It was important to speak to the victim as soon as possible and the officers made the short drive to Roszsa Toth's home.

As Hower and Lynch pulled into the driveway of the Seaford home, a young man who looked to be in his late teens came out to meet them. As the officers got out of the van, he introduced himself as Roszsa Toth's son. On the way to the house he explained that his mother had been attacked as she walked along Railway Parade.

Michael Lynch's first impression of Roszsa Toth was that of an attractive woman with long black hair, who looked to be in her early thirties. He was mildly surprised when she said she was forty-one. Immediately obvious to the officers was the fact that Mrs Toth, with her thick Hungarian accent, was very difficult to understand. Danny Hower noted that she was sitting calmly on a chair and it was at first difficult for him to grasp the severity of the attack. She did most of her speaking through her son who translated for the police officers.

Mrs Toth indicated the graze to her knee and told them she thought the man could have been someone desperate for money. She had calmed down considerably once she got home and she explained that the man hadn't really hurt her although she knew that the matter must be brought to the attention of the police. She didn't want to make a fuss.

As the interview progressed, Lynch took down the details. Mrs Toth described her attacker as being between eighteen and twenty years of age, wearing a black jacket. She told the officers that he was around one hundred and eighty centimetres tall with a round face and blue eyes. He had been wearing a light coloured beanie.

Painstakingly leading her through her statement, Hower heard Mrs Toth mention a gun. Through her son, he learnt that the attacker told her that he had a gun and that she had felt something hard pushed against her head. She explained that it may not have actually been a gun because it didn't have the cold feeling of metal. This put a different light on the attack. In most of these types of offences, it was common for the attacker to be either unarmed, or armed with a knife. A gun was different. Danny Hower considered bringing in a police dog, but he realised that by the time the nearest dog could attend, it would be too late for it to be of any assistance. One thing that disturbed Michael Lynch was the fact that Roszsa Toth had offered the attacker her expensive ring during the attack and he had refused it. If the attacker was a drug addict after money, it was strange that he hadn't taken the opportunity to grab the ring and run. Most attacks that Lynch had investigated were snatch and grab types. He had anything up to five or six a month. This seemed different. There seemed to be no reason for such a violent attack on the woman.

Hower and Lynch stayed at Roszsa Toth's house taking her statement for an hour then headed back to the Frankston police station to fill in the reports and alert the CIB detectives of the attack.

9

A Young Mother Vanishes

ON the night of Thursday 8 July 1993, Russell Hayes had a dinner invitation. His friend Debbie Fream had just given birth to a son and she had invited him over for dinner to catch up and to see the new baby. Russell had worked with Debbie whom he called 'Dee' and they had established a close platonic friendship. They talked regularly both at work and on the telephone and would often go to the same nightclubs together: Russell could drink and Debbie, who rarely drank, would drive them both home.

Debbie Fream had left the small country town where she had grown up to take a job as a data entry worker at a business in Clayton. Her boyfriend, Garry Blair, had stayed behind while Debbie had opted for the city with its bright lights and good job prospects. Initially Debbie shared a flat with a friend in Mordialloc and then Garry joined her and they both moved to Kananook Avenue, Seaford. She often spoke about how happy she was with Garry.

Not long after Debbie Fream began the job in Clayton, she discovered she was pregnant. A doctor had told her that she might have problems conceiving and although the pregnancy came as a surprise, it was a happy one. Debbie continued working into the fifth month of her pregnancy, but fatigue soon overcame her and she had resigned to await the birth of her baby.

Russell Hayes had not seen Debbie since before the birth of her son Jake in Frankston Hospital. Finishing work in Clayton around 5 pm, he clocked off and drove straight to Seaford. When he arrived at Kananook Avenue, Debbie's car wasn't in the driveway and the house lights weren't on so he waited in his car. Debbie had told him that she had a bit of shopping to do and he knew that she wouldn't be long.

Five minutes later, when Debbie's grey Pulsar pulled into the driveway, Russell got out of his car and gave his friend a congratulatory hug. Russell unloaded the shopping, leaving Debbie to carry baby Jake into the house. She joked about how many extra things she needed to carry around since the baby arrived.

Twelve-day-old Jake was asleep and Debbie gently lifted him out of the baby capsule, showed him to Russell and then carried him to his cradle in the bedroom.

Alone in the lounge room, Debbie and Russell chatted about the baby, life in general and the omelette Debbie was going to make for dinner. Debbie was in good spirits. She told Russell that although a lot of people had told her it was difficult coping with a new baby, she was finding it really easy. Debbie also explained that Garry was working an afternoon shift. As the time went on, the two friends moved into the kitchen and Debbie began peeling vegetables and cracking eggs for the omelette. The telephone rang and Russell heard Debbie answer, 'Hi Mum, how are you?' Debbie's mother had come down from the country when Jake was born and had kept in regular contact by telephone when she returned home.

They discussed the baby and Debbie told her mother that if Garry wanted another one, they would get married. She told her mother how wonderful her cousin Sara had been since Jake's arrival and then noticing that her mother sounded tired, voiced her concerns. They chatted a couple of minutes more before Debbie told her mother she had to go because Russell was visiting for dinner. While dinner was cooking, the two friends went out onto the front veranda for a smoke.

Back inside the house, Debbie told Russell that she needed some milk and would just pop down to the local shop. She said she would only be a couple of minutes. Searching for her keys, she grabbed her purse out of her handbag and, finally finding the keys, headed out the door after assuring Russell that Jake was asleep and would be fine until she got home.

Settled comfortably in front of the television, Russell heard the Pulsar pull out of the driveway as he switched the channel to watch *Home and Away*. Engrossed in his favourite television program, Russell barely noticed the time pass and suddenly it occurred to him that Debbie had been gone a lot longer than a couple of minutes. He wandered out into the kitchen and turned off the vegetables that she had left boiling on the stove.

After half an hour, he wondered where Debbie was and even wandered outside, walking to the end of the driveway to see if he could see her car coming. Soon after, Russell Hayes really began to worry, He didn't know Seaford very well and didn't know which shop Debbie would have gone to. At any rate he couldn't go and look for her because of the tiny baby asleep in the bedroom. He couldn't just leave Jake and drive off.

An hour after Debbie had left, Russell rang the Frankston police station to ask if any accidents had been reported in the area. A police-woman he spoke to suggested telephoning Frankston Hospital because, she explained, there was often a delay between an accident and the police receiving the report. Russell rang the hospital and they told him that no-one by the name of Debbie Fream had been admitted and that they had no unidentified accident victims. Russell then tried a girlfriend of Debbie's who lived in Seaford. If this woman could come and mind Jake, he could go out and look for Debbie. The friend wasn't home.

Finally, Russell telephoned Garry Blair at work. Garry told Russell not to worry and that Debbie had probably just run out of petrol, but it didn't put his mind to rest. Surely Debbie would have telephoned him if that were the case. Garry suggested Russell ring another friend, Jeanette Maizey, who lived locally. Jeanette agreed to come around immediately and told Russell she would look out for Debbie on the way over.

Ten minutes later, Garry rang back to say he had organised to leave work early and was on his way home. Jeanette arrived a few minutes later; she had seen no trace of Debbie or her car. She told Russell she would drive up to the Seaford Safeway and look around there but she was back ten minutes later. She had not seen Debbie. When Garry Blair arrived home just before 9 pm, Debbie Fream had been gone nearly two hours.

Garry asked Russell to drive around to the Food Plus store on the Frankston-Dandenong Road, which he did. Debbie's grey Pulsar wasn't there and Russell searched surrounding streets before returning to the house in Kananook Avenue.

Leaving Jeanette to babysit, Russell and Garry drove to the Frankston police station to report Debbie missing. The police wanted a photo of the missing woman so the two men returned home, found a recent photo and drove back to the police station. By the time they finally returned home, it was nearly midnight and still Debbie hadn't come back. Russell stayed for a while before reluctantly leaving. He had to work the next day but he gave Garry his telephone number and made him promise to call as soon as Debbie appeared.

Garry telephoned Debbie's brother Troy. Both men had worked together that afternoon and he had told Troy that Debbie was missing as soon as Russell had called. Troy had finished work around 10.30 pm and telephoned Garry asking him to ring him if Debbie wasn't back by midnight. When Garry finally called, Troy was so worried about his sister he came around immediately. Garry asked him to drive to the handy bank in Seaford to check the balance of his account to see if Debbie had withdrawn any money. Troy drove to the Westpac automatic teller machine in Frankston and got a print-out of Garry's balance. Back at the Kananook Avenue house, Garry figured that there was around fifty dollars less in the account than there should have been but that Debbie had probably withdrawn the money for shopping with Jeanette. There was still over two hundred dollars left in the account.

Garry, Troy and Jeanette spent an anxious all-night vigil waiting for Debbie to come home.

Russell Hayes was woken early the next morning when an officer from the Frankston police station telephoned to ask him if he had heard from Debbie. He hadn't.

Milk bar proprietors in the area also received early morning visits by detectives. The closest shop to Debbie Fream's home was on the corner of her street and McCulloch Avenue. The proprietor, however, said he couldn't remember whether he had served her or not.

10

The Four Day Wait

GARRY Blair couldn't understand it. Where was Debbie? The previous day he had slept late in anticipation of working that night. Debbie had given Jake his four-hourly feeds and he had noticed that she seemed a bit weary but she hadn't complained, in fact she had chatted about visiting her friend Jeanette Maizey and about how both women had planned to go shopping. Debbie also spoke about Russell coming for dinner that evening.

Jeanette Maizey and her two children had called in around 11.30 am for a half hour visit, promising to return in the early afternoon for the shopping trip.

Cradling Jake in her arms, Debbie had kissed Garry goodbye on the front porch as he'd left for work just after one in the afternoon. She seemed cheerful and she told him she would see him after work. Now she was gone and no-one knew where.

They were both on a high after bringing Jake home from hospital and he couldn't understand her disappearance. It seemed like a nightmare. Where was she?

Early Friday morning, Senior Detective Michael Glowaski drove to the house on Kananook Avenue to talk to Garry. The distraught young father repeated the information about Debbie going to buy milk around 7 pm the previous evening and that no-one had heard from her since.

Glowaski took down Debbie's description and Garry described the black skirt and white windcheater she had been wearing the day before. He also gave the detective a description of Debbie's grey Pulsar and the registration number. Glowaski returned to his office at the Frankston police station and began to make inquiries.

In light of the young mother's disappearance, the attack on Roszsa Toth the night before was seen in a more sinister light. Senior Detective Andy King had begun work at 6.30 am on Friday morning in preparation for an early morning drug raid. When he arrived back at the CIB offices, he checked the crime reports in-tray and read the report detailing Debbie Fream's disappearance and Roszsa Toth's attempted abduction.

Thinking that there could be a connection, King, together with an officer from the Frankston community policing squad called around to interview Roszsa Toth again. The morning after the attack, the woman looked ragged. She told King that she walked along Railway Parade every night and nothing like this had ever happened before. Mrs Toth repeated details of her ordeal and accompanied the two officers to the toilet block at the Seaford Reserve to reconstruct the events of the night before. She showed them where the man had been standing when she had first seen him and where he had grabbed her.

Mrs Toth was then driven to the St Kilda Road police complex where she was assisted to compile a photo-fit picture of her attacker. Her injuries were also photographed for police records and she was examined again, this time by a police doctor who knew what to look for in this type of attack.

To Andy King, the odds of one woman being attacked close to Seaford railway station around 6 pm and another vanishing from near Kananook station an hour later, were long — unless the same offender was involved. Foremost in his mind was the disappearance of Sarah McDiarmid from Kananook station in 1990. Every police officer in the district remembered the McDiarmid case. Debbie Fream's disappearance from the same area was alarming.

Also concerned for the safety of Debbie Fream was Detective Inspector John Noonan from Frankston. As head of D District's six detective divisions, Noonan was informed on Friday morning that the young mother had vanished. He too made the link between the assault on Roszsa Toth and the disappearance of Debbie Fream. Noonan put all his available resources into finding the missing woman.

Senior Sergeant Chris Jones from the missing persons squad was lecturing new recruits on Friday morning at the police academy when his beeper sounded. Another officer from his squad, Henry Van, informed him that they had a missing woman in the Frankston area last seen around 7 o'clock the night before. Van explained that the woman had left a twelve-day-old baby with a friend and gone to the local milk bar in the middle of cooking dinner. Both the woman and her car were missing. Jones headed straight to Frankston, thinking about the case he was about to investigate. Since his squad had been set up a year earlier, they had dealt exclusively with old files, trying to find a new perspective. This was their first call to investigate a fresh disappearance.

Arriving at Frankston police station, Chris Jones met with Inspector John Noonan for a briefing session and, together with other detectives, had a round table discussion about the various possibilities. Debbie Fream was missing and so was her car. She could have suffered post-natal depression and sought refuge with a friend. She could have had a nervous breakdown, or she could have vanished in some sort of suicide bid. More sinister was the possibility that she had been abducted.

Chris Jones knew that the missing person squad worked at a disadvantage compared to a normal homicide investigation. When a body is discovered, detectives can look for evidence to match the clues found on and around the body. If the victim is shot, the detectives look for bullets, bullet holes and a gun. But when a person is missing, there may be no evidence of a crime even when a crime is the most likely explanation.

Chris Jones remembered his boss Chief Inspector Peter Halloran's favourite saying: always go back to the facts. The facts in this case were: Debbie Fream was missing, her car was missing and she left a twelve-day-old baby in the middle of cooking dinner. After dismissing the more innocent possibilities, it didn't take long to conclude that the most likely explanation was that something untoward had happened to the missing mother.

The first priority was to co-ordinate a search for Debbie Fream. John Noonan telephoned Brian McMannis at the State Emergency Service office, ironically located on McCulloch Avenue not far from the milk bar closest to Debbie Fream's home. Brian McMannis had been an SES volunteer for seventeen years and had been in charge of the Frankston branch for the past eight. Inspector Noonan had great respect for the work the volunteers did and had called on them often to assist in searches and to provide lighting for crime scenes and road accidents.

With sixty-two volunteers, the Frankston SES could provide greatly needed assistance to the police. Various police experts would lecture the volunteers at their Monday night training sessions to keep their methods up to date. What Noonan appreciated most was the enthusiasm of the volunteers. If he asked them to search an area, they did it immediately and thoroughly. They also brought with them much needed equipment and even food and hot coffee. Partly funded by the local council, SES volunteers spent much of their time raising money themselves in order to continue to provide the free service. McMannis offered one of their caravans for a command post as well as volunteers to hand out pamphlets alerting the public to the missing woman.

John Noonan asked Brian McMannis to organise a search of Kananook Creek and its surrounding areas. Although a daunting task with its thick surrounding scrub, McMannis had 230 volunteers ready within hours, calling in extras from surrounding SES units. After a briefing at the SES offices in McCulloch Avenue, the searchers in their bright orange overalls were transported to various points along the creek. McMannis also called in members of the Doncaster unit who were trained divers. They launched a rubber dinghy and searched the waist-deep creek and its banks while the other volunteers concentrated on the surrounding scrub. The search of the creek was an exact duplication of the one the SES had done three years before for Sarah McDiarmid. But this time, as with the earlier search, they found nothing.

Together with his partner Michael Glowaski, who had earlier interviewed Garry Blair, left the office on another call. Returning to the police station around 2.30 pm along the Frankston-Dandenong Road, Glowaski noticed a grey Pulsar parked outside the New Life Christian Centre in Madden Street, just off the main road. Thinking it may be the car they were looking for, the detectives turned around and headed to Madden Street. The registration checked out. It was Debbie Fream's car.

Without touching it, they examined the car and saw that the front passenger side door was unlocked and there was a dent in the centre of the bonnet. The damage seemed to be recent. Notifying Inspector Noonan at the Frankston police station, the detectives guarded the grey Pulsar until the crime scene examiners arrived and the car could be examined, photographed and impounded for evidence.

John Noonan and Chris Jones immediately drove to Madden Street and the first thing they checked was the driver's seat. According to the description, Debbie Fream was short in stature and they both noticed the seat pushed all the way back to the last notch to indicate that a much taller person had driven the car. From the moment the car was found, the disappearance was definitely viewed as sinister; where was the missing woman? If the car had broken down, she could have walked home from Madden Street. Dabbing around inside the car with sticks designed to react to blood by changing colour, examiners found traces of blood.

Noonan and Jones had another meeting to discuss tactics for the investigation. Jones offered the services of the missing persons squad and he also offered to co-ordinate the vast amount of information that was sure to come flooding in. One person needed to sift through all the information reports and direct detectives towards further avenues of inquiry.

Jeanette Maizey gave a statement to police at Frankston in the early afternoon. She told officers that she had called to see Debbie the previous morning around 11.30 am and that she had returned for the shopping trip around two in the afternoon. Debbie had told Jeanette that she had felt a bit dizzy earlier in the day and that she also felt tired. The two women had left the Kananook Avenue house as soon as Debbie finished breastfeeding. After shopping they visited Jeanette's mother, giving Debbie an opportunity to show off the baby.

On duty that afternoon at the Frankston community policing squad, Sergeant Jo Lomas was worried about the missing woman, especially when she received the news that the car had been found with the keys in the ignition and the seat pushed right back as if a tall person had driven it. Debbie Fream was only 158 centimetres tall and drove with the seat well forward. A number of community policing squad officers decided to stay in the police station rather than going out to make their usual checks and visits. If the young mother was found, then their services would be required one way or the other.

Community policing squad officers had discussed the woman's disappearance. They too had swapped theories suggesting the possibility of post-natal depression and leaving the baby with a friend; she may have disappeared on purpose. News of the car being found however, put a different light on the case. Comparisons with the Sarah McDiarmid disappearance from the Kananook railway station in July 1990 were again inevitable.

Chris Jones from missing persons had his work cut out for him. As he expected, members of the public came forward with hundreds of leads which were entered painstakingly into a central data bank. Each lead was checked by detectives, a huge task considering that they were coming in at a rate of around one hundred per day. The difficulty was that detectives didn't know what they were looking for. Was it a murder or a disappearance? They weren't even sure whether an offence had been committed. It wasn't against the law to vanish.

Most important of all the leads were those involving the grey Pulsar and the times that people had first seen it parked outside the Christian

Centre. Two women reported seeing the car at 7.50 pm on the night Debbie Fream disappeared. What had happened to her in the fifty minutes between leaving to buy milk and her car being parked in Madden Street?

Two days after Debbie Fream's disappearance, information came to light from Ann Smith, Debbie's mother, about a telephone death threat that Debbie had received not long after she and Garry had moved to the house in Seaford. Ann Smith informed detectives that Debbie had told her that a man had telephoned her saying he was going to kill her. Mrs Smith had not been overly concerned. She knew her daughter had a way of dramatising things and had assured her that it was probably a crank call.

In light of Debbie's disappearance, the call was now taken seriously.

The following day, the *Sunday Herald Sun* ran with the front page story: 'Murder Threats to Missing Mother'. The link between the telephone call and Debbie's disappearance seemed obvious. It was a lead that had to be followed. If the man who had threatened her was responsible for her disappearance, then there had to be a connection somewhere. Investigating officers began looking for someone who may have held a grudge against the young mother, although it seemed unlikely. Who could have hated Debbie enough to kill her?

That afternoon, Jeanette Maizey was again questioned by detectives. They asked her what she knew about Garry Blair. It was routine; people closest to victims are usually the ones responsible for any harm that comes to them. Stranger killings are relatively rare and detectives wanted to get a picture of Debbie Fream's de facto.

Jeanette Maizey told Senior Detective Geoff McLean that she had met Garry Blair when they all lived in Casterton. Explaining about life in the country with its huge unemployment problems for young people, Jeanette confessed that they had all 'partied' quite a bit and it wasn't unusual for many of them to indulge not only in alcohol, but also marijuana. She described Garry as a 'moderate' marijuana user but she assured McLean that she had never seen him violent. Not long after Jeanette met Garry, he had started dating Debbie Fream.

Debbie and Jeanette had become close friends and confided in each other. Debbie would often tell Jeanette how much she loved Garry. When Jeanette moved to Frankston, Debbie followed soon afterwards. Her reasons, she had explained to Jeanette, were twofold: she wanted to find a job and she also wanted to get Garry away from the group in Casterton whom she believed were a bad influence on him.

Early in the pregnancy, Debbie and Garry experienced a rough patch in their relationship. Garry, it seemed, had been spending a lot of time with Debbie's brother, Troy, who had temporarily moved into the Kananook Avenue house. Troy and Garry had spent a lot of nights out partying, leaving Debbie alone with the effects of her pregnancy sickness.

Jeanette told McLean she had advised Debbie to tell Troy to move out, and by the eighth month of her pregnancy, Debbie's patience had run out. Telling her brother to leave hadn't been easy. She reported to Jeanette that Troy had been really angry and that her brother's anger had scared her. The decision, however was for the best. Garry started coming straight home from work and Debbie was a lot happier.

Following Jake's birth, Jeanette explained, Debbie had 'been over the moon.' Garry was supportive and everything had worked out well. Debbie even expressed milk so Garry could feed the baby at night.

Jeanette again repeated the events of the day Debbie vanished. She added that while shopping, Debbie had mentioned she needed milk but the two women had spent their time looking at fabrics and Debbie hadn't bought milk in the time they had been together.

Jeanette told of minding the baby the night Debbie had failed to return from the shops and how Troy had arrived around 1.30 am.

McLean asked Jeanette if Debbie had mentioned the threatening telephone call. She described how, about three or four months before, Debbie had told her that someone had threatened her over the telephone. Debbie had said the man had sounded drunk but had referred to her by name. At the time, Debbie couldn't think of who she might have upset enough for them to have threatened her in such a way.

Debbie's brother Troy was also questioned by police. Jeanette had mentioned the friction caused by him living at Kananook Avenue and it became important to speak to him. Troy told detectives that he had a close relationship with his sister and they spoke often, although he did admit that as they had both got older, they tended to fight, 'probably because we're both stubborn,' he explained. He described Garry Blair as 'pretty easy going and gets on well with everyone. I've never heard anyone say anything bad about Garry.'

Questioned about drugs, Troy said, 'When Garry and Debbie were living in Casterton, they got into a bit of shit with the coppers over marijuana. Basically growing and possession of the plants, but nothing big. Garry got done for having four or five plants but they were seedlings really and if mates rocked around and asked for a smoke then he'd give them one. He wasn't selling if that's what you want to know.

'Around October, November 1992, Debbie got done by a copper from Casterton with a gram of marijuana.' Troy explained that the car that Debbie and Garry were passengers in was pulled over by police. 'Garry had already been in the shit for drugs so Debbie said it was hers to keep him out of trouble. I think Garry had been to, or was going to, court for the other drug charges so he didn't need this one as well. Since they've been down in Frankston, Debbie has really gone anti-drugs and gets right up Garry when he smokes. I think it was more the money side of it 'cause Garry was spending too much on drugs and they had a kid on the way.

'I know that since Garry and Debbie have been in Frankston, Garry has bought marijuana from some seedy joints and he said he's been to some weird places to score, but he always kept Debbie out of it 'cause she just didn't want to think about it and wanted nothing to do with it.'

Troy explained how Garry had told him at work that Debbie had gone to the shop and hadn't come back. The first thing that had occurred to Troy was the threatening phone call that Debbie had got months earlier.

With the information regarding Garry Blair's use of marijuana, another avenue of investigation presented itself to the detectives working on Debbie Fream's disappearance. Could there be a drug connection? Even though Garry Blair was just a casual user and Debbie was against the use of marijuana, violence in the drug world was certainly common enough.

Once the media got wind of the story of a missing young mother of a newborn baby, they flocked to Garry Blair. Grateful that his appeals for Debbie to return or be returned were spread to such a wide audience, his photograph was printed in the newspapers and splashed across television screens nation-wide, holding baby Jake wrapped in a white blanket.

As soon as she heard her cousin was missing, Sara Smith, who had grown up with Debbie in Casterton, told her boss she needed to take time off work. She packed a bag and moved into the little house on Kananook Avenue, along with a number of other relatives and friends, to help care for the baby and to wait for news of Debbie. In the days following Debbie's disappearance, the house was kept perfectly clean by the restless family members, unable to leave and unable to sit still. They carefully avoided any mention that anything terrible might have happened to Debbie, almost as if to say it might make it true. The only possibility they discussed was that Debbie might have had an accident and could be wandering around in a daze. Eventually she would come home.

11

Taylors Road

FRED Michelmore had lived with his family on Taylors Road for seven years. He was by trade both a fencing contractor and a farmer, running cows, sheep and agistment horses on his farm in Carrum Downs. His eighty acre farm had been in the family since 1933 and he came from a long line of farmers. Although only a short drive from the built-up areas of Carrum Downs and Seaford, Michelmore's farm seemed as if it were in the middle of nowhere. Access was only by bumpy unmade roads and the whole place had a definite country feel.

On Monday 12 July 1993, Fred Michelmore had worked on the motor of his tractor until lunchtime. After lunch, he went about repairing the electric fence behind his truck shed and fixed a broken insulator. He then decided to move ten horses from beside the house to a paddock alongside Taylors Road. After wheeling his motorbike from the shed, Michelmore set off to round up the horses. Travelling slowly behind them down a stock lane towards Taylors Road, he kept an eye on the waist-high electric fence as he went, knowing that one gap or breakage could result in the loss of valuable stock.

Shutting the paddock gate behind the horses, Michelmore began riding along the eastern boundary, checking his fences. About twenty metres from where the southern fence began, he noticed what looked from the distance like a pile of rubbish among an isolated clump of metre-high ferns growing by the side of Taylors Road. He rode past but something didn't seem right so he swung the motorbike around and rode back once more. Pulling to a halt, he looked through the fence. The object was not a pile of rubbish; it looked more like a shop mannequin lying amongst the ferns. Fred half smiled to himself. The blokes up the road were obviously playing some kind of joke on him. Moving closer however, Michelmore realised that it wasn't a mannequin — it was a woman's body.

It didn't take Fred Michelmore long to realise that the dead woman was Debbie Fream. He had seen the intense television and newspaper coverage of the missing young mother and that very morning, over a cup of coffee, he had read another story about her on the front page of the newspaper. Michelmore knew instinctively that he had found her. He looked at the dead woman and saw her half-closed eyes and noticed that she was wearing a white bra and that she had a black belt loosely around her midriff with a gold buckle. She had white underwear beneath a pair of flesh coloured pantyhose and she was wearing a pair of black boots. Blood and dirt had washed through her damp blond hair.

Michelmore took in the flattened ferns nearby, figuring that somebody had pushed them flat to try and conceal her body.

The farmer sat quietly on his bike for a couple of minutes, trying to take in the scene before him. He was stunned. A day so far filled with mundane farm duties had suddenly taken on a new light and now, for a short time, he was the only person on earth who knew the whereabouts of Debbie Fream — apart of course from her killer. He didn't get off his bike to look more closely, aware that it would be best not to disturb anything.

Finally coming to his senses, Fred Michelmore turned his motorbike towards the house and rode home to tell his wife Beverley and to telephone the Cranbourne police station.

Senior Constable Debbie Jago answered the call at 3.50 pm.

'I think I've found the body of that girl,' he told her without preamble. Senior Constable Jago asked his name and address.

'Are you positive it's a body?' she asked.

'Yes, I think so,' the farmer replied. 'I thought it was a mannequin. She doesn't look too good. It's hidden in some ferns outside my property on the side of the road.'

Jago asked Michelmore to hold the line while she put him through to homicide. Senior Detective Colin Clark took the call. Colin Clark had been with the Frankston CIB for fifteen years and he had been seconded to work with Rob Hardie and Charlie Bezzina in the homicide investigation into the murder of Elizabeth Stevens. Clark had been seconded once before to the homicide squad, assisting in the 1980–1981 investigations of the so-called Tynong North killings. Being a local, homicide investigators relied upon Clark's parochial knowledge of the district and its criminal element. Working out of the Cranbourne CIB offices, Clark had followed Debbie Fream's disappearance with interest because of its similarities to the Stevens case. Both women had disappeared around the same time of the evening in the Frankston area within a month of each other. Colin Clark had also investigated the Sarah McDiarmid disappearance in 1990 and that case was always in the back of his mind.

Speaking to Detective Clark, Michelmore again described his find, agreeing to wait at his house until the police arrived. Fifteen minutes later, Michelmore jumped into a police car with detectives Clark, Graeme Arthur and Andrew Patterson and directed them to the body on Taylors Road. Telling Michelmore to wait by the car, the detectives walked over to near where Debbie Fream lay and took a couple of photographs with a Polaroid camera. On a branch of one of the trees that concealed her from the road, detectives saw a white windcheater, heavily bloodstained around the neck area. They too, were careful not to get too close. Evidence must not be lost or tainted, although Fred Michelmore explained that Taylors Road was a popular track for horse riders who had their horses agisted at surrounding properties. He guessed that twenty or thirty could have ridden past in the last four days.

Leaving Andrew Patterson guarding the scene, Clark and Arthur drove Fred Michelmore back to his house. Checking his diary, the farmer told the detectives that he was last in the paddock on July 7, when he had moved some cows out. Debbie Fream had gone missing the following day.

The detectives telephoned for back-up and then returned to the scene, blocking off Taylors Road with Clark standing at one end of the road, and the police car parked sideways at the other end to prevent traffic entering the area. Soon after, uniformed officers and marked police vehicles converged on the scene.

Detective Inspector John Noonan arrived to take charge of the crime scene. Connecting the murder of Elizabeth Stevens with the attempted abduction of Roszsa Toth and the disappearance of Debbie Fream, Inspector Noonan had a strong suspicion that he could have a serial killer operating in his district. He had put every available detective onto the investigation — named Taskforce Pulsar — and now he stood on the isolated stretch of Taylors Road staring down at the body of the young mother. Although he had a strong feeling from the moment she disappeared that she would never be found alive, it was nonetheless disturbing to know for sure. Instinctively, the inspector looked at the dead woman's hands. Defence wounds, in the form of cuts and stab wounds, told him that she had fought her killer.

Officers from the state forensic science laboratory arrived and Graeme Arthur called the State Emergency Services personnel to provide lighting while the crime scene examiners worked into the night, combing the area for clues to the identity of Debbie Fream's killer.

Procuring a large stepladder from the SES to straddle the barbed wire electric fence bordering Fred Michelmore's property, detectives climbed back and forth viewing the body both from Taylors Road and from the farmland where it was more easily seen.

Crime scene examiner Senior Constable Tony Kealy had extensive crime scene experience having notched up thirty years in the force, thirteen of which had been spent at the Victoria police state forensic science laboratory. He worked originally from the huge laboratory complex in Macleod and had helped set up the outer branch two years before in Hastings. Kealy had been around long enough to remember the old city morgue with bodies stacked in every available space, and he still remembered the smell of death associated with the poorly ventilated building. Memories of standing in blood and water on the concrete floors at the morgue in the small hours of the morning now seemed like scenes from a B-grade Frankenstein movie. Kealy had done what he considered an apprenticeship as a crime scene photographer for three years before he became a crime scene examiner. He had seen so much death.

At the crime scene, Kealy's job was to look for solid forensic evidence to aid the detectives in their investigation. Police now had the car and the body and it seemed all of the dead woman's clothing was accounted for. But her purse and any items she may have purchased were still missing and there was no trace of the murder weapon.

Kealy bent over close to the body. He had to get an idea of the type of wounds that the woman had suffered in order to know what type of weapon the searchers should look for. To the seasoned crime scene examiner, it looked like a frenzied attack with a large knife. Scanning the surrounding area, Kealy began to get a picture of the murder scene. There was blood around the area in which Debbie Fream lay, and in smaller patches nearby. No drag marks were evident, suggesting that the woman had been murdered in the area where she now lay rather than killed elsewhere and dragged to this spot. Kealy also noted that the woman's underwear was still in place, discounting theories of a sexual attack. If it wasn't a sexually motivated killing, then it could be the work of a thrill killer or, considering the missing purse, it could have been a robbery gone wrong.

The branch used to partially cover the body came from a tree a few metres away. Kealy carefully held the broken end of the branch next to a corresponding fresh break on the trunk of the nearby tree. It seemed to match. But little else fell into place. After a long search, they found little of any evidentiary value. Line searchers failed to find either the knife or the purse.

Tony Kealy took particular notice of the soil and mud on Taylors Road. He had examined Debbie Fream's Pulsar on the day it had been found and had painstakingly scraped mud and dirt from the tyres and undercarriage. Initially, the soil samples had looked sandy, but a soil expert told him that the sample contained no shell fragments so it probably wasn't from near the coast and it didn't match this spot on Taylors Road. Kealy would spend a considerable amount of time driving around the general area looking for matching soil that could lead them to the missing purse or the murder weapon.

All afternoon Fred Michelmore and his wife Beverley sat with a detective giving statements with painstaking detail. Beverley remembered driving her son to work along Taylors Road on the night Debbie Fream disappeared and then picking him up later. She had driven four times back and forth up the dirt road but couldn't remember seeing anyone. Fred explained that he would normally have gone into the paddock on Friday but he had gone on a hunting trip for the weekend. When the couple discussed their movements with the detective, Beverley realised that she had seen Debbie Fream's body on Saturday. A woman who agisted her horse on the farm had reported a dead sheep in a paddock adjoining that by which the body had been found. Beverley and the young woman had walked with the farm dogs to find the sheep carcass and one of the dogs had run over to the clump of ferns on Taylors Road. The two women had veered off to the right towards the dead sheep and Beverley had called to the dog, wondering what it was sniffing at. From the distance, Beverley could make out something white through the ferns and assumed it was a piece of paper caught in the trees. She called the dog over and thought nothing more of it. What she had seen from a distance was Debbie Fream's white nursing bra.

Around 7.30 pm homicide detectives Senior Sergeant Rod Wilson and Sergeant Mick Hughes arrived at Taylors Road. In his mid-thirties, Senior Sergeant Wilson had done his apprenticeship as a detective with the Carlton CIB and transferred to the homicide squad in 1981. He got his first murder case only two days into his new job. In his long career in the homicide squad, Wilson had met many murderers. They were all different; some had lengthy police records while others had no priors at all. Rod Wilson had followed Debbie Fream's disappearance although he hadn't been called in until her body was located. Along with the other detectives, Wilson wasn't surprised Debbie Fream had been found dead. It was unlikely that she would have left a twelve-day-old baby, and in the middle of cooking dinner.

Mick Hughes and Rod Wilson were briefed by Inspector Noonan and took charge of the scene and the investigation. They made their way in through the clump of bushes to view the body. The dead woman had been stabbed a number of times in the throat and once in the stomach. Wide stab wounds suggested a very large knife had been used. Dried blood had blackened the left side of her face and vegetation was matted through her hair. A long purple line around her neck suggested that the killer had strangled her, while defence wounds on the dead woman's hands told the detectives that she had struggled with her killer.

Comparisons with the Stevens murder were inevitable but even a cursory examination told Wilson and Hughes that while the two murders were certainly similar, they may not necessarily be connected. Elizabeth Stevens's throat had been slashed, as had her chest, with a small pocket type knife, the blade of which had later been found. Debbie Fream's body only had stab wounds, which looked like they had come from a large knife. Similarities were that both woman had disappeared off the streets at night and both were found dumped with only a token attempt to conceal the bodies. Both women had sustained severe injuries to the neck. Initial investigations into the disappearance of Debbie Fream had revealed no connection between the two women; they hadn't known each other and they hadn't moved in the same circles.

A decision was made to investigate the two murders separately, using different crews from the homicide squad. Even considering the strong possibility that the murders were linked, they had to be investigated separately in case they weren't. The danger in assuming that the same killer was responsible for both murders was that this could be a copy-cat killing where the only connection was that the murders were within a month of each other, or perhaps a mere coincidence. If all the information was pooled and they were not linked, vital evidence could be confused and lost.

Around 10.30 pm Debbie Fream's body was removed from where it had lain for the last four days. Colin Clark had stood in Fred Michelmore's paddock guarding the body before its removal. It was dark and eerie and isolated. The command post had been set up further down the road to keep police traffic away from the crime scene and Clark stood as a solitary sentinel in the darkness, battling the urge to turn to the dead woman and whisper, 'Tell me who killed you.'

Undertakers manoeuvred a white stretcher covered in a sheet into the narrow space between the body and the barbed wire fence and gently lifted the body onto the sheet. Police photographers and a video operator caught the proceedings on film with the aid of flashes and SES lighting. For the benefit of the camera, two undertakers lifted the body, rolling it slightly so the camera could film tiny pinpoint stab wounds to her back. When the footage was taken, they carefully placed her back down and covered her with the folds of the sheet.

In an undertaker's van escorted by officers from the Frankston traffic operations group, the body was taken to the city mortuary via the casualty section of the Alfred Hospital where life was pronounced extinct at 11.41 pm. After completing the necessary paperwork the body was placed in the homicide fridge a little after midnight.

John Noonan arrived at the little house on Kananook Avenue to tell Garry Blair that Debbie had been found. The young man opened the door and invited the inspector inside to a lounge room full of concerned relatives and friends. Noonan had spoken to Garry at length during the last four days and the two men had developed a good rapport.

'Sit down Garry,' Noonan said quietly, and Garry Blair knew.

·'Unfortunately, we have bad news for you. We have identified the body. The girl we found was Debbie.'

Garry Blair broke down with the enormity of Noonan's words. The four day limbo was over and now he knew that Jake's mother would never come home. Everyone in the room immediately began to cry. They all grabbed those closest to them, clutching together in their grief. Every day, relatives had visited; some had stayed camped out on the floor, waiting. For four days, they had all avoided mentioning the possibility that Debbie was dead. She must have hurt herself, they thought, and was wandering around in a daze. Now they knew.

John Noonan was well aware of the media interest in the case and gently asked whether Garry wanted to make a statement. If he didn't

Noonan would arrange for the media to be kept away. The distraught young man said that he would make one plea for anyone who knew anything to come forward. Noonan arranged a press conference with the understanding that the media would leave the young man alone afterwards. It was agreed and Garry made one last appearance before the television cameras.

12

Another Post-mortem

AT 8.15 am on Tuesday 13 July, Professor Stephen Cordner's services were again required to perform the post-mortem examination on the body of Deborah Ann Fream. It was exactly a month to the day that he had performed a similar examination on another murder victim, Elizabeth Stevens.

Dressed in the customary surgical gown and white plastic apron, Cordner looked at the young woman on the mortuary table. He could see at a glance that the woman had recently given birth; her breasts were swollen to suggest that she had been breastfeeding an infant. He mentioned this fact to his assistants. It helped bring a sense of gravity and reality to what could seem to them like an endless stretch of nameless bodies. This woman was obviously young and she was obviously a mum. Professor Cordner had read reports of the missing mother in the papers and now that she lay before him dead, he was acutely aware of what her loss would mean to her son who was barely two weeks old.

Cordner performed the external examination first by noting the appearance of the dead woman. He dictated his observations into his hand-held tape-recorder which he would later transcribe into a written report for the homicide detectives and the coroner's files.

Noting the blood which blackened one side of her face, he said, 'There is a moderate amount of dried blood extending from the left side of the mouth and from both nostrils over the left side of the face. In addition there is blood staining, more marked over the front and left side of the neck and left shoulder than was present over the right. There is no blood staining associated with the stab wound to the upper abdomen.'

Cordner noted the presence of petechial haemorrhages around the eyes and the eyelids, normally associated with asphyxiation or strangulation. A thin, deep-red ligature mark around her neck confirmed that the killer had strangled her.

Debbie Fream had been stabbed in the neck and stomach with a knife with a wide blade. Cordner measured each injury and dictated the results into the tape-recorder.

An abrasion on her right cheek obscured a stab wound beneath it while another stab wound had penetrated her left ear lobe and continued downwards into her neck. On the dead woman's face, Cordner counted twenty-eight abrasions.

Examining her neck, Cordner recorded three stab wounds on the left side and ten parallel stab wounds to the front. He also noted a number of dark marks around Debbie Fream's neck, suggestive to him of a ligature being applied and then reapplied to count for the series of lines. There was another stab wound on the right side of the neck.

Cordner found that Debbie Fream had been stabbed twice in the chest and once in the abdomen.

Suggestive that Debbie Fream had fought her attacker, Cordner found numerous cuts and abrasions and stab wounds to her hands and arms. Particularly vicious were the cuts between the webs of her fingers suggesting that she had tried to grab the knife away from her attacker.

Turning the body over, Cordner recorded six pinpoint stab wounds in her back, ranging in depth from two to four centimetres. They had been made with a smaller weapon than the stab wounds to the dead woman's neck.

After completing the external examination, Professor Cordner proceeded to check the internal damage caused by each of the wounds by opening the body. Of interest when later examining sections of the heart under the microscope, Cordner noted the presence of a collection of chronic inflammatory cells in association with myocardial fibre damage. This type of inflammation could be the result of an infection and it could disappear without the person ever knowing they had it, or it could develop into a life threatening heart disease. Considering the horrendous injuries the young woman had sustained, the professor concluded that in this case, it had in no way contributed to the cause of death.

In his summing up, Cordner wrote:

1. The body was that of a well nourished young woman showing the signs of recent delivery...

2. The deceased shows the general signs of mechanical asphyxia...

Taken with the ligature mark around the neck, this means that the deceased has had an episode of neck compression during life.

3. There are twenty-four stab wounds mainly concentrated around the neck but also on the head, chest and arms. The stab wound to the abdomen is a post-mortem injury.

4. The stab wounds to the hands are defence injuries.

5. There are also pinpoint stab wounds to the back which have been caused by a different weapon.

6. The stab wounds have caused haemorrhage and blood had also been aspirated into the severely damaged trachea.

7. In my opinion, the cause of death is: Aspiration of blood and haemorrhage from multiple stab wounds to the neck in a woman who has had an episode of ligature strangulation.

After the post-mortem examination of his granddaughter's body, Dr William Fream performed the formal identification at the Coroner's Court mortuary.

His statement read: 'On the 13th day of July, 1993 at the Coroner's Court, I identified the body of Debbie Ann Fream... who was twenty-two years old.

Her occupation was home duties. The deceased was my granddaughter. I have known the deceased for twenty-two years.'

13

Scant Evidence

INSPECTOR John Noonan arranged for all investigators working on the murders of Elizabeth Stevens, Debbie Fream, Sarah McDiarmid and Michelle Brown, as well as those connected with the attack on Mrs Toth, to meet at the Frankston police station to discuss the investigation. Noonan had headed a taskforce before and knew the importance of pooling information and using the expertise of all those involved.

The inspector was devoting much of his available resources to finding the man he believed to be a serial killer. He had pushed for a central data bank to be set up with a full-time typist entering all the available data on each of the investigations. Every lead and information report and the follow up information was entered into the data bank, which was designed to assist in the matching of data in relation to the murders. If a suspect's name was keyed in, the computer could tell whether the suspect had been entered before. If someone was checked in a particular spot where a murder had taken place, the computer could recall the details. Up until now, information like this could have been lost under mountains of written files and its significance may not have become apparent until someone got around to checking it by hand. A central data bank was able to solve these problems and make sure that all the information gathered by the hundreds of officers working on the investigations was given equal priority.

John Noonan had worked in the district for ten years and knew the area well. He had a strong feeling that the Toth attempted abduction and Debbie Fream's murder were linked because the coincidence of two women being attacked on the same night near adjoining stations was too great to ignore. He also had a strong feeling that the attack of Roszsa Toth and the murder of Debbie Fream were connected to the murder of Elizabeth Stevens.

To John Noonan, the similarities with the McDiarmid case were also too many to be ignored. Sarah McDiarmid had disappeared from the Kananook railway station in July 1990. The amount of blood found on the ground next to her car suggested that her throat had been cut. The location of the railway station was also too significant to be ignored; the attack on Roszsa Toth had occurred near the Seaford station and Debbie Fream had been taken from the general area as well. The chance of this happening at random were long. Sarah McDiarmid was in her early twenties, so she fit the general age pattern of the victims and her attack had been random. She didn't normally catch the train at that time of night so it was unlikely someone was waiting for her. Debbie Fream didn't normally go out at night for milk and Elizabeth Stevens wasn't usually that late coming home on the bus. The only difference between the McDiarmid case and the cases of Stevens and Fream was that Sarah McDiarmid's body had never been found. The case of Michelle Brown, who was murdered in Frankston in 1992, was different because her body was found naked, unlike Elizabeth Stevens and Debbie Fream. Because of decomposition, her cause of death was never exactly established. She did, however, fit the general pattern of the victims.

When Debbie Fream's body was discovered in Taylors Road, detectives knew that she had met her killer somewhere between her home and wherever she had gone to buy milk. From there, one of them had driven to Taylors Road. Appeals through the media brought forward a number of people who had noticed a grey Pulsar driving erratically on the night she disappeared, flashing high beams at oncoming vehicles. Detectives assumed that if the grey Pulsar was Debbie Fream's then it must have been Debbie driving as the killer would hardly have wanted to draw attention to himself.

Initial confusion as to which milk bar Debbie Fream had gone to on the night she disappeared occurred when the proprietor of the McCulloch Road shop said he didn't recognise the woman in a photograph shown to him by police. Michael Stuart opened his shop at 6.30 am on the Friday following Debbie's disappearance and soon after was visited by police showing him the photograph of Debbie in hospital after having Jake. Stuart told the officers that he didn't recognise her and he didn't think she had been in his shop. The police officers gave no details about the woman but in the following days, Michael Stuart saw the photograph many times on the news. Detectives visited him a second time a couple of days later and asked him again but he still said he didn't recognise Debbie Fream as a customer.

It wasn't until July 26 that Michael Stuart finally admitted that he had indeed served the murdered woman in his shop. Receiving that week's edition of *Who Weekly*, Stuart read an article about the Frankston murders entitled 'A City Now Lives in Fear'. Photographs of Debbie Fream were featured that were different from the hospital photo Stuart had seen. Debbie was pictured before the birth of her son wearing her hair down. Stuart studied the photo and realised that she had indeed been a regular customer at his shop. Then he suddenly remembered a woman coming into his shop to buy milk and eggs on the night Debbie Fream had been murdered. Though it was two weeks after the event, Stuart specifically remembered the woman buying eggs because they were kept behind the counter and he had to get them for her. Although not a hundred per cent certain it was Debbie Fream he had served, the photo certainly looked like the woman he remembered. Detectives wondered why he hadn't recalled the woman when they had spoken to him on the morning after Debbie disappeared. She would have been the last customer he had served the night before.

The time lapse between the murder and the detectives knowing for certain that Debbie Fream had gone to the McCulloch Avenue milk bar wasted valuable police hours. If they had known which milk bar Debbie had gone to in the initial days following her disappearance, they could have focussed their resources by canvassing that particular area. As it was, they had to concentrate on every possible place she could have gone to buy milk in the general area, including two supermarkets in Seaford, a number of other milk bars and the Food Plus store on the Frankston-Dandenong Road which was a short distance from where her car was found.

After Debbie Fream's body was found a Seaford couple, Michael and Lynne, decided that the car they had seen the previous week on their way to the Seaford Hotel might have some bearing on the case. The couple contacted detectives and told them that they had left home around 7 pm to go to the pokies. Driving down Brunel Road, Michael noticed a small grey car travelling towards them. It was driving almost in the middle of the road, swerving slightly, and the driver had flashed the high beams. Just as the car was about to pass them, the driver turned the high beams on and left them on. Lynne saw the car slow down to turn into Maple Street without indicating, almost swerving in front of them. She briefly saw a man in the car, turned right around so that his arm was resting on the dash board. He had looked at Lynne and she saw him laughing. Lynne could see that the man was fat with a chubby face and dark hair.

Lynne thought that it was young men skylarking and she figured they were probably drunk. In her rear vision mirror, she saw that the car didn't turn into Maple Street, it kept going down Brunel Road.

Another lead that hit the press was a taxi driver who telephoned Crime Stoppers anonymously to report that he had seen a man at a toilet block in Seaford washing blood from his face and hands on the night Debbie Fream was murdered. He gave police the man's registration number. Through the media, Senior Sergeant Rod Wilson appealed for the man to contact police again. He didn't, but a number of other people described the same man and detectives were able to trace him. The man had no prior convictions and also had an alibi for the night Debbie Fream disappeared.

Another suspect initially looked promising. A local man had a prior conviction for a violent assault after breaking into a home and bashing a woman. Although the man had a shaky alibi for the time of Debbie's disappearance, detectives had no firm evidence, and they released him. However, they kept him under close surveillance.

Then came a break. A local resident, Darren, had actually seen a man at the car very early in the morning after Debbie Fream had vanished. Darren and a work mate had driven along Madden Street around 6.40 am on Friday 9 July. The weather was cloudy and overcast and Darren guessed that visibility was around 200 metres as the grey dawn broke. As the two men approached the Christian Centre, they noticed headlights go off on a small silver car parked on the side of the road. Darren watched as a man got out of the driver's seat and ran across the road away from the car. At the time, Darren had thought it strange because the man got out so quickly that he wouldn't have had time to lock the door. His mate commented that it looked suspicious and the two discussed the possibility that they may have just witnessed some sort of drug deal. When they passed the man, he seemed to turn his head away to hide his face.

Darren described the man as being over six feet tall, of medium build, fair complexion and wearing a dark jacket. In the early morning light, Darren thought the man had dark hair with a pony tail. He didn't know the man or where he lived, but he was almost certain he had seen him before.

Uppermost on the agenda of all the investigators was to reduce the number of potential victims available to the killer and it was in their emotive accounts of the crimes that the media served an important role. Such was the fear in the Frankston community that many women stopped going out at night and took measures to enforce personal protection. But detectives were well aware that it only took one woman to ignore the warnings and the killer would have another victim.

The hunt spread to known sex offenders living in the area. Studies in the United States suggested that serial killers often killed within a small radius of their home so the detectives had the onerous task of checking anyone in the area who had prior convictions for sexual or violent attacks against women. Their task was daunting when a computer check of known offenders in the Frankston–Seaford area came up with 500 names. Eventually, homicide detectives narrowed the field to the thirty most likely suspects.

14
Hunting a Serial Killer

OBVIOUS similarities between the murder of Debbie Fream and the murder of Elizabeth Stevens were many. The two young women were killed within a month of each other and both murders had happened at night. Both murders had occurred within a short drive of each other and both victims had been strangled and had sustained knife injuries to their throats. Neither had been sexually assaulted. Both women had been killed and dumped in isolated locations.

Rob Hardie and Charlie Bezzina worked on the Elizabeth Stevens investigation while Debbie Fream's case was given to homicide detectives Rod Wilson, Mark Woolfe and Mick Hughes.

While the media immediately dubbed the murders the work of a serial killer, such offenders are extremely rare in Australia. With this in mind, homicide detectives called upon the expertise of Inspector Claude Minisini.

Claude Minisini had been a detective with the rape squad in the late 1980s and was interested in finding the most effective ways of investigating sex crimes. He had begun looking at profiling as a way to better understand offenders, their motives, and factors which would ultimately aid in the identification of such offenders. After a visit from experts in criminal investigative analysis from the FBI's Behavioural Science Unit, Minisini made enquiries about studying behavioural analysis techniques with the FBI in the United States, but it wasn't until 1989 that the course became available to international students. In 1990, Minisini applied and was accepted to the fourteen month course at the sprawling FBI academy in Quantico, Virginia.

Totally self-contained, the two hundred acre property set in dense forests at Quantico had been designed by J Edgar Hoover as the ultimate learning facility. It had the capacity to house 1000 people, had its own shops, bank, gyms and firearm ranges. Covered walk ways connected all the buildings and in theory one could live there permanently and never leave the buildings.

Most of Minisini's classes were held in the Behavioural Science Unit housed two storeys underground. To get into the facility, students caught an elevator down and passed through two huge reinforced metal doors. Designed ostensibly as a secure bunker in case of nuclear attack, rumour had it that Hoover would have used the underground area to protect himself. His monument to self-preservation was now fully utilised by the Behavioural Science Unit.

At the end of his fourteen months at the FBI academy, Claude Minisini became accredited as a criminal investigative analyst, one of only thirty-two such experts in the world.

Of essence to profiling, or criminal investigative analysis, was the use of huge banks of statistical data gained by interviewing serial killers and violent offenders. The extensive interviews gave the FBI great insights into the minds and methods of such offenders. Using the data bank, experts could profile or analyse crimes and offenders, often giving police accurate descriptions of the type of offender they were looking for. Experts in the field learnt to look at the serial crimes from the interpretation of evidence rather than just the solid facts.

Extensive studies of serial killers suggested that they were preferential in their victim selection — usually choosing similar types of victims. If a killer murdered young women then he — for nearly all serial killers were men — possibly held a grudge against women of that age because of a real or perceived injustice. John Glover, the Sydney granny killer had preyed upon elderly women while the so-called 'Mr Cruel' preyed exclusively on children.

In the United States, the FBI had interviewed around thirty serial killers and then continued by interviewing other categories of serial offenders such as rapists, arsonists and child molesters, to build up an impressive data base of facts and statistics. Many serial killers had admitted to torturing and killing animals before they moved on to human victims. Many had suffered head injuries as children or were the victims of physical or sexual abuse and many abused drugs or alcohol. The type of victim was considered a strong indicator of the type of warped hatreds the killer had formed in childhood and adolescence. A killer who chose young women may have suffered at the hands of a similar type of woman as a child. The abuse may have been as simple as being ignored or laughed at.

Serial killer Ted Bundy had murdered attractive young women; all his victims were brunettes who wore their hair parted down the middle. They all bore a striking resemblance to his fiance who had jilted him. In 1980, African American Carlton Gary killed nine rich southern white women — the type his mother used to work for as a servant, who ignored him completely and whose whims could affect his family's livelihood.

Serial killers were creatures of habit. Once a method of killing proved successful, they tended to stick with it. If the Frankston murders were the work of one man, he had found his two victims alone at night and he had pounced. Chances were that he would continue to hunt at night although it wasn't unusual for a killer to become cocky and careless. His attacks appeared to be random and he did not appear to stalk his victims for any appreciable length of time. The women were in the wrong place at the wrong time.

Another frightening reality was that cooling down periods between murders were invariably shortened as time went on. If the killer had only waited a month between the Stevens and Fream murders, the next one could be in three weeks or less. Serial killers rarely stopped killing of their own volition. Capture or death were usually the only ways to stop them.

Experts had identified significant phases through which serial killers moved. In his mind, the killer rehearses the murder over and over again, sometimes for years. When the fantasy becomes inadequate as a form of pleasure, the killer begins searching likely places in which to find a victim. If the Frankston murders were connected, the killer had so far preyed on women not generally regarded to be at high risk of being a victim of violent crime. His preferred areas were the streets of Frankston and its surrounding suburbs. He moved around darkened streets looking for victims of opportunity, staking out areas searching for vulnerable women.

The killer sometimes retained the ability to ingratiate himself with his victims — perhaps by asking directions or luring them with a plausible tale. It was the experience of researchers in the United States that many victims had gone willingly with their killers under a false pretext. Ted Bundy would put his arm in a sling and ask for help carrying books or loading his boat onto a trailer. He was charming and helpless and women were only too pleased to offer him their assistance. Once cornered, the killer pounced.

Knowledge of the phase where the killer stalks his victims is perhaps the most disturbing aspect for police. While they were investigating the two murders, they knew that if they were hunting a single killer, there was every likelihood that he had set his sights on a third victim. Media exposure could work against them because the killer could be following their investigations and might alter his patterns to throw them off the trail. He could kill in a different location or at a different time of day or night. The widespread use of the term 'serial killer' could also stoke his ego.

Typically, a serial killer ensures that his victims are in a vulnerable position before turning on them. After capture, he acts out his fantasy on them, culminating in the murder. The victim becomes the killer's focus of revenge. Some experts say that the murder becomes a ritual re-enactment of disastrous experiences in the killer's childhood, only this time, the killer reverses the roles, re-establishing his power. Many serial killers spoke of an intense emotional high as the victim died, indeed some reported a spontaneous orgasm. Although Debbie Fream and Elizabeth Stevens had not been sexually assaulted, it didn't necessarily mean that the killings hadn't been sexually motivated.

Coming down from the emotional high, the killer would want to prolong the pleasure of the kill and it was not uncommon for them to take something from their victims as a memento. Debbie Fream's purse and bag of shopping weren't found in her abandoned car and they could have been taken in order to remind the killer of the act. The murder weapon was missing too.

After the murder, the serial killer feels let down by the experience which quickly fades in intensity. He becomes depressed and since he was merely acting out a healing ritual, he realises that the reality did not equal his fantasy and nothing has changed. He had given the victim the false identity of someone who had wronged him in the past and the victim ceases to represent who he thought she represented. Nothing in his life has changed and he sinks into a depression. This lasts until the killer begins once again fantasising about recreating the murderous high and thus begins the cycle all over again. Like a drug addict, the incidents become more frequent in order to satisfy the addiction and the serial killer becomes more daring and often more violent.

If the Frankston murders were connected, the killer had shown a preference for young women although if he was the same man who had tried to abduct 41-year-old Roszsa Toth, then he may have been willing to settle for an older victim if a younger one was not available when he felt the urge to kill. He may be an opportunistic killer holding a murderous grudge against all women. Another consideration was that Roszsa Toth didn't look her age and could have been mistaken for a younger woman, especially at night.

Given access to all the available data, Claude Minisini was asked to profile the Frankston killer. From the evidence, he had little doubt that the same killer was responsible for both murders. It was highly unlikely that two separate killers both killed in the same geographical area within a month of each other, both taking their victims to isolated spots, both using strangulation as a form of control and both inflicting knife wounds to the neck and face areas.

Minisini was taken on a guided tour through all the relevant locations to get a feel for the area where the killings and Debbie Fream's abduction had taken place. Studying the information, the expert began to get a picture of the killer. Each killer has an individual signature about his crimes and Minisini worked to identify this killer's signature.

Considering the murder of Elizabeth Stevens, especially the strange marks carved into her chest, Minisini deduced that the killer had fulfilled a strong fantasy that could have been festering for years. Fantasies are the first in a number of stages through which the killer passes. When the fantasy of killing is no longer fulfilling, the killer begins selecting then stalking women before moving into the fourth phase, which is the actual killing. Because serial killers in the United States had reported their fantasies as overwhelmingly intense, Minisini suggested that the Frankston killer wouldn't be able to hold down a job or that if he did, it would be a menial one. Like children who daydream at school and spend much of their time staring out the window, killers with such a strong fantasy life could concentrate on little else. All his energies would go into planning the next murder. He would probably have a sporadic work record and killing was the only thing he was serious about.

The evidence suggested the killer showed a great familiarity with the areas of Frankston and Langwarrin and Minisini supposed that he walked comfortably around those areas without standing out. He would probably be an average looking person — not sinister or threatening otherwise people would notice him. It was also likely that the killer would live alone or not be accountable for his time. Because he inflicted neck wounds to his victims, he would be covered in a substantial amount of blood after each killing. Minisini figured that the killer would need to live in a place where he could arrive home covered in blood and remain undetected.

It was important for Claude Minisini to consider why Elizabeth Stevens had become a victim. He knew that she had left her home in Langwarrin, had been seen in Frankston and that her body had been found the following day at Lloyd Park after heavy rains. Minisini discounted theories that Elizabeth hitched a ride back to Langwarrin. It was contrary to her known victimology. Her relatives said that she would never have hitched a ride so Minisini concluded that Elizabeth Stevens did catch the bus back to Langwarrin and that she was probably targeted as she got off the bus by someone on foot who followed her as she walked.

Minisini also surmised that the weather conditions were important to the crime and the killer. The area wasn't isolated; the bus stop was near a group of shops. Not only would the rain wash away any forensic evidence after the murder, but when the killer first approached the victim, anyone around would take little notice. People caught in heavy rain tend to hurry along with their heads bowed. In the rain, people could pass the killer on the street and the chances of anyone looking closely at him would be slim.

If this summation was correct, then Elizabeth Stevens was a victim of opportunity. The killer had passed out of his fantasy stage and was obviously ready to act out his fantasies and kill. He had armed himself with his weapon of choice, a knife, and had walked around prepared should the right victim present herself.

Significant to Claude Minisini was the fact that both Elizabeth Stevens and Debbie Fream had petechial or pinpoint haemorrhages around their eyes suggestive of strangulation, yet neither woman had been strangled to death. If strangulation was used in both cases yet not to cause death, Minisini figured that it was part of the killer's pattern. He used strangulation to control his victims before inflicting the fatal injuries. Both women had defence wounds which meant they had fought their killer so perhaps he had subdued them initially but still took pleasure in the women being conscious for the fatal blows. It all formed part of his signature.

Of interest to Minisini was the fact that Debbie Fream had a cord mark around her neck and Elizabeth Stevens didn't, yet both women had been strangled. It was likely that the killer had used his hands to strangle his first victim and had worked to refine his killing techniques by bringing a cord to the next murder.

Another facet of the control favoured by the killer was the isolated locations to which he took his victims. He could virtually do what he wanted and his victims were powerless to fight against him. He had the opportunity to spend time with his victims undisturbed.

Minisini studied the strange criss-cross patterns made on Elizabeth Stevens's chest. Of great significance to the expert was the fact that the markings were post-mortem and that the neck area of Elizabeth's grey windcheater was blood soaked. He had obviously cut her throat while she was still fully clothed. Feeling inadequate with women, the killer only removed her top after death and used his victim in a voyeuristic, almost childlike way. He may have had a bad experience with women in the past and was intimidated by them. Sexually motivated nonetheless, the killer had chosen a non-traditional way to show it — as a voyeur.

When Minisini first looked at the crime scene photographs of Debbie Fream's murder, he was momentarily confused. He saw the stab wound in her chest and the fact that her top was off. Had the killer lifted her top before she died? It could alter his theory about the killer only feeling comfortable with his victims after they were dead. But when Minisini examined the bloodstained windcheater carefully, he noticed a knife cut in the middle corresponding exactly with the stab wound to her chest. His theory still held. The killer had stabbed her first and then, after she was dead, had removed her top.

Looking for an approximate age of the killer, Minisini thought that he would probably be between eighteen and twenty-four. Most serial killers began killing in this age group. In this case, Minisini considered it likely that the killer would be around the same age as his victims; late teens, early twenties. It was unlikely that the killer was older and had killed before because there were no other unsolved murders with the same signature.

Another significant factor of the crimes was the way the killer concealed his victims. It was unlikely that the killer knew the women prior to killing them as the concealment was superficial. In each case he had broken a couple of branches from nearby trees making little attempt to hide the victims. In other words, he only felt it necessary to hide his victims long enough for him to leave the crime scene safely. Elizabeth Stevens was found the day after she was killed and Debbie Fream would also have been had Fred Michelmore checked his paddock as he usually did on a Friday. If a killer made little effort in concealment, it meant he wasn't concerned if the bodies were found. He didn't necessarily want to shock by leaving them in the open, he just wanted to get away safely. He may even have wanted his victims to be found so he could bask in the glory of yet more screaming headlines.

Minisini believed that the killer lived in the Frankston area and that he had most likely been on foot for both the crimes. He wouldn't want to walk any great distance covered in blood and it would be important for him to get home as soon as possible after the murders.

Using a map and marking the spot where Elizabeth Stevens was found as well as the milk bar from which Debbie Fream was taken, the location where her car was dumped, and Taylors Road, Minisini marked an area which was the likely primary location of the killer's home. He figured that the killer would live close to Madden Street where the car was dumped and he marked a triangle on the map from a little south of Madden Street to the freeway exit towards Skye Road. Minisini figured that the killer wouldn't drive the car past the area where he lived; he would pull up short and walk the rest of the way, thus discounting the area of the Frankston-Dandenong Road north of Madden Street. On the other side of the triangle, the Frankston Freeway formed a natural border confining the possible location to a smaller area. A second likely area for him to live was the other side of the freeway closer to Kananook railway station.

Because most of the activity had taken place in the Frankston area, Minisini figured that the killer had been drawn to Langwarrin for either family or business and if he had been stopped or challenged, he would have a reasonable explanation as to why he was in the area. He had killed Elizabeth Stevens because the opportunity had presented itself and, because he would have been covered in blood, he could have used a series of back streets and lanes to make his way back to Frankston. Minisini figured that he would know that area well also because of the unlikelihood of a killer grabbing a victim without a clear idea of where he was going to take her.

Looking at the crimes from such an analytical perspective, Minisini aimed to narrow the pool of suspects. Directing police to be alert to an unemployed man in his late teens or early twenties who lived, possibly alone or not accountable for his time, in the general area near where Debbie Fream's car was found. The advice was only an aid; it wouldn't replace the other investigations but it could be used as a statistical guide. Minisini was careful however, to advise detectives not to discount anyone if they didn't fit the exact profile.

15

Operation Reassurance

FROM the moment Debbie Fream's body was discovered, the media had a field day. To frightened Frankston residents it seemed that every edition of the *Herald Sun* featured yet another aspect of the murders. Not only was the community under siege with a killer in its midst, but it was also under siege from the media. One young man was walking along a street in the Pines Estate in Seaford when a car of journalists slowed down beside him. 'Did you know her?' one yelled out the window. The man ignored them and walked on in disgust.

The fear was palpable and residents were faced with little choice but to lock themselves in their houses and only go out at night if absolutely necessary. Journalists chose young mothers to feature in their articles with titles like 'The Face of Fear,' writing emotively about women whose life styles had been grossly altered in light of the murders.

The media barrage gathered momentum and almost a fortnight after the discovery of Debbie Fream's body, a full page story in the *Herald Sun* cried 'Neighbourhood in the Grip of Terror,' featuring an unnamed mother photographed peering tentatively out through her Venetian blinds. The article began, 'Imagine being so gripped with fear you don't feel safe to walk past your front gate. You are suspicious of every stranger you pass walking down a street you've been down a thousand times before. Feeling on edge, you constantly look over your shoulder at an unfamiliar car driving slowly down your street, you no longer feel safe catching the train, you shelter in your house...' While it made good reading, it did nothing to comfort the residents of Frankston and its surrounding suburbs.

Some people were so afraid that they put their houses up for sale and made immediate plans to leave the area. Real estate agents noticed an immediate drop in sales, rentals and prices. Frankston was not a popular place. Once known for its large shopping malls, its cinemas, restaurants and pubs, it now became the place of the serial killer. Where once neighbours would chat about the mosquito problems or the new McDonalds store in Seaford, they now talked about how the killer had changed their habits and their lives. Where once people would browse over the new releases in the video stores, they now looked sideways at the man browsing down the aisle and wondered: was it him?

Inspector John Noonan was sitting in his small, cluttered upstairs office at the Frankston police station when the phone rang. On the other end of the line, a woman sounded worried. She explained that she had been put through to him because she had been enquiring about personal protection for the women's group she represented. She and her friends, she explained, were terrified in the present climate, and they all wanted to know what they could do to keep themselves safe. John Noonan invited her to come to his office to discuss the issues of concern. When he finished talking to the woman, he telephoned the Frankston mayor, Dennis Shaw and asked him to come to the meeting too.

Later, when the three met, they discussed personal safety and the importance for women to do everything possible not to put themselves at risk. Ideas about martial arts and carrying weapons came up, but John Noonan assured the woman that the best weapon was a scream. If any woman was grabbed, it was best to scream and struggle before anything happened. To give in to a man with a weapon, to go quietly, could spell disaster — especially with this killer. Nobody knew if Elizabeth Stevens or Debbie Fream had put up a fight. As far as the police knew, Roszsa Toth, the only victim to escape the killer, had struggled and screamed and the killer had run away. Weapons, the inspector explained, could be taken from the victim and used against her.

Parking at night in places that were well lit was important as was locking an unattended car and always checking the back seat before you got in. The woman was so impressed with the simple but sensible advice that she suggested John Noonan speak to her group to reassure them as well. The idea was good. There was an obvious need in the community for reassurance and a more public meeting could help quell the growing fears. It was from this hour-long meeting with one concerned woman that Operation Reassurance was born.

John Noonan discussed possible locations for such a public meeting with the mayor and they decided on the Seaford Community Hall.

Going downstairs for a press conference which had been scheduled for that afternoon, Noonan offered the woman the opportunity to announce the public meeting to the bank of television cameras in the foyer. Initially reluctant, she soon saw the importance of the decision that had just been made and agreed to appear on camera.

This was the first time that a meeting of this nature was to be held in Victoria. Then again, it was the first time there had been such a spate of killings.

Chief Superintendent John Balloch returned from an overseas holiday on Sunday 18 July. Planning another week off, he envisaged himself recovering from jet lag with leisure. It was not to be. Telephoning his temporary replacement, Laurie Merrigan, Balloch was briefed about Debbie Fream's murder and the forthcoming public meeting. He returned to work the following day and was briefed further by Rod Wilson and his fellow homicide detectives working from the offices of Taskforce Pulsar at the Frankston police station. Balloch called in mayor Dennis Shaw to discuss the best way to handle the public meeting. From the beginning, the two men decided that it was best to be as candid with the public as possible.

The meeting was held on Wednesday 21 July, John Balloch and Dennis Shaw had envisaged a small public forum to discuss their investigation and public safety. Balloch had wondered that very afternoon whether the meeting would be a fizzer. Eight hundred people turned up to the small venue and another two hundred had to be turned away. A recurring sentiment from the huge crowd was that people felt it necessary to lock themselves in after dark and not go out for any reason. John Balloch tried to explain that those kind of measures were unrealistic. It was safe to walk the main streets in Frankston after dark as long as people stayed in crowded places. It was unsafe to walk around lonely streets at night, but the reality was that it was always unsafe. To the chief superintendent, the huge irony was that many people only thought about personal safety when something like this happened. Security measures such as locking car doors and checking the back seat before you got into a car were things that should be done all the time.

One member of the assembly called for the re-introduction of the death penalty but Balloch explained that it wouldn't help police solve this case and more importantly, it wouldn't stop this killer — he had already killed twice; more victims would mean nothing in that respect.

When Balloch told the assembly that he had all available officers working on the case, one woman stood up and said that she had seen a speed camera on the way to the meeting and asked why the camera operator wasn't helping in the hunt for the killer. Another irony. The road toll in Frankston was twenty-seven in 1993. The killer had killed two victims. The fact escaped the scared crowd that they had more chance of being killed in a car accident than of being murdered. The humble camera operator was trying to save their lives as much as the hundred detectives working on the serial killer case.

It was at this meeting that John Balloch first heard a strange rumour that was spreading at an alarming rate. Someone said that a friend's sister had been shopping and returned to her car to find an old woman sitting in the passenger seat. Apparently the friend's sister had spoken to the old woman before realising that it was in fact a man dressed as a woman. She had run off to get a shopping centre security guard but when they both returned the old 'woman' was gone. The story went that police had fingerprinted the car and the prints belonged to the notorious Mr Cruel. John Balloch assured the woman that he had heard of no such story, but it was one of those rumours which persisted and Balloch felt that the public didn't believe the police denials. He had a strong feeling that people believed that the police were trying to conceal the facts from them.

So huge was the turn-out that another meeting was scheduled for the following day. People attending Wednesday's meeting donated fifteen hundred dollars to the fund set up for baby Jake.

Ten days after the first public meeting, a policewoman telephoned John Balloch at his office and repeated the Mr Cruel story. It too had happened to the elusive 'friend of a friend' and Balloch decided to chase it so it could rest once and for all. He rang the friend who said that it was another friend of a friend and so the chase began. It was always two friends removed but it concerned the chief superintendent that the rumour had gained such force even among police officers. It was always difficult to quell such rumours. The simple fact that the police didn't even have Mr Cruel's fingerprints on file did little to dampen people's enthusiasm for spreading the story.

From the meetings, it became obvious that people needed to be reassured by an increased police presence. Police from surrounding districts were seconded to work in the Frankston area to supply a visible police presence and increased patrols, especially at night. Door knocks were organised and suspect people and vehicles were checked, and all the information was entered into the growing data bank.

16
Corridor of Death

ON 12 December 1876 the decomposed body of 56-year-old Anne Hastings was discovered among ti-trees in Mt Eliza. Her husband William was charged with her murder and went to the gallows protesting his innocence. A year earlier Frankston publican Henry Howard had murdered his business partner Elizabeth Wright and her friend Thomas Harman. Howard had stabbed them both to death, himself going to the gallows without emotion and unrepentant. By the time Anne Hastings was murdered, *The Age* regularly ran long articles entitled, 'The Frankston Murders.' Over a century later, the headlines were the same.

It wasn't long before the media linked up almost every unsolved murder in the peninsula area to the murder of Elizabeth Stevens and Debbie Fream and newspapers began calling Frankston and its surrounding suburbs 'the corridor of death.'

The murders of Allison Rooke, fifty-nine, who disappeared on 30 May 1980 and Joy Summers, fifty-five, who disappeared on 9 October 1981 were once again looked into by both the police and the media. Allison Rooke and Joy Summers both vanished while waiting for buses on the Frankston-Dandenong Road. Allison Rooke's naked body was found on 5 July 1980 in scrub on McClelland Drive in Frankston. Because she had been dead for over a month, pathologists couldn't establish a cause of death. Joy Summers had also been dead over a month when her naked body was found in scrub along Skye Road.

There were seventeen months between the Rooke and Summers murders but in the intervening time, four women had vanished from around Melbourne. Their bodies would later be found buried in scrub land in Tynong North. Bertha Miller was the first victim of the Tynong North killer. Aged seventy-four, she had vanished from Glen Iris on 10 August 1980. Fourteen-year-old Catherine Headland disappeared from a bus stop in Berwick on 28 August 1980. The next victim was eighteen-year-old Ann Marie Sargent who disappeared while hitch-hiking from Cranbourne to Dandenong on 6 October 1980. A month and a half later the final victim, Narumol Stephenson, thirty-four, vanished on 28 November from Brunswick.

In early December, the bodies of Bertha Miller, Catherine Headland and Ann Marie Sargent were found in bushland off Brew Road in Tynong North. The body of Narumol Stephenson wasn't found until February 1983. The killer had dumped her remains adjacent to the Princes Highway in Tynong.

At the time, detectives had followed thousands of leads in an attempt to find the killer. Whether the same killer was responsible for both the Tynong North murders and the killings of Allison Rooke and Joy Summers, was still a mystery but police lost no time interviewing suspects from the earlier investigations when bodies of young women began appearing in Frankston over a decade later.

More recently was the Sarah McDiarmid disappearance and the unsolved murder of Michelle Brown. Sarah McDiarmid disappeared from the Kananook railway station on 11 July 1990. Her body had never been found although a pool of blood near her car led detectives to believe she had been murdered. On 1 March 1992, Michelle Brown had telephoned her mother from the Food Plus store on Frankston Dandenong Road asking to be picked up from the Frankston railway station at 8 pm. When her mother arrived, Michelle was nowhere to be seen. Her naked body was found two weeks later in a shed behind a gun shop in Playne Street, Frankston.

Sarah McDiarmid was the most likely to be connected to the murders of Elizabeth Stevens and Debbie Fream. She was around the same age as the latest victims and she had disappeared from a railway station. Sarah McDiarmid had never been found but if the same killer was responsible, he could have been lucky in the disposal of her body. Elizabeth Stevens and Debbie Fream had been dumped with little attempt to hide them. It was likely that if the same killer was responsible, he would have made no greater an attempt to hide her body, but he may have hidden it in a place that wasn't searched. But only the killer knew for sure.

17

The Peninsula Country Club

THE Long Island golf club opened in December 1937. Its neighbour, the Peninsula golf club, was known as the millionaire's club and it catered to Frankston's early elite residents who wished to live in quality rural homes in a seaside setting.

In 1993 Norman White was the security manager of the Peninsula Country Club in Skye Road. Having worked at the club for five years, his duties included patrolling the club house, the golf course and the boundaries of the property.

The boundary fence line of the golf club was mainly cyclone wire, part of it adjoining the Pines housing estate and the other part adjacent to Monterey Technical School. A bike track ran along one of its borders down to Monterey Tech, separating it from the adjoining Long Island Country Golf Club.

Norman White inspected the fences most days, sometimes in his four-wheel drive and sometimes on foot, depending on the weather. The western boundary adjacent to the bike track usually presented the most problems. Vandals frequently cut through the cyclone wire to gain access to the golf club grounds, often to vandalise club equipment. It was part of his job to note any damage to the fences and report it immediately for repairs. The track was mostly used as a shortcut by kids from John Paul College who lived in the Pines estate and students from Monterey Tech.

The track was overgrown on both sides by overhanging trees pushing against the wire mesh and its dirt path quickly turned to a series of muddy puddles whenever it rained.

On Thursday 29 July, White carried out his regular inspection late in the afternoon, patrolling the southern and western boundaries. He could see the Long Island Country Golf Club fence line as well as his own and although he noticed a three metre wide hole had been cut in the Long Island fence, the Peninsula fence was intact.

Caught up with other duties, White was unable to patrol the fence line the following day — Friday 30 July.

18

A Schoolgirl Disappears

RIDING her Australia Post motorbike slowly down the footpath adjacent to Skye Road on Friday 30 July, a postwoman was delivering mail along her normal daily route. She had started work at six that morning and her shift was nearing its end. It was around half past two in the afternoon.

From the footpath, the postie noticed a car that in normal circumstances she would probably have ignored, but in Frankston in July 1993 with newspapers screaming headlines about the serial killer, every car — not to mention almost every man — was suspicious. The post officer wasn't the only woman in the community to be looking over her shoulder.

The car was an old, rusted, yellow Toyota Corona and it didn't have a front or a back number plate. But what caused feelings of unease in the woman was the fact that a man wearing a dark coloured cap was sitting slouched down in the driver's seat. She noticed that the man's arms were folded and he seemed to be looking down Skye Road. When she passed him, the man looked over at her and seemed to slouch down even further until the top of his head was level with the top of the steering wheel. In the current climate of fear, this man was definitely suspicious.

The postie was so suspicious, in fact, that she brought her motorbike to a halt, deciding to go into the nearest house to telephone the police. Just as she turned into a nearby driveway, she saw a schoolgirl crossing Skye Road and continuing along towards the bike track.

Knocking on a front door, the postie asked to use a telephone. The owners of the house recognised her by sight and quickly acceded to her request. She explained the circumstances and told the home owner that it was part of her job to report any suspicious things she saw while delivering the mail.

The postie spoke to an officer at D-24 and told him about the yellow car and the man with a chubby face sitting in it. The officer told her that he would send a car around to check it out.

Natalie Russell left John Paul College at the end of fifth period around 2.30 pm on Friday. She wanted to get home early to do some reading for school. Natalie was an attractive girl with long dark hair and large expressive brown-green eyes. Into her third term of year twelve, she had spent most of the day at school with her friend Carly and the two had chatted between classes about the weekend. During biology, Natalie had been bored. She wrote a two page letter to a friend saying that her parents were going to Sydney for a week, leaving the following Monday. She wrote enthusiastically about the diet she was about to start and perhaps even some aerobics classes. She wondered if she would stick to her guns, but she hoped to because she had convinced another friend to diet with her and they could both encourage each other.

After class, Natalie told Carly that she intended staying home that night to study. There was only a couple of months left of VCE and the pressure was on. Natalie also mentioned the geography excursion on Monday. She told Carly that she was looking forward to it.

Her final period for the week had been religion and she had spent a little while in the library finishing an English essay before heading out the school gates. As she left, she waved to a bunch of boys she knew. Although she usually rode her bike, she was walking home today because it had rained that morning and her mother had given her a ride to school. Although Natalie was a fit young woman who rode her bike everywhere and played netball, she had earlier grumbled to Carly about the prospect of walking home. It was a cold, wet day and her bag, filled with study books, weighed a ton.

Many students at John Paul College had stopped riding to school since the killings had begun. Bikes were swapped for the relative safety of cars and buses. Some had bought hand-held alarms after the school had warned them about personal safety. But the serial killer was far from the minds of the students as they headed home for the weekend.

Natalie wore her tartan school skirt and dark blue school jumper with its red crest, specially designed for year twelve students. The logo read: John Paul College, With Him is the Fullness of Life. She walked down McMahons Road and crossed Skye road, heading towards the bike track she regularly used as a quick way home — failing to heed the principal's warning two days earlier at the school assembly when he had told them it would be safer to avoid the bike track until the killer was caught. However, the track was straight and, apart from some overgrown trees, visible from both ends, and local kids had continued to use it.

Walking across the road, Natalie was seen by two other John Paul College students chatting on the opposite side of the road to the bike track entrance. They had both seen the dirty, yellow car parked near the entrance to the track and they both watched Natalie disappear past the car and up along the track. They had no reason to suspect that Natalie had only minutes to live and that they would be the last people to see her alive — apart of course, from her killer.

Working his second day of duty on Operation Reassurance in the Frankston area, Sergeant Richard Brown had patrolled the suburbs since eleven that morning. The directive from homicide detective Rod Wilson was to 'show the flag' by providing a visible police presence. Nobody really considered that the day shifts would come up with anything because Elizabeth Stevens and Debbie Fream had both been murdered at night but the public needed visible reassurance. Ironically, Brown had noticed a distinct anti-police feeling whilst on patrol and it was obvious to him that some members of the public viewed the extra police presence as an intrusion.

The previous day, Brown had worked with an officer who had grown up in the Frankston area who had shown him many of the out of the way places such as the virtual labyrinth of paths and tracks connecting many of the main roads, used mainly by school kids. He had checked many cars and recorded their registration numbers on his running sheet which, if required, would help provide detectives with a list of vehicles in any given area.

Working with Constable Joseph Aiello who had just graduated from the police academy, Brown was being especially thorough showing the new recruit the ropes of checking and listing suspect vehicles.

Earlier in the day, Brown and Aiello had driven into the carpark of the Flora and Fauna Reserve in Langwarrin and seen a yellow Toyota Corona with no registration plates, although a closer check revealed the Roads Corporation registration receipt affixed to the front windscreen on the passenger side.

Used in the past as a training ground for army reserve soldiers, the reserve was dotted with foxholes which over the years had filled with heavy native foliage. Paths wound around the area and it was popular area for joggers who could complete a five kilometre run within the confines of the reserve. When the army reserves stopped using the park for training, it was renamed the Flora and Fauna Reserve, attracting a surprising number of visitors.

The carpark was busy considering its out of the way location on McClelland Drive in Langwarrin and Brown had checked it half a dozen times during his patrols. There was no-one in the yellow Toyota so Brown noted the vehicle on his running sheet and radioed an 'if listed' check to D-24 to see if it was listed as stolen. D-24 responded that it wasn't listed.

A couple of other calls to suspect loiterers had proved to be merely people delivering pamphlets, so Brown and Aiello kept patrolling. Just after 3 pm they had been following a car to Skye Road when a D-24 call came over the radio to check a suspect person in a vehicle parked on Skye Road. Brown radioed that he would do the check since he was only minutes away. When they arrived, the two officers saw the yellow Toyota Corona and recognised it as the same vehicle they had checked earlier at the Flora and Fauna Reserve. Again, the car was empty.

Looking through the window, Brown could see a red Dolphin torch on the front passenger seat lying next to a pair of sunglasses and a screwdriver. The general interior of the car was dirty and messy. Earlier, Brown had noticed a plastic shopping bag containing two loaves of bread. It was now gone. There was an old portable radio cassette player which appeared to be wired to the dashboard.

Considering the possibility that the driver of this car was visiting a nearby house, the two officers checked the five closest homes to where the car was parked. They questioned each occupant until one woman told the officers that she had seen a man dressed in black walk up towards a house with a high fence. She thought he had gone in through the gate. Since it was possible the man could be a burglar, Brown and Aiello checked each front and rear yard in case the man had entered surreptitiously. Back at the yellow Toyota Corona, a local council officer from Frankston stopped and spoke to the police officers. He told them he had driven past around 2 pm and the car hadn't been there then. The two officers walked around the adjoining streets and saw a man dressed in black. They questioned him and found out that he lived in the house with the high fence.

Brown thanked him and checked one more house. A woman told him that she had seen the car earlier and a man had got out and opened the bonnet to look at the motor. When he finished, he had walked off but she couldn't tell the officers which direction the man had taken. Sergeant Brown looked under the car at the front and saw a small puddle of water and assumed that the radiator or the hoses were leaking and the car had broken down.

Looking across Skye Road, Brown saw the entrance to the bike track and was considering walking its length when a call came over the radio that an armed robbery had taken place in nearby Carrum Downs. Brown radioed for a divisional van from Frankston to patrol the area around Skye Road to look for the driver of the yellow Toyota. He didn't really consider that the driver had gone down the bike track; there were hundreds of kids leaving John Paul College and walking along Skye Road. The area was extremely busy. The yellow car and the bike track faded from his mind as he and Aiello raced to the scene of the armed robbery.

A little over half an hour after Natalie Russell walked into the entrance of the bike track, a fifteen-year-old schoolboy named Simon rode his bike down the same path. Three-quarters of the way along the track, Simon noticed a black shoe lying in the middle of the path. He slowed down to take a closer look; it was almost exactly like one of his sister's, with silver metal on the side and silver lace holes. The afternoon sun shone on the silver making it glint. But the shoe wasn't his sister's so he kept riding. He did however notice the shoe's position; it lay next to a large hole in the cyclone wire fence of the golf course.

A couple of minutes after Simon rode down the bike track, a thirteen-year-old boy named Sam also entered the track from Skye Road. About halfway along, he saw a man walking towards him. The man was walking quickly and Sam felt, rather than saw, the man looking at him.

Out of the corner of his eye, Sam watched the man, who had his hands thrust deep in his pockets. A vague feeling of unease came over the young teenager. He thought that the man approaching was somehow trying to act natural. If anything happened, thought Sam, no-one would hear. The area was then deserted. Luckily the man hurried past him without speaking. Sam caught a look at the man's face as he passed, more through fear than simple curiosity. The man was big and sort of fat. He was wearing a black top and dark pants. He had dark hair. After he passed, Sam turned around and looked back at the man who kept his head down and continued walking. Sam walked a little quicker trying to shake the uneasy feeling he had.

Natalie Russell's family reported her missing around eight in the evening. Her mother Carmel couldn't understand where her daughter could be. As the mother of four children of her own as well as two stepchildren, she didn't panic when Natalie was a bit late from school, but considering the pervading community fear, Carmel went over the morning in her mind. She had driven Natalie and her brother, Damien to John Paul College at quarter past eight. Just before they had left home Natalie had told her that she might go into Frankston after school. But when Carmel had dropped her daughter off, Natalie had said she might just walk straight home from school.

Carmel hadn't really taken much notice but in hindsight it sounded like Natalie had changed her mind about going into Frankston and that she would have been coming straight home. Carmel had driven past John Paul College at 2.40 pm on her way home from shopping and had looked out for Natalie but figured that if her daughter had finished at 2.30 pm, she had missed her by five or ten minutes. Carmel had half expected a phone call from Natalie around three o'clock asking for a ride home but when she didn't hear from her, she assumed that her seventeen-year-old had changed her mind and gone to Frankston after all.

Not long after, Damien came home from school and Carmel drove him to football training, returning to collect him just before six o'clock. They called into McDonalds on the way home and bought an easy tea.

Ten minutes after she arrived home with her son, Carmel heard a bus go past their house. She looked to see if Natalie was among the passengers getting off, but she wasn't. Before long, Carmel really started to worry. Natalie always telephoned her if she planned to be home after dark and it was dark now. Damien offered to check the bike track to see if his sister was there. When Carmel disagreed, Damien said, 'But she could have fallen over and hurt herself, Mum.'

When Natalie's father Brian arrived home at 6.45 pm, Carmel voiced her concerns. Brian volunteered to drive to Frankston and have a look for his daughter; he had some errands to run so he told his wife he would keep an eye out for her. Carmel telephoned her daughter Janine in Sydney and told her that Natalie was late home. Janine was worried. She knew her sister hated to worry their mother and it was unlike her to be late. Carmel mentioned the trip to Sydney planned for the following Monday. She and Brian were leaving Natalie and Damien home by themselves. Natalie had jokingly threatened to have a party while her parents were away, but Carmel knew she wouldn't.

Looking out for the 7.15 pm bus, Carmel heard it coming up the road and went outside, but it passed without stopping. She rang Natalie's aunt, Pat Smith and told her that she was worried. Pat agreed that it was unlike her niece not to let her parents know where she was. When Brian got home ten minutes later, Carmel insisted they call the police.

At the Frankston police station, the Russell's call to report their daughter missing was taken very seriously. The missing persons report was passed on to all the officers working Operation Reassurance.

Sergeant Phil Atkins from the protective security group had been working Operation Reassurance for two weeks. He was the supervising sergeant for the other PSG members who had also been assigned temporary duties as part of the operation. Atkins sent two of his men immediately to the Russell's home in the Pines estate. He told them to get a full description of the girl, a list of any places she could possibly be and an idea of her character — was she the type to be late home or go to visit a friend?

A short time later, the two officers arrived at the Russell house and spoke to Carmel and Brian. It looked serious and they telephoned Inspector Ron Cooke at the Frankston police station. As the duty officer for that shift, it was Cooke's responsibility to co-ordinate the search for the missing schoolgirl.

Inspector Cooke sent Phil Atkins over to the Russell house to evaluate the situation. Carmel Russell had already given the officers a school photograph of her daughter. Natalie had been captured on film half blinking, but the photo was a recent likeness. When Atkins arrived, he questioned Mr and Mrs Russell again.

'Nat always rings me to let me know where she is.' Carmel Russell looked the police officer straight in the eye. 'She knows how much I always worry about her. I know that if she could get to a phone and ring me, she would.'

The worried parents stressed over and over that not only did Natalie always ring to let them know where she was, she was always home before dark. If she had gone into Frankston with friends, she would have been home by six o'clock.

Following correct procedure, it was essential to establish whether Natalie had come home, changed and gone out again. Atkins went outside and shone his powerful torch around the front and back yard to see if he could find Natalie's school bag anywhere. Finding nothing, he went back inside and asked Mrs Russell to check Natalie's bedroom to see if any of her clothes were missing. The four police officers and the Russells found no sign that Natalie had been home and left again and Atkins became really concerned when he saw how worried Natalie's parents were.

The first thing to be done was to establish the route Natalie would have taken from John Paul College. Carmel Russell told the officers that Natalie was walking home because she had driven her that morning. She would probably take the short cut along the bike track. Phil Atkins knew the bike track well from his years working at Frankston before transferring to the PSG. It was one of many possibilities to be checked.

The Russell family were stricken with fear. Uniformed police officers in their living room made their daughter's disappearance real. The officers left them to wait while they went to search for Natalie.

Back at the Frankston police station, Inspector Ron Cooke was also treating Natalie Russell's disappearance seriously. It was distressingly similar to that of Elizabeth Stevens. Neither girl was the type to disappear without letting her family know where she was and both had been on their way home from school; both girls had disappeared on a Friday.

Cooke telephoned Chief Superintendent John Balloch, who had only been home half an hour, and told him that another young woman had gone missing. For the chief superintendent, the news was alarming. His district was in terror and he had all available officers working gruelling hours to catch the killer. The media would go wild; indeed hours earlier, it had — with a third body. Balloch had been in his office that morning when Frankston mayor Dennis Shaw had telephoned asking about a third body. Balloch denied the rumour but the phone calls persisted. Was there a third body in Frankston? Balloch kept saying no. Finally, he was informed that a third body had indeed been found but in this case, it had no bearing on the recent spate of killings.

As the story unfolded through a series of telephone calls, Balloch found out that a body of a young woman had been found on a property in Mt Eliza early in June. Apparently, a young woman had been reported missing three years earlier by her family in Perth. Questioned at the time, her boyfriend told detectives that he had dropped her off at Melbourne airport and hadn't seen her since. Another man in Mt Eliza had been questioned initially, but failed to mention that he was storing some things belonging to the woman's boyfriend while he moved to the United States. Looking into the case again, detectives questioned the friend a second time. He casually mentioned that the boyfriend had left a barrel of computer parts in his garage. Homicide detectives made their way to Mt Eliza.

Enclosed in a barrel of lime, detectives found the body of the missing woman. They made a decision to keep the find secret: if the boyfriend returned from the United States of his own volition, detectives would have a good chance of picking him up for questioning. However, if the news became public, the young man could disappear and might not be found. But keeping a body secret in Frankston in July 1993 was virtually impossible. While John Balloch was overseas, his temporary replacement had been informed of the find, but Debbie Fream was murdered shortly afterwards and in the confusion, he had forgotten to mention the body in the barrel to his boss. John Balloch then had to telephone all the people who had enquired and tell them that there was indeed a body but it wasn't connected. It had been a very difficult day and now the news of another woman going missing — a seventeen-year-old student — made him despair at the problem he and his officers faced. He waited by the phone for further news, feeling that somehow he had let the community down.

When the officers reported back from the Russell house, Inspector Cooke radioed for the police helicopter to begin an aerial search of the area. He also called in the mounted branch. The search began as Phil Atkins and Ron Cooke drove to the John Paul College in McMahons Road. Cooke requested the SES to provide a command post at the school as well as lighting.

Knocking on the door of a house on the college grounds, Phil Atkins spoke to two nuns who lived there. He asked them if they had seen Natalie Russell. They hadn't but they were able to tell Atkins the names of some of Natalie's friends who the sergeant telephoned from the house. It wasn't long before Atkins found out about a party that many of the year twelve students had gone to. One of the senior officers at Frankston went personally to check the party but Natalie Russell wasn't there.

Atkins asked the nuns to remain inside their house while Inspector Cooke called in the dog squad to make a check of the area. The police dogs were so well trained that they could detect a person — living or dead — better than a group of twenty officers searching. Steve Smith arrived at the school together with his Rottweiler, and began the search. The dog found no traces of anyone in the school grounds.

Atkins then radioed for four units to backtrack from the school to the Russell's home and two units to check all the pubs and wine bars in the Seaford, Frankston and Langwarrin areas. The bike track also needed to be looked at for any signs that Natalie may have walked down there. The track was bordered on both sides by cyclone wire fences which Atkins knew were often cut or broken. Atkins and Cooke discussed the situation with Brian McMannis, the head of the State Emergency Services who had been celebrating his birthday at a Frankston restaurant when he received the call. They asked him to send a couple of SES members down the track. They were to pay close attention to any breaks in the fence and report on how thick the bushes were on either side for a line search to begin as soon as possible.

Inspector Cooke spoke to two members from the mounted branch who had arrived earlier and directed them to join the search of the track and the golf courses. Their advantage of height on horseback could aid in spotting something which might otherwise be missed.

Brian McMannis dispatched two SES volunteers to make a cursory search of the bike track.

19

The Bike Track

ROY Stevens, a volunteer with the State Emergency Service, had been paged to the SES headquarters at 9.55 pm on Friday evening. He arrived around a half hour later and immediately boarded one of the SES vehicles heading for the command post at John Paul College. On arrival, little time was wasted. Stevens was instructed to check the bike track between the Peninsula and the Long Island golf clubs for a missing seventeen-year-old John Paul College student. He and a fellow SES officer, David Male, set off with their powerful torches.

Although technically wide enough for a car to travel its length, the bike track was so overgrown with trees pushing against the wire fences on each side that travel was only possible on a bike or on foot. Bracing themselves against the cold and the rain, the two men began the long walk up the dirt track.

Stevens searched the right hand side of the track, while Male searched the left. They had both been told to pay particular attention to areas where the fence had holes or gaps. About halfway along the track, Stevens saw the first of a number of the holes in the fence and he and his partner climbed through it and began to search in the text-book circular way. They found nothing and returned to the main track. At another gap, both men shone their torches through the fence only to see vegetation so thick it would have been impossible for anyone to get through. They continued on.

Further down, Male and Stevens found a third hole in the cyclone wire. They climbed through and began searching again. Almost immediately, Stevens's torch beam illuminated a pair of legs wearing what looked like black tights. He moved a little closer and saw a young woman lying on her side. He could see her left hand facing palm up. It was smeared with blood. He couldn't see her face, only the back of her head. He took a couple of steps back and yelled to his partner in a voice that betrayed his shock, 'Come over here, have a look at this. I think I've found something!'

David Male pushed through the scrub to where Stevens was standing and stared down at the girl's body. The two men were horrified. They were volunteers and, unlike police, their experience of finding dead bodies was limited. Both men quickly scrambled out through the hole in the fence. Understandably, neither wanted to stay alone while the other went to summon help. The worst fears of all the searchers had been realised — there was some sort of maniac on the loose and the two had just seen first-hand the results of his work. They headed quickly towards a pair of flashing torches they could see on the golf course. Responding to their calls, two police officers from the mounted branch rode over.

Senior Constable Cynthia Cameron checked the time. It was 10.45 pm when Stevens and Male called to her and her partner Helen Seymour. They had been searching the golf course on horseback for around forty-five minutes. Cynthia Cameron asked her partner to hold her mount while she followed the two SES workers into the bushes to confirm their find. She saw the black-stockinged legs and the body through the cover of the bushes and immediately radioed for senior officers to attend. The time was 10.54 pm and the body had been found.

Phil Atkins was at the command post at John Paul College directing officers in the search when the call came over the radio.

'Someone's calling you and it's urgent,' he was told.

Atkins grabbed the radio.

'Could we have assistance at our location urgently,' said the breathless voice, describing the location on the bike track.

Inspector Cooke was talking to members of the homicide squad on the mobile phone in the command post caravan when Phil Atkins ran in and grabbed him by the jacket. Cooke almost threw the phone down and raced with Atkins to a police car. They drove to the scene using the Monterey Technical School entrance.

'What have you got?' asked the sergeant over the radio en route, praying that the searchers had made a mistake.

'We don't know whether it's a mannequin or not,' came the reply. But Atkins knew that mannequins were not dumped in the scrub — bodies were.

Cooke and Atkins looked at each other. They both knew.

Atkins was angry. *Right under our goddamned noses*, he thought.

Hundreds of police officers had been patrolling the Frankston area and it seemed that the killer had sailed right through them to kill again. Atkins thought of the officers he had sent out searching just after Natalie Russell had been reported missing; they hadn't complained, in fact they had been unusually silent, grabbing their kits and hitting the road as soon as their orders came through. There had been no dinner breaks, no coffee breaks, no-one had wanted to waste a minute. Now he knew that the missing school girl wouldn't be found alive.

Parking the police car in the school grounds adjacent to the tennis courts, Cooke and Atkins hurried through the rain down the muddy path of the bike track to the area where the SES volunteers waited. They were both shaking and Atkins knew that the freezing temperature had little to do with it. They were probably both in shock.

The sergeant shone his torch at the hole cut in the cyclone wire. His breath fogged in the torch beam and he had to turn his head slightly so as not to reduce his visibility. He ducked through the fence and made his way through the bent branches. He hoped fervently that the SES workers had made a mistake but a couple of metres in he saw a school bag and further along was the crumpled figure dressed in a school uniform lying face down in the dirt under a canopy of ti-trees. He swore loudly, breaking the eerie silence of the freezing winter's night.

Atkins was careful not to get too close and he didn't touch the schoolgirl's body but he had to make sure she was dead. Shining the torch in the direction of her head, he could see the vivid red colour of blood washed through her thick black hair. From that angle, it looked to Atkins as if she had been bludgeoned to death. In the torchlight, no steam was visible from her nose or mouth to indicate she was breathing. Her black tights were ripped and her hands bore the defence wounds common to victims who had fought with their attackers. Around her feet, dirt had been kicked into piles and Atkins knew the struggle had been violent. The words 'killing field' came into his mind. Next to him, Inspector Cooke too stared down at the victim. Overhead, the police helicopter arrived, shining its powerful night sun along the area of the bike track. It had been called in earlier to assist in the search and now its light was utilised on the crime scene.

Atkins pressed the button down on his portable radio. 'Our worst fears have been realised; notify the members of the taskforce.' Atkins also asked D-24 to organise for the command post to be moved to the carpark of Monterey Technical School. Ron Cooke telephoned Chief

Superintendent John Balloch to tell him that they had found the missing schoolgirl, dead.

Everyone knew instinctively that it was the same killer and everyone wanted him caught. The terrible tragedy was that for the police to get enough evidence to catch him, more women had to die. The first two murders had turned up no forensic evidence of any value and Phil Atkins hoped that this time the killer had slipped up and that this scene would provide the clues needed to identify him. It became his job to guard the immediate area. Inspector Cooke organised other officers to guard both entrances to the bike track and set a media point — he knew that it wouldn't be long before they caught wind of this latest murder over their police scanners.

Phil Atkins remained outside the hole in the fence while other officers converged on the scene. He was wearing a police issue white raincoat over his leather jacket but in the confusion immediately following the find, he had left his police hat in the car and he was soon soaked through by the persistent drizzling rain. The weather was freezing cold as Atkins remained at his solitary post and he was thankful for the police helicopter hovering perfectly still directly above him. The jet wash from the powerful engines was forced downwards in warm gusts which almost stopped his teeth from chattering.

Atkins thought about the girl's final moments. Was her death swift or did her killer torment her? She must have known. The media had focussed daily on the Fream murder. Information caravans had been set up in both the Frankston and Seaford areas and nobody in either suburb and indeed all of Melbourne had missed the image of Debbie Fream as a new mother lying in a hospital bed proudly holding her newborn son. What must Natalie Russell have thought when she was grabbed?

She must have known.

The Russell family were 'lucky' in one sense — they didn't have to go through the agonising four day wait experienced by the family of Debbie Fream. At least for Natalie Russell's family and friends the period of agonising limbo would soon be over. Eight hours between disappearance and discovery was a small blessing.

Atkins knew that the killer was getting a taste for blood. Where was he when the police were hurrying to the scene? Was he at home watching television? Sitting with a wife? Children? Was he like an animal fresh from the kill? Was he dreaming in ecstasy about her cries, her blood? Probably. Did he feel any remorse? Probably not.

Out of the darkness, Atkins made out a figure walking across the marshy school grounds. He shone his torch onto a teenager coming towards the bike track. Inspector Cooke also saw the figure and sent two detectives to get her. From his post, Atkins was furious at the danger the girl had put herself in by walking alone at night. He yelled out to her that a girl had just been murdered and what on earth was she doing here. 'What killer?' the girl called back. The detectives took the girl to the command post and questioned her thoroughly about what she was doing out on her own. The girl told them that she was on her way home so Cooke organised for her to be escorted.

Sergeant Mick Barry arrived at work an hour early for his 11 pm shift. Before he entered the Frankston police complex, two colleagues having a 'smoko' at the back entrance waved him over.

'Another one's gone missing, mate,' one of the men told the sergeant. 'Walking home from John Paul College. Just a school kid.'

'God, this place is going to be jumping,' said the other, voicing the opinion of all three officers. The public fear was almost tangible. Seconded from CIBs all over Melbourne to assist in investigations and door-knocks around the area, Frankston police station had almost two hundred detectives working on the murders.

The three police officers discussed the disappearance of the seventeen-year-old student. The details were sketchy but they considered the possibility that she had merely gone shopping or to visit friends without letting her family know. They didn't know much about her.

Inside the station, more police officers were discussing the disappearance. It didn't look good.

The senior sergeant in charge of the station, Peter Bull, was also on duty that night shift. He was gearing up to join the search, handing out photocopies of the photograph of the missing girl to all the cars and vans heading out to look for her.

Minutes later an officer entered the duty sergeant's office.

'They've found her and she's dead,' he announced emotionlessly.

His colleagues looked at him and for a moment thought he was joking. But they soon knew he wasn't when senior officers began rushing into the office grabbing hats, coats and kits before heading for their respective cars.

Mick Barry and his partner did likewise; they rushed to their police car, screeching their tyres on the concrete as they emerged from the basement carpark. They didn't use lights and sirens; they weren't advertising this one.

Mick Barry's partner radioed D-24 for the location of the body find. Such details over the radio were coded so as to not give information to those listening in with radio scanners. The last thing investigators needed was an hysterical audience.

En route to Silvertop Drive, Sergeant Barry was informed via police radio that he was to help set up a command post in the back carpark of the school. His car was the eighth police vehicle at the scene. As they pulled up, Barry's partner dropped the photo of Natalie Russell onto the back seat saying, 'Guess we don't need this any more.'

More members of the State Emergency Service arrived at the same time as Sergeant Barry and his partner and set up powerful lights illuminating the carpark area adjacent to the school's two tennis courts. Down the track, they saw the police helicopter maintaining a perfect hover over the crime scene.

Police swarmed around the area, but only a few ventured down the narrow path behind the tennis courts to where the young woman's body lay. The area had become a crime scene and homicide detectives were on their way. Evidence must be protected, hence the girl's body lay alone in the icy night with a light drizzle of rain falling down upon her — the sensation of which she was no longer capable of feeling. Her seventeen and a half years on earth had ended in this lonely place.

Detective Sergeant Tony Jay was working a district response shift from Springvale when the call came through that the missing schoolgirl had been found murdered. He and his partner raced to the scene to offer their assistance. When Jay arrived, he learned that nobody had made a physical description of the crime scene. In order to begin investigating, detectives needed to know as much about the nature of the crime as possible. Jay spoke to Inspector John Noonan and the two decided to view the scene. They walked down the bike track to where Phil Atkins stood.

Following John Noonan, Jay crouched through the cut wire and made his way down the narrow corridor of foliage to the body. Noonan dictated a description of the victim, while Jay scribbled it in his notebook:

Blue jumper
Black tights

Skirt — green/blue check
    — maroon stripes
    — lifted up to waist
Tights not disarranged
Jumper lifted up to expose shirt
On right hand side, left arm twisted up
Blood on left hand
Right arm to side, hand up
Blue/grey long sleeve shirt
No shoes
Left leg folded back
Right leg outstretched under left leg
Damage to rear of hand
Tear on left stocking on thigh

Time almost stood still for the officers standing under the ti-tree canopy, discussing how the schoolgirl met her death. They didn't touch her or disturb the scene and they too thought that she may have been bludgeoned or bashed because of the blood in her hair. They couldn't see her face at all.

Tony Jay had been a uniformed officer at Frankston when Bertha Miller and Joy Summers were murdered in the early 1980s and as he walked out through the wire fence, he thought of all the suspects interviewed back then and wondered if this killer was anyone he had come across before.

Jay arranged to speak to SES member Roy Stevens who had found the body. Two hours after shining his torch on the dead schoolgirl, Stevens was still shaking and emotional. Jay realised that he must have been suffering from shock.

At 12.40 am a briefing was held in the woodwork classroom and the detectives all gathered to listen to Inspector Noonan bring them up to date. Knowledge of the cause of death was limited to what Noonan and Jay had seen earlier. They were reasonably certain that the body was that of Natalie Russell. Tasks were allocated and Jay met up with an old workmate, Detective Colin Clark. The two discussed the murder and Jay asked Clark, who had worked on the Stevens murder, what the similarities were. But before the cause of death in this case was identified, any discussion of similarities with the first two murders was merely educated guessing.

Crime scene examiners Sergeant Brian Gamble and Senior

Constable Tony Kealy arrived at Monterey Technical School just after 1 am. Kealy was a local and it was difficult for him to witness yet another young woman's body. He had searched the area surrounding Taylors Road where Debbie Fream's body had been discovered and now he had to look down on another victim of the same killer.

For Gamble and Kealy, the first job was to work out how far the crime scene extended in order to plan the methodical and slow search for evidence. Walking up the bike track, the two crime scene examiners noted the holes in the cyclone wire fence which the SES searchers had seen earlier. They also noticed blood around the hole through which the body had been found.

Measuring and recording the dimensions of each of the holes, Gamble and Kealy then focussed their attention on the hole near where the body had been found. It showed signs of being recently cut. Brian Gamble carefully cut samples of the wire for evidence. If a suspect was caught, the cuts could often be matched by forensic experts to pliers or wire cutters just as certainly as fingerprints could be matched to a particular person.

Using a small jar of distilled water and a tiny piece of sterile gauze, Gamble held the gauze with a pair of tweezers and moistened it before rubbing it carefully over the blood stain on the pole supporting the wire fence. He wiped the blood off the pole and then sealed the gauze for evidence. Tests would show whether the blood was from Natalie Russell or her killer.

Regarding the area immediately surrounding the body of the schoolgirl, the two crime scene examiners decided that it shouldn't be examined before dawn. There could be fibres or other pieces of minute evidence that could be lost in the dark if the police were in too much of a hurry. They also decided not to bring the SES lights into the crime scene area; any additional human traffic would contaminate it unnecessarily. Drizzling rain presented a potential problem, but Kealy judged that it was light enough to not disturb the ti-tree covered crime scene. He discussed this with homicide detectives who agreed to wait. Before the sun rose, Gamble and Kealy concentrated their efforts on the bike track itself.

The helicopter stayed until it had just enough fuel to get back to Essendon airport and then it flew away leaving Phil Atkins with the eerie silence and darkness that he had first noticed. He stayed for four hours until he was relieved at 3 am to return to the relative warmth of the command post.

As many of the police officers left to interview people, Natalie Russell lay dead all night alone under the ti-trees while rain drizzled around her in a gentle mist in the eerie silence.

20

The Long Night

CONSTABLE Angela Butts was working an 11 pm shift out of Frankston police station. When she arrived at work, the station was buzzing with the news of the body find. Teaming up with Senior Sergeant Peter Bull, the two raced to the Monterey Technical School where they were told that the body was that of a schoolgirl. It was impossible to get a positive ID because she was lying face down and she wouldn't be moved until daylight when crime scene and forensic officers could make a more thorough examination of the scene.

Inspector Ron Cooke made the decision to notify the Russell family before they heard the news that a body had been found through the media. Cooke, Peter Bull and Angela Butts made the short drive to the modest home in the Pines estate. Angela Butts didn't know quite what to expect. A new police officer, barely three months out of the police academy, she knew that the Pines estate had a tough reputation. She wondered what the family would be like.

Carmel Russell greeted the officers and led them into the lounge room. They stood before the worried mother, hats in hand and told her that a body had been discovered along the bike track.

'Is it female?' Carmel asked in her quiet voice.

'Yes, I'm afraid it is,' answered Inspector Cooke.

'Is she wearing a school uniform?'

'Yes,' the inspector nodded sadly.

Carmel Russell considered the information for a moment and looked squarely at the officers. 'It can't be Nat,' she told them. 'Nat is too strong, she would never let anyone kill her. She would fight or run away. No, no, it can't be Nat.'

The officers exchanged glances as the distraught mother completely dismissed the possibility. Peter Bull was almost certain that the body would be that of Natalie Russell, and he decided to leave Angela Butts at the house until further news came through. As they left to return to the crime scene, Peter Bull told Angela to answer the phone in case the media tried to call, and to keep an eye out for reporters if they should start knocking on the door. If there were any problems, she was to use her police radio to call them at the crime scene.

Angela Butts evaluated Mrs Russell as the two women settled themselves on the couch in the warm lounge room. The young police officer was impressed. Slight in build, the fair haired woman showed a strength not always seen under such circumstances. Not that Angela had any experience with this kind of thing. The police academy had taught her procedure, then she had spent four weeks on a booze bus, two weeks directing traffic and two weeks at driving school. She had not even done a death notification and now she sat in the lounge room with a woman whose daughter may have just been murdered by a vicious serial killer.

'There's no way it's Natalie,' Carmel Russell told Angela. 'She's too clever.'

Angela Butts knew enough about grief to realise that denial was the first stage. The mother sitting opposite her would refuse to believe that her daughter was dead until the body was identified.

Carmel's husband Brian sat quietly in another chair while his wife did most of the talking. Carmel told Angela what Natalie was like and how popular she was, her face occasionally lighting up in a radiant smile as she recalled some of the funny things Natalie had done.

Noticing a beautiful bunch of flowers, the policewoman asked whose they were. Carmel said they were from her daughter Lisa who lived in Perth. 'It was my birthday last week,' she explained.

Carmel's second eldest daughter, Janine, had called her mother a number of times during the evening to be told the same thing: she's not home yet.

Janine's fiance Martin was watching the Steve Vizard show on television a little before midnight. Janine was lying down in the bedroom. The program was interrupted by a news break saying that the body of another young woman had been found in the Frankston area. Martin went in and told Janine who rang her mother immediately. Angela Butts answered the phone.

'Is she home yet?' asked Janine, her voice shaking.

Angela told her that there was still no news. Janine remembered talking to Natalie on the phone two days earlier. She had been watching an episode of 'Australia's Most Wanted' and there had been a feature on the Frankston serial killer. Janine had telephoned her sister in Melbourne just to tell her to be careful. Now Natalie was missing and a body had been found.

Soon after midnight, there was a knock at the front door. Angela Butts opened it to a friend of Natalie's and her father. The friend had heard that Natalie hadn't returned home from school and that a body had been found. The young girl was frantic and Carmel Russell comforted her. 'They don't know if it is Natalie,' she said. 'It may not be her.'

After the girl and her father left, Carmel paced the lounge room floor talking about how wonderful her daughter was. The worried mother was shaking slightly and Angela Butts was overwhelmed by the unfairness of it all. This girl was clearly loved and cherished. These parents really cared. In her short time in the police force, the young policewoman had already seen so many parents who didn't care. Carmel told her how Natalie went to work each Saturday with Brian, helping him fix brake pads. She would come home covered in grease, smiling. She loved the work and got to spend time with her dad as a bonus.

Angela looked over at Brian. He was a big man, but he seemed to have shrunk as he sat hunched in his chair. Angela thought he looked as though the life had drained out of him and the two women encouraged him to get some rest. He went into the bedroom and slept for a couple of hours while the women talked over cups of hot coffee. As light dawned on the house in Forest Drive, Carmel turned to Angela and said, 'It's light now, they'll be able to identify the body and they will tell us.'

To the policewoman, Carmel Russell now seemed more willing to accept that the body could be that of her daughter. It seemed to be the only way to explain why Natalie hadn't come home or phoned to say where she was.

Angela was in a difficult situation. She understood the desperate need for the family to know, one way or the other, whether their daughter was dead or alive. But she also knew that the police would be in no hurry to identify the body. Not only did they have to wait until it was light to make a thorough search of the scene, but they needed to leave the body in its exact location for a forensic pathologist to examine it for evidence. The police were desperate to catch this killer: if someone turned the body over, evidence could be lost.

But in front of her stood a mother just wanting to know. Crime scenes, forensics and evidence meant little to Carmel Russell. Was her daughter alive or dead?

Brian woke up and came back into the lounge room. In a quiet moment between husband and wife, he turned to Carmel and said, 'I think we're in trouble.'

21

A Small Piece of Skin

AROUND 1.15 am, Detective Sergeant Brad Penno arrived at Monterey Technical School. He and other officers from homicide were briefed by the head of the squad, Chief Inspector Peter Halloran. Since the victim was wearing a John Paul College uniform and fit Natalie Russell's description, detectives were working under the assumption that they had found the missing girl, even though formal identification wouldn't be made until the body was taken to the city mortuary.

Half an hour after he arrived, Brad Penno together with Peter Halloran and John Noonan walked past the tennis courts and through the entrance of the bike track where two uniformed police officers wearing raincoats stood guard. They walked along the track and climbed through the hole in the fence to where the schoolgirl's body lay. With the aid of their torches, the officers could see her lying on her side, face down. Large quantities of blood were clearly visible around her head and shoulders. Her school bag lay a short distance away.

At 6 am, homicide detective Sergeant Mick Hughes received a telephone call from Rod Wilson. Whatever Hughes's plans were for his Saturday morning, they were soon shelved when his senior sergeant told him that a body had been found which was believed to be that of missing student Natalie Russell. Wilson himself had been called in the middle of the night by Peter Halloran who had briefed him on the latest murder. Halloran told him to get a couple of hours sleep. They would all have a long haul in front of them. However, Rod Wilson had not been able to sleep and he finally gave up trying. He got dressed and drove to Frankston.

Hughes met Wilson and other homicide squad members at Monterey Technical School and they were soon briefed by Brad Penno. The detectives walked down the bike track, through the hole in the cyclone wire fence and stared down at the body of the young woman in the early morning light.

Brad Penno was on hand at 9.30 am when pathologist Dr Tony Landgren arrived to perform a preliminary examination of the deceased in situ. Crime scene examiners Brian Gamble and Tony Kealy had been working around the immediate crime scene since first light to collect samples and anything that might be regarded as evidence before the body could finally be moved. They had found both her shoes and collected her heavy school bag. On overhead vegetation, Kealy's trained eye noticed a single fibre which he bagged and labelled. Around a metre from the dead girl's head, Kealy and Gamble found a leather strap stained with what appeared to be blood. On the other side of her body was another leather strap which looked as if it had been broken off from the first.

Manoeuvring through the undergrowth, Dr Landgren gently turned the body and for the first time, the extent of her injuries became obvious. She had received multiple stab wounds to her face and neck and her throat had been cut. The doctor certified death at 9.35 am.

Just before 11 am, Constable Scott Jasper was directed by homicide detectives to escort the body of Natalie Russell to the Institute of Forensic Pathology mortuary. Jasper had been at the crime scene since five that morning maintaining a log of everyone who entered the area of the bike track. The constable watched as the government undertakers placed the body onto a stretcher which they carried to the end of the track and placed in the rear of an SES four-wheel drive. The body was driven to the command post and transferred to the undertaker's van. The whole procedure took five minutes and Jasper followed the van in a police car to the South Melbourne mortuary.

When the body of Natalie Russell arrived at the mortuary, attendants placed it in a fridge specially allocated to homicide victims. Adjacent to the brightly lit post-mortem examination operating room, the body rested behind the heavy stainless steel door awaiting the pathologist.

Dr Landgren had made the cursory examination at the scene and half an hour after the arrival of the body of the schoolgirl, he prepared to perform the post-mortem examination. He dressed in blue surgical clothing and covered himself in a white plastic apron. Natalie Russell's body was transferred onto a stainless steel trolley and photographed by crime scene photographer, Howard Hopper. Her school uniform was dirty and blood stained and Tony Landgren began dictating his observations into a tape-recorder. He described her school uniform, noting the insignia on her school jumper — *John Paul College, With Him is the Fullness of Life* — was heavily stained with her blood. The irony didn't escape those watching.

Also attending the post-mortem was Inspector Claude Minisini who had profiled the killer. He studied the wounds to the dead schoolgirl carefully and had no doubt that her murderer was the same person who had killed Elizabeth Stevens and Debbie Fream. Minisini was particularly struck by in the long cut down her left cheek and noted that the savagery against Natalie Russell was much worse than the other two victims. What had she done to make the killer so mad? Minisini wondered if she had fought him or angered him by something she said.

Beginning with her head and neck area, Landgren described her long brown hair, her earrings and her brown-green eyes before beginning on the injuries. Injury number one was a long cut extending from the right-hand corner of her mouth upwards to her hairline opposite her right eye. Landgren measured it at 10 centimetres. He counted four other shorter cuts on her face. Natalie Russell's throat had been savagely cut and the pathologist measured the horizontal throat wound at 12.5 centimetres.

Steadying his camera, Howard Hopper, bent over the pathologist while Landgren gently washed around the neck injuries with a white cloth. Both men saw a small piece of skin came away onto the cloth. It looked like a piece of skin from someone's finger.

Dr Landgren gently removed the piece of skin from the cloth with a pair of tweezers. Measuring it, Landgren noted that it was 2.7 centimetres by 0.6 centimetres. If the skin didn't belong to Natalie Russell, then there was a very strong possibility that the killer had cut himself while cutting her throat and had left the tiny piece of skin behind. It was just the type of clue that detectives needed.

DNA tests could match the skin and blood type with an offender once he was caught. It wouldn't help find him, but once he was found, it could be used to prove he was the killer. It was difficult for a suspect to explain how a piece of skin from his finger was found inside the throat of a murder victim. Importantly, if a suspect was interviewed in the next week or so, detectives would be looking out for a wound matching the size of the piece of skin he had found. Landgren carefully sealed the piece of skin in a small jar and continued the examination. He listed and described eleven injuries to the head and neck before moving to the chest and abdomen. A tiny one-centimetre area of skin loss over the sternal notch was the only injury he found there.

In her right hand, Landgren found five dark hairs measuring up to five centimetres in length. Since her own hair was long, there was a chance that she had grabbed her killer's hair and pulled out the few strands. In her left hand, the pathologist found ten similar short dark hairs. They too could help link an offender to the crime. The evidence was mounting.

Natalie Russell's hands showed cuts and grazes suggesting that she fought her attacker before he had a chance to inflict the fatal injuries.

When Dr Landgren performed the internal examination, he found that the right carotid artery and both external jugular veins were horizontally transected. The left carotid artery and the left internal jugular vein were intact, suggesting that the killer held her head to the left thereby exposing the right veins and arteries. The killer could have stood behind her, holding her head with one hand and cutting with the other. That could have been how he cut himself.

If the killer was right handed, he had probably held her head with his left hand while he cut with his right. This would account for the main damage to the right side of her neck. If the skin was indeed from the killer, detectives could look for a suspect with a cut to his left hand, probably one of his fingers.

When he finished the examination, Dr Landgren and his assistants bagged the clothing and jewellery for forensic testing. Samples taken from the body during the examination as well as the piece of skin were labelled for further testing.

Dr Landgren listed the cause of death as 'Multiple neck and facial injuries.' He commented at the close of his official report:

'There was no significant natural disease. The features of the facial and neck injuries suggest the use of a knife or other sharp instrument. The injuries to the hands could represent attempts at defence.' The examination had taken a little over two hours.

22

Piecing the Puzzle

TWELVE hours after his arrival at the bike track, homicide detective Brad Penno drove to the Frankston police station, leaving the scene to the forensic experts. Catching Natalie Russell's killer was top priority for all the detectives working on the investigation. It was hard staring down at the body of the teenager — still in her school uniform. Dead. Seeing her so brutally injured only spurred investigators on. This time, hopefully, the killer had slipped up. Penno was on hand when Tony Kealy and Sergeant Brian Gamble had discovered the two strips of leather near the body. The straps could have been used to strangle the victim and if so, then it would be the first piece of solid forensic evidence obtained that could point to the killer.

Tony Kealy and Brian Gamble, with the aid of some other police officers, whipper snippers and rakes, began clearing the area around where Natalie Russell's body had lain. They cut down all the long grass and began the laborious task of raking through the clippings in the attempt to find any additional evidence. They would work until late afternoon finding little more than two tiny silver earring clasps. But the blood, the cuts in the wire and the leather straps were like hitting the jackpot after the failure to turn up virtually anything at the other two murder scenes.

Within the spacious offices of the new Frankston police station, homicide detectives pieced together Natalie's last movements. People had seen her leave school and enter the bike track where her body was found. Chances were that she was killed within minutes of entering the track and the time of death was probably between 2.45 and 3 pm.

Constable Joseph Aiello walked into the temporary homicide squad office and told Mark Woolfe about the yellow Toyota Corona he had checked near the bike track the previous day at 3 pm. Woolfe sent him to get the running sheet and looked over the details of the check. The postal worker was called to the police station and she repeated her story about seeing a man slouching down in the yellow Corona.

Mark Woolfe asked her if she would recognise the man if she saw him again and she said she would. Woolfe showed her a blue school bag which she identified as being similar to the one she had seen the schoolgirl carrying as she crossed the road.

Brown and Aiello had taken details of the registration from the sticker on the windscreen of the yellow Toyota Corona, and Mark Woolfe ran a check on the owner of the vehicle. Within seconds, the computer gave him the name of the registered owner. Paul Charles Denyer.

According to the computer information, Denyer lived in a block of flats on the Frankston-Dandenong Road. Woolfe entered Denyer's name into the data base and learned instantly that the car had been checked before — once at Kananook railway station and earlier Friday morning at the Flora and Fauna Reserve in Langwarrin.

At 3.40 pm, Mick Hughes and Charlie Bezzina went to pay a visit on Paul Charles Denyer. Receiving no reply to their knocking, Hughes left a card which explained that police officers were conducting a door knock in the area and requested that the occupants telephone the Frankston police station when they returned home.

The only thing now was to wait. The pieces seemed to be falling into place. At last detectives had a suspect whom they could place at the scene at the time of the murder. He had been in his car minutes before Natalie Russell entered the bike track and his car had been empty fifteen minutes later when Brown and Aiello had checked it. If Paul Denyer was the killer, he would have been down the bike track at the same time that the officers were checking his car. But the wisdom of hindsight couldn't save Natalie Russell now.

At 5.15 pm, Mick Hughes received the telephone call he had been waiting for. A young woman named Sharon Johnson explained that she had found the calling card in her door and Hughes told her that detectives would be around shortly to speak with her.

Ten minutes later, Hughes, Rod Wilson, CIB detective Darren O'Loughlin and a number of other detectives converged upon the modest block of flats at 186 Frankston Dandenong Road.

Sharon Johnson was walking out towards the letter box when they arrived. Hughes identified himself to her and after a quick introduction, left the surprised young woman and proceeded to flat 1.

Hughes approached the flimsy, wooden wire door and knocked. A tall, overweight young man with a round face appeared in the doorway. Hughes could see him through the wire.

'I'm Detective Sergeant Hughes from the homicide squad,' he said. 'We are conducting investigations into the murders of Deborah Ann Fream and Natalie Jayne Russell. Do you mind if we come in and have a talk to you?'

'Yeah sure, come in.' Paul Denyer pushed open the wire door.

'I got your card but I didn't expect a whole heap of you,' he said smiling, looking at the group of detectives who followed him into the lounge room. The flat was messy and sparsely furnished and the lounge room was small with a worn green modular lounge suite and a cluttered coffee table.

Hughes began by asking Denyer his full name and date of birth which the suspect gave willingly.

'Who do you live here with?' Hughes asked him.

'My girlfriend, Sharon Johnson,' Denyer replied.

Mick Hughes asked Denyer if he and Sharon were living in a de facto relationship.

'What does that mean?' he asked. 'I've heard people say de facto before but I've never really known what it means.'

'It just means 'in fact',' Hughes explained patiently. 'Are you in fact living with Sharon as husband and wife when you are not married? That's all it means.'

Denyer told the detectives that he did have a de facto relationship with Sharon. Hughes then asked the young man if he had a job. Denyer spoke in a quiet, confident voice, explaining that he didn't have a job and hadn't had one since he had worked at Pro Marine in Seaford a couple of months back. Without further preamble, Mick Hughes asked Denyer to account for his movements on the previous day.

'Can you tell me what you did yesterday?'

'When yesterday?'

'Just run through what you did all day.'

'From when I got up you mean?'

Hughes nodded and Denyer began telling the detectives that he had got up around 7.30 am and driven Sharon to work because she was running late. Arriving at Sharon's work at a quarter to nine, he had dropped her off and then gone to the automatic teller machine in Hartnett Drive in Seaford to withdraw forty dollars. He had then driven the old Corona around Brunel Road to the car wreckers to hunt for a spare wheel for his car. He found one and it had cost thirty dollars.

Denyer guessed that he had arrived at the wreckers around 10 am. Back home around 11 am, he said he had telephoned Sharon at work to tell her he had bought a wheel.

Denyer told the detectives that he had worked on his car and then gone to another wreckers in Langwarrin to look for a speedo cable, calling in to visit his mother on the way. Denyer said that his mother wasn't home so he had a coffee with her boyfriend, Jim Dale.

As he was heading to the Langwarrin car wreckers, Denyer told the detectives, his car had overheated and he had to pull over into the carpark of the Langwarrin Flora and Fauna Reserve to top the water up. While Denyer had waited for the radiator to cool, he had smoked a cigarette and gone for a walk.

'Where did you walk?' asked Hughes.

'Not far,' replied Denyer, `just around the general area where I was stopped.'

'Did you see any police cars in the area?' asked Hughes, who knew that Brown and Aiello had checked the car at the reserve and hadn't seen anyone near it.

Denyer said he hadn't, although he did recall a number of other cars in the carpark. He said that when his car engine cooled, he filled the radiator, started the car and headed home along Skye Road, but that the car had overheated again, forcing him to pull over across from the golf course.

Mick Hughes asked him what he had done after the car overheated. Denyer explained that he had checked under the bonnet and noticed that a hose had come loose and that the hose needed a Phillips head screwdriver to attach it back on again. Not having a Phillips head screwdriver among the other tools in his car, he had to walk home and get one and then walk back to his car. Hughes asked him why he didn't just fill up the radiator with water and make the short drive home before the car overheated a third time. Denyer said that although he carried a couple of plastic bottles of water, he had used them back at the Flora and Fauna Reserve.

'Why didn't you just go to someone's house and get some water to fill your car up?'

'I don't like going into other people's houses,' Denyer replied, and when Mick Hughes asked him why he didn't get some water from the golf course, Denyer said that he hadn't thought of it.

Asked why he didn't just drive the car the short distance home,

Denyer said that he wouldn't have driven the car without filling the radiator.

'When you were in Skye Road, did you see any police cars?' asked Hughes.

Denyer said that he hadn't and then explained that by the time he had walked home, picked up the screwdriver and bottled water and finally returned home with the car, it would have been around 3.30 or 4 o'clock in the afternoon.

Later in the afternoon, Denyer told them, he had driven to Sharon's work in Highett to pick up her pay cheque and then drove to a bank in Rowans Road in Highett to cash it. After withdrawing some money, he had collected Sharon from her other job and the two had driven to Sharon's mother's house in Karingal, stopping at the Edithvale McDonalds to grab a bite to eat on the way.

They had arrived at Sharon's mother's house around seven o'clock and stayed until nearly midnight.

Senior Sergeant Rod Wilson spoke to Denyer for the first time. Wilson couldn't fail to notice the plethora of scratches on Paul Denyer's hands and asked him about them. Denyer held up his hands and the detectives all saw several cuts on his fingers and thumbs as well as a larger cut on the inside middle finger of his left hand.

'Paul, how did you get those cuts?' Wilson asked.

'Working on my car, and when I was pulling parts off the cars at the wreckers,' he replied.

'That's a decent cut on your middle finger. How did you do that?'

Denyer was evasive. 'I don't remember, I'm cutting myself all the time.'

Hughes asked Denyer what clothes he had been wearing the previous day and the suspect told him that he had worn black tracksuit pants, a red polo shirt and a green jumper.

'Did you have any type of hat on?'

'Yeah, a blue baseball cap.'

'What type of shoes were you wearing?'

'Black Aerosport runners.'

Hughes asked to see the runners and Denyer obliged by getting them from the front passage.

Then Hughes cut to the chase. 'Paul, Deborah Fream disappeared on the night of the eighth of July 1993, and her body was found the following Monday. Can you remember what you were doing on the eighth of July?'

Without hesitation, Denyer replied, 'Yeah, that was a Thursday night wasn't it?'

'Yes, as a matter of fact it was. What made you remember that?' Hughes was alert to the fact that most people don't usually remember their movements, especially three weeks later. It was highly suspicious that Denyer remembered the date down pat. The fact also didn't escape the detectives that Denyer hadn't once protested about their presence. Usually, people begin with, 'What do you want?' or 'You don't think I had anything to do with this?' But Denyer sat calmly answering questions with the confidence of someone enjoying the attention.

'I remember the night because I was supposed to meet Sharon and I missed the train so I met her at the Kananook railway station.'

Hughes asked Denyer what he knew about Debbie Fream's disappearance.

'Just that she was abducted from the Food Plus and taken up to Taylors Road and murdered.'

'How do you know that?'

'Just from the news and that.'

'Do you remember what you were doing that night?'

'Yeah.'

Hughes knew that it was time to take Paul Denyer to the Frankston police station. He wanted the interview to be properly recorded. They had a suspect with cut hands who had, by his own admission, put himself at the scene of two murders. He and the other detectives had a strong feeling that they had finally caught their killer. It must be done by the book.

'Paul, I would like you to come back to the Frankston police station with us now as I have some further questions I would like to ask you and it may take a while. Are you prepared to come with us to answer some further questions?'

'Yeah, sure,' Denyer told them.

'Before we go, I think I should advise you of the following rights. It is my intention to interview you in relation to the deaths of Natalie Jayne Russell and Deborah Ann Fream. I must inform you that you are not obliged to say or do anything but anything you say or do may be given in evidence. Do you understand that?'

'Yes,' replied Denyer without emotion.

Hughes had to make sure. 'What do you understand that to mean?'

'I don't have to answer your questions or do anything unless I want to.'

'That's right,' said Hughes. 'You may communicate with a friend or relative to inform that person of your whereabouts. Is there anyone you want to ring to let them know where you are going to be?'

'Can I let Sharon know where I'm going?'

'Sharon knows. She has already gone back to the police station. Is there anyone else you wish to notify?'

'No.'

Hughes then explained that Denyer could call a legal practitioner if he wished but he declined. The young man put on a dark jumper with a coloured pattern on the sleeves but when he went to put on the black runners that he had shown the detectives earlier, Hughes asked him if he would mind wearing some other shoes as the police might need to examine the black runners later on.

At 6.20 pm, Wilson, O'Loughlin, Hughes and Denyer drove to the Frankston police station to begin a formal interview that would last until the next morning. Within hours the detectives knew for certain that their hunt for the Frankston serial killer was finally over.

23

The Initial Interview

LESS than twenty-four hours after he had video-taped Natalie Russell's body and the surrounding crime scene, Senior Constable Stephen Batten set up his camera in one of the interview rooms at the Frankston police station. As a member of the state forensic science laboratory audiovisual section, it was Batten's job to make a video recording to back up the audio recording that was made as a matter of course during an interview.

Three hours after Paul Denyer was brought to the Frankston police station, Sergeant Rod Wilson and Senior Constable Mark Woolfe from the homicide squad began the formal interview. In the intervening time, Wilson had organised the audiovisual unit, and the detectives had worked out a tactic for the interview. As soon as Mark Woolfe had seen the suspect brought into the police station, he checked his hands and saw the cuts, noting in particular the skin missing from Denyer's middle finger. 'Look at his hands,' he had whispered to Wilson. Even though they weren't experts, it looked like the piece of skin missing from Denyer's finger was very close in size to the piece Tony Landgren had taken from the throat of Natalie Russell.

Beginning at 9.22 pm, Rod Wilson explained to the suspect that he and Mark Woolfe would conduct the interview and that the two other officers present were from the audiovisual branch. Denyer nodded.

For the record, Denyer was asked to state his name, address and employment status. Wilson restated Denyer's rights to contact a legal practitioner or a friend and that he wasn't obliged to answer any question. Paul Denyer told Wilson that he did not wish to exercise any of his rights.

Formalities over, Wilson began the questioning. He asked Denyer to run through his movements again starting from the previous day. Glancing at the camera, Denyer hesitated, half smiled and said that he had never been in front of a camera before. Wilson told him to take his time and offered him a cigarette.

Denyer repeated the story that he had told the detectives at the flat. He had got up around 7.30 am and driven Sharon to work. Wilson asked him what kind of car he drove and Denyer told him that he drove a Toyota Corona Mark II which he had bought a couple of months earlier. Initially it was unroadworthy and unable to be driven but Denyer had worked on the car since he bought it. A couple of weeks ago he had obtained a permit to drive the car provided that he register it within twenty-eight days.

It was in this car that he had driven Sharon to her job at a charitable organisation in Springvale where she worked as a telemarketer from 8.30 am until three each afternoon. On Friday morning, they had both slept in and they had arrived in Springvale around nine o'clock. Denyer also repeated how he had gone to the automatic teller machine in Seaford on his way home and then to the wreckers to buy the spare wheel. He guessed that it must have been around a quarter to eleven by the time he finished at the wreckers.

Denyer described returning home and telephoning Sharon and then her mother Pauline with whom he chatted for around twenty minutes. After topping up the oil and water in the car, Denyer said, he went out around 11.30 am to visit his mother who wasn't home. He had stopped to chat with his mother's boyfriend, Jim. After that, he went to Harvey's Wreckers.

Denyer again described the car overheating and stopping at the Flora and Fauna Reserve carpark to top up the water with one of the two bottles he had in the boot. Wilson asked a lot of questions to establish the exact course of events and backtracked often to make certain of times and motives. Why did you visit your mother? Does she work? Why did you think she'd be home? Did you think Jim would be there? Why did you stop at the flora reserve?

Denyer answered all the questions calmly, painstakingly going over details of the previous morning.

He told Wilson that after leaving the flora reserve, he had driven down Skye Road and the temperature gauge again registered that the engine was overheating. He described pulling the car over near a bus stop opposite the golf course. Wilson questioned him in great detail about the car and the hose that had come loose: the details were vital because the split hose and its loose clamp put their suspect at the scene of Natalie Russell's murder.

Wilson asked Denyer what type of screwdrivers he carried in his car and why he couldn't have used one he had instead of walking home. Denyer said that he wasn't very good with tools and decided to make the twenty minute walk to his house. Wilson ascertained that Denyer had in fact worked in a garage a couple of years before and that part of his job had been to fix cars. Now Denyer was telling him that he couldn't improvise with a screwdriver to tighten a hose clamp? Wilson pressed the point.

'You don't think you're qualified enough to tighten a clamp?' he asked.

'Yeah, yeah,' Denyer contradicted himself.

'But you just said you didn't know much about tools.'

'Well, I wanted to get the proper tool for the proper job.'

'But it's only a screwdriver,' persisted Wilson in a quiet, even voice.

'Well I've got two sizes. I've got a small one and a big one,' Denyer continued, saying that the small screwdriver was bent and the other one was unsuitable. Wilson asked about two red-handled ones he had seen on Denyer's dashboard earlier outside the flat. Denyer told him that they weren't in the car when it overheated.

Questioning him about the water in the radiator, Wilson asked Denyer again why he hadn't filled the bottles from the golf course or from someone's house.

'I just didn't feel right about it,' Denyer told him and then described walking home, getting a screwdriver and a bottle of water and walking back. He guessed he would have been gone for around an hour. When Denyer guessed that he was in Skye Road around 2.30 pm, Wilson knew the times didn't match. Denyer had said that he had stopped at the flora reserve around midday and stayed for twenty minutes while the engine cooled. It was only a ten minute drive from the reserve to Skye Road. The detective again took him back over the day's events to try to clarify the times that Denyer had been at various places.

Bringing the questioning back to when Denyer would have been parked opposite the bike track, Wilson told him that it would have been more like 12.30 pm when he had pulled up opposite the bike track.

'Is there somewhere else you might have gone?' he asked.

'No, I don't think I went anywhere else.'

Replying to further questions by Wilson, Denyer described walking back to the car and fixing the hose clamp. Wilson asked Denyer that if he had indeed arrived around 2.30 pm, walked to his house and back and then fixed the car, would it be fair to guess that it would have been around 3.30 pm when Denyer finally got into the car to drive home. Denyer agreed.

Step by step, Wilson led Denyer over the events of the rest of the afternoon; collecting Sharon's wage cheque from her second job, going to the bank and then picking up Sharon from work. Wilson asked if the car had overheated when he drove it in the afternoon. Denyer said that the temperature gauge had gone half way but the car hadn't overheated again. Wilson again pressed the point.

'Having started the car from your mother's place, it overheated and it overheated between the reserve and Skye Road. But it didn't overheat on a forty minute trip to Highett?'

Denyer implied that the repairs he had made to the clamp had fixed the problem but admitted that he had topped up the water when he arrived at Sharon's work.

'I had to go borrow a tap from the factory but there was no-one there so—'

'But you were a little bit apprehensive about getting tap water from residents,' Wilson interrupted, alluding to Denyer's earlier statement.

'Yeah, well,' admitted Denyer, 'in a residential area, especially at this time, I mean people get suspicious of anything so I really don't like doing that.'

'Rod Wilson decided to bring the questions to the murder of Natalie Russell. He asked Denyer if he was aware that a girl had been murdered in Frankston yesterday.

'Yeah,' replied Denyer, 'I've heard a lot about it.'

'When did you first become aware of it?' asked Wilson.

'Well, I saw some police cars and everything when I was driving up Skye Road this morning, and SES workers. And I spoke to Sharon's mum just before that. You know, she told me they found—'

'Sorry, you said you saw SES workers? In Skye Road?'

'Yeah, and they had some white tape across the walkway.'

'Mm'hm,' nodded Wilson.

'And I saw you,' said Denyer.

'Sorry, you saw me?' asked Wilson, surprised.

'Yeah, I saw you and I saw the other guy who I was talking to in there. I saw you guys standing next to a van.'

Wilson asked Denyer what he had been wearing the previous day and the suspect repeated what he had told him in the flat. Wilson asked again about the cuts on Denyer's hands — in particular the large cut on the middle finger of his left hand. He asked Denyer to put his hand flat on the table, giving a better view to both himself and the video camera. Denyer obliged. Wilson asked him about the large cut and Denyer told him that he had got it yesterday working on the car. Wilson quickly asked which occasion: at the flora reserve, Skye Road or at his flat? Denyer began to say that he had cut his finger on the fan when he was topping up the water but Wilson reminded him that he had said the engine wasn't running when he topped up the water. Denyer backtracked, explaining that when he filled the radiator at home he had left the motor running while he checked the alternator and it was then that he had cut his hand.

Denyer gestured with his hands to show how the injury had occurred, describing reaching into the car's engine and catching it on the fan. Wilson asked him why he had the left the motor running and Denyer simply replied that he was a clumsy worker where cars were concerned and that he had cut himself heaps of times.

Mark Woolfe wasn't satisfied. He knew something about engines. He also knew that fans were designed to flick away anything that came into contact with them to avoid people injuring themselves. They persisted with the questioning, mentioning all the cuts that covered his hands.

Denyer became evasive saying that he didn't remember when he did all of them. He said that he cut himself so frequently, he hardly noticed how he did it. The detectives persisted. Wilson pointed to the deep cut in Denyer's thumb which looked recent. 'Do you know how that occurred?'

'No, I don't recall how that happened.'

Wilson asked him to put his thumb up toward the camera to record the deep cut on video. 'You can see it's deeper at the top and then it's got thinner at the bottom. It's not as open, is it? Do you see what I mean?'

Studying the cut on his thumb, Denyer agreed.

'How did you do that?' Wilson asked.

'I think I was sharpening a knife at home,' Denyer explained, saying that he had cut himself a number of times while sharpening a knife to cut Sharon some apple pie to take to work. He told the detectives that he had sharpened the knife by pushing it in and out of the stay-sharp scabbard and showed them the movements with his hands. Both detectives could see that there was no way that Denyer could have cut himself on the thumb if he was sharpening the knife the way he illustrated. Denyer too could see that his explanation was not working and tried twisting his thumb around to show how the cut could have been made. Finally, he shrugged and said, 'Well, that's the only explanation I have for it.'

'That's opened up quite appreciably. You would have had to have bled.'

'I don't bleed very much. I don't bleed hard. Like, I cut myself and it won't bleed.'

'But Paul, that would bleed.'

'Oh well, it would have bled.'

'You'd have to remember that bleeding.'

'It would've bled but not too, you know, quick.'

Denyer said that he had dabbed the cut with toilet paper and blown on it and the blood flow had stopped.

'That cut?' asked Wilson.

'Yeah, yeah.'

'Are you telling the truth?'

Denyer began to lose his cool. He could see that his explanation wasn't holding water and Wilson wasn't letting up.

'And you're trying to tell me that when you first mentioned it, you did it with your right hand because you're right-handed. Then when I challenged you on it, you turned around and said it was your left hand. You couldn't have cut your thumb that way because the sharp edge is underneath.'

Denyer tried to explain again, but Wilson interrupted him saying that it was impossible to get such a straight cut in his thumb in the way he was describing. Denyer shrugged and said that it was the way he remembered it. Wilson moved on to discuss the other cuts that covered his hands.

'Did Sharon ask you how you got the cuts?'

'Yeah, she asked me.'

'What did you tell her?'

'I told her, you know, it happened when I was working on the car.'

'Wilson indicated the large cut. 'What did you tell her about this one?'

'Well, she — the only one she really saw was this one. She asked me about that 'cause my hand was on the steering wheel today. She went, "Oh, what was that?" And I said, "Oh, did it while I was working on the car." '

'So you're sure she never asked you about these cuts?'

'No, no. She didn't ask me at all.'

Wilson changed tack. 'When your car was parked in Skye Road, it was checked by the police.'

'Oh.'

'Were you aware of that?'

'No.'

'You were not aware of that?'

'No. Well, I — when a friend of mine told me they heard my name over a scanner yesterday—'

'Sorry?' asked Wilson.

'A friend of mine told me — I spoke to her this morning. She said she heard my name mentioned over — and my address and details of my car — mentioned over a police scanner but—'

'Who was that?'

'Oh, her name's Donna Vanes.' Denyer explained that he had spoken to Donna Vanes around midday and she had told him that a friend of hers had a scanner and she was sitting in the car with the friend the previous day and had heard Denyer's name mentioned.

'So you became aware today at midday that your car was checked by police yesterday in Skye Road?'

'Yeah.'

'In view of the fact that we had a caravan, and you've told us all here before how you saw me in the caravan, did you think that it might have been important that your car was seen in Skye Road yesterday, and having knowledge that it was checked, that you might have wanted to come forward?' asked Wilson.

'No, I didn't think it would be important to, you know, talk or anything 'til I got home today and I saw that card in the door.'

'Did you hear any of the appeals on the radio?'

'No.'

'Did you hear on the radio that a body had been found in that area of Skye Road?'

'No, not today. I've been listening to the radio in the car but—'

'I thought you said when I asked you before when you became aware of it, you said you *had* become aware of it.'

'Mm, I read something in the paper this morning about a girl going missing and when I spoke to Sharon's mum today before I—'

'When did you read that in the paper? Today?'

'This morning.'

'In what paper?'

'*Herald Sun*. It was on the front cover.'

'You read something about a girl going missing?'

'Yeah, it was just a small paragraph...'

Rod Wilson persisted with establishing just when Denyer had heard of the murder of the schoolgirl. Denyer again described driving up Skye Road and seeing Wilson.

'You'd never seen me before?' asked the detective.

'Oh, I saw you on the telly a couple of weeks ago but then—'

'Well, when did you see me on the telly? Who did you think I was?'

'A policeman. It would've had your name and everything underneath.'

'Well, where was I from? Did you know that?'

'No, I just saw your name.'

'So you saw me this morning and you saw a van set up. You knew that your name had been read out over the scanner with details of your car. You saw a caravan set up but you didn't think it would be relevant to say that you had your car parked there, knowing that the police had checked it?'

'Well, I thought, you know, if the police, you know, checked my car out sitting there, it would be, you know, routine for them to come around and see me so—'

'So you expected the police to come and see you?'

'Yeah, I just thought, you know, you guys would come around, yeah.'

Wilson nodded and then Denyer said, 'I didn't expect a whole heap of 'em but...'

'Yeah, I appreciate that.'

'You know what I mean.'

'But when the police left a card just saying that there'd been a door knock in the area, did you find that a bit of a surprise?'

'No, no, 'cause Sharon's mum told me. She said, "Have yous had a door knock yet?" I said, "No, we haven't been home today." '

Wilson asked again what Denyer had known about his car being checked. 'Did you have any idea where it had been checked?'

'Well, it must have been checked when I left it...'

'Why was that?'

'Because, I mean, the police couldn't have remembered the rego number just by looking at it from a distance. They'd have walked up to the window and had a look at the permit on the window 'cause—'

'But why wouldn't they have checked it at the park in Langwarrin or at any other stage?'

'Don't know.'

'Why would you assume they checked it in Skye Road?'

'Because I was with the car in Langwarrin and they — I didn't see any police except, you know, when I dropped the car off and I walked home. I mean, I couldn't have been there to see it.'

Wilson questioned Denyer on this point. He knew that the car had been checked in both Skye Road and the Flora and Fauna Reserve. Denyer was saying that he never left the car while it was parked in the reserve and he didn't see any police. He must be lying. Wilson had exhausted preliminary questions about Natalie Russell's murder and their suspect couldn't account for his movements apart from his story about leaving the car and walking home to get water and a screwdriver. Wilson moved the questioning around to the murder of Debbie Fream.

'Do you recall another murder prior to Natalie Russell being found yesterday?'

'Debbie Fream.'

'Yeah,' said Wilson.

'That caused a lot of publicity.'

'Right,' agreed Wilson, 'What do you know about that?'

'Oh well, I know about — I think she was abducted from the Food Plus and driven down Taylors Road where she was murdered there and then the killer drove her car back and dumped it in a street in Seaford.'

'Do you know what street?'

'Madden Street.'

'Can you remember when it was?'

'A couple of weeks ago or something. It was a Thursday night wasn't it? Yeah, Thursday night.' Denyer couldn't remember the exact date but when Rod Wilson asked him what his movements were on the night, Denyer remembered immediately.

'Yep, I was at my brother's place during the day between 2.30 and 3.30. I was there for a while... the only thing I remember about that day is I was out the front of my place having a cigarette. My brothers drove past. They turned back around and came back to my place. I owed Richard some money, so I walked down to the Ampol and got some money out for him. When I got back home they said, you know, they're going to go up to his place, which is just up the road, and they're going to come back in about ten minutes. So it was like half an hour later they hadn't come back and I was sitting there waiting. Then Richard came back by himself in Steven's car and said, "Oh, have you got your money?" I said, "Yeah." I said, "Look, where's Steven?" and he said, "Oh, he's gone home." And I wanted to go to Steve's place that afternoon 'cause sitting at home all afternoon by yourself is boring, you know. And Richard said, "No, no, I don't know if... you'd have to ask Steven, and you can't ask him when he's already on his way there." So I said, you know, I was a bit annoyed about that and I said, "Well, I don't want to hang around here all day." So he took me to his place and dropped me off there.'

Denyer gave the detectives his brother's address and continued describing his movements on the day Debbie Fream was murdered.

'I was there for a little while. I was talking to, you know, a couple of guys that he lives there with. I don't know their real names but I just know 'em by their nicknames. I had a beer while I was there. I left — I can't remember exactly what time I left there, but I stopped at a bottle shop just down the corner and I bought a cask of wine 'cause Sharon asked me to get something to drink that night for tea. I got back home and started cooking the dinner, listened to some music, played some guitar, done some housework. I was there 'til about twenty past seven. I started walking down to Kananook station at about, you know, twenty past seven or so to catch the 7.36 train.'

'Why did you have to catch the 7.36 train?' asked Wilson, knowing that Debbie Fream had gone missing around 7 pm.

'Because me and Sharon had a schedule that I would meet her at Moorabbin station when she got dropped off there at night time so she wouldn't have to come home alone.'

Wilson asked again where Sharon worked and Denyer explained that she worked at Multifit between 4.30 and 8 pm. Their arrangement was that Denyer would catch a train and meet her at Moorabbin railway station at 8 pm. Denyer reiterated that he left home around 7.20 and walked down the Frankston-Dandenong Road to Hannah Street and turned left into Claude Street. He kept walking until he came to the railway bridge. When he got to the bridge he saw the train had pulled into the station; he was too late. Denyer told Rod Wilson that he turned around and walked straight back home. He telephoned Multifit around 7.55 pm to leave a message for Sharon that he would meet her at Kananook station rather than Moorabbin. Sharon caught the 8.15 train from Moorabbin and Denyer was at Kananook station to meet her when the train pulled in at 8.40 pm. Wilson had Denyer restate all his movements; going to his brother's house, buying the cask of wine, missing the train and finally meeting Sharon.

As far as Wilson was concerned, the times fit. Denyer normally picked Sharon up at Moorabbin station, but on Thursday 8 July, he didn't. Not only that, he admitted to walking around streets that were relatively close to the McCulloch Avenue milk bar where Debbie Fream had bought eggs and milk. Denyer said that he walked to the station rather than drove because his car wasn't working at the time.

Wilson broached the subject of the murder of Elizabeth Stevens, asking Denyer if he remembered it.

'Well, I saw a big commotion on the telly, you know, stopping cars and giving out leaflets and everything like that.'

'Do you recall where you were on the night she disappeared?'

'I was home during the day. I can't exactly remember what I was doing or anything. Sharon was working at Multifit, you know, until eight o'clock. The usual time. I went up to Sharon's mum's that day. I caught a cab up there. I sat around and watched a bit of telly with her mother and had a cup of tea and coffee and something to eat. Then I told her mother that I wanted to go up to mum's place to check out this battery that I had left there.'

Denyer explained that he had first taken Sharon's mum's dog for a walk then left to make a two or three kilometre walk to his mother's house to look at an old car battery. It had been around twilight when he left to walk to Langwarrin. Denyer couldn't remember the exact date, but he remembered that it was a Friday and there had been a bad storm that day which had knocked down some trees in the area. Denyer said that it was still raining when he set out to walk to his mother's house.

Denyer said that the walk to his mother's had taken him around an hour and he had got wet in the rain.

So when you got to your mum's place, did you find this battery?' asked Wilson.

'I couldn't find it in the front lawn where it was supposed to be. That's where I left it last.'

'What, just lying in the weather?'

'Oh, lying with — amongst the garbage bins and rubbish and things like that.'

'What, you thought this battery might've been a good one for your car?'

'Yeah.'

'Kept in that condition?'

'Yeah.'

'Lying amongst the rubbish bins?'

'Well, I didn't know. I just wanted to test it, that's all, but I couldn't find it there.'

'But you would imagine that you — you're a man that's worked for months tuning cars at service stations...'

'But I don't know a lot about batteries though.'

Denyer said that he hadn't looked in the shed for the battery and he hadn't gone into the house because there were no cars out the front and no lights on. His younger brother had in fact been home and had told Paul the following day that he was there, however Denyer hadn't knocked.

Wilson persisted with his questioning. 'Paul,' he said, 'let me understand that you've walked in the dark three kilometres for an hour to check to see if there's a battery for your car and you didn't even have a look for it?'

'I had a look in the front lawn 'cause that's the only place where I thought it would be.'

'But it might've been... you could have knocked on the door and said, "Does someone know where the battery's gone?" I mean you just walked an hour to find that battery and you didn't want to check if it was anywhere else?'

'No, didn't think it would be anywhere else. Thought it might—'

'But when did you last see it in the front garden, as you just said before, in amongst the rubbish bins?'

'Last time I saw it — just trying to think the last time I was living there — about a year and a half ago, bit over a year and a half.'

'So a year and a half ago, there was a battery sitting amongst the rubbish bins and you're honestly trying to tell me that you thought it might have been okay?'

Denyer tried to say that when he was working in the garage, they used old batteries all the time and that he honestly thought this old one could be charged up.

'Do you know the area where Elizabeth Stevens was found?'

'I know the park, but I don't know whereabouts in the park.'

'Okay, do you know the name of the park?'

'Yeah, Lloyd Park.'

'How do you know Lloyd Park?'

'Well, I used to live in the area and I used to drive down there with my brothers and drive back. And we know Lloyd Park. I used to smoke dope in there,' Denyer grinned.

'Well on this Friday night, how do you know that we're talking about the night that you walked down there?'

'Because the body was found the next day.'

'How do you know that? How do you remember that?' asked Wilson.

'Oh, it was on the news. I was sitting at home with Sharon that night round six o'clock or something. Saturday, it was on the news.'

'So when you walked from Sharon's mother's place all that way in the drizzling rain to look for this battery that had been sitting in the rubbish for a year and a half, that you never even looked for in the end, and no-one was home when you got there, how close were you to Lloyd Park on that night?'

'Denyer said that the closest point he got to Lloyd Park was about a fifteen minute walk.

Rod Wilson decided it was time to lay the evidence before the man sitting opposite him. The detective went over Denyer's accounts of his movements: his car had been parked opposite the bike track where Natalie Russell was murdered, he had been walking the streets near Kananook railway station the night Debbie Fream was killed and he was walking near Lloyd Park on the night Elizabeth Stevens was murdered.

Wilson asked Denyer if he carried a knife and the suspect admitted that he usually carried a knife in his sock for protection. But, he added, he had forgotten to carry it on the night that Debbie Fream was murdered.

'Are you responsible for the deaths of any of these women?'

'No.' Denyer was beginning to look uncomfortable and defensive.

Wilson asked him what he knew about the women and Denyer replied that he knew how they died. He had seen it on the telly.

'Elizabeth Stevens had her throat cut and the other girl, Debbie Fream, had multiple stab wounds or something to her body and upper body, up here.' Denyer gestured to the right side of his neck. Debbie Fream had been stabbed in the right side of her neck and Rod Wilson quickly asked, 'Why did you indicate that exact area?'

'I was just pointing, that's all,' said Denyer, looking even more uncomfortable.

'But why did you point there?' persisted Wilson.

Denyer looked embarrassed and said it was a lucky guess.

Rod Wilson asked him what else he knew about the murders. Denyer then said that he knew Debbie Fream was the mother of a twelve-day-old baby called Jake, and that she had lived with a de facto husband. Elizabeth Stevens had been a student at the Frankston TAFE. He remembered that Elizabeth Stevens was eighteen and that Debbie Fream was twenty-two.

Rod Wilson asked Denyer if he had discussed the murders with anyone else.

'Oh well, just with Sharon. We just talked about it, you know, taking precautions...'

'Did you ever discuss the injuries that we're just discussing with anyone else?'

'Well, Sharon heard a rumour that the killer cut her, played noughts and crosses with a knife on the bodies and I heard that—'

'On which body?' interrupted Wilson.

'On both, two bodies,' Denyer said.

'And Sharon told you that?'

'A girl from Sharon's work, her husband is a detective working on this case. That's what I was told. This lady told her — you know how husband and wife tell each other everything.'

Rod Wilson wondered if Paul Denyer told Sharon everything.

Mark Woolfe took over and went over all the details again. Woolfe's style of questioning was different to that of his senior sergeant. He fired questions thick and fast, challenging Denyer on the smallest details about the car; which tools he carried. He suggested that Denyer was lying about the severity of the water leak problem. It would have only cost around thirty dollars to fix the problem and Woolfe suggested that if the leaks were that bad, Denyer would have fixed them rather than putting up with his car overheating all the time. The suspect sat leaning back against the wall of the interview room, his arms crossed defensively in front of him.

When Denyer said he only once missed picking Sharon up from work — on the night Debbie Fream went missing — Mark Woolfe pressed the point and Denyer backtracked. He then said there were other nights, but he couldn't remember which ones. Mark Woolfe asked what the arrangements had been for Sharon the night that Elizabeth Stevens was murdered. All along, Denyer had stressed that he had picked Sharon up or met her at the station every night, and yet, on the night of the first murder, Paul Denyer had visited Sharon's mother and stayed there, waiting for Sharon to get home. Denyer explained that her sister would pick her up or else she would catch a taxi. In the end, he said, she had caught a taxi.

'Why did you pick a storm to go for a two hour walk to have a look at a battery?' Woolfe asked him.

'I don't know. I just felt like walking.'

'Well, I suggest to you that's a lie. What do you say to that?'

'Well, I don't reckon it's a lie.'

'I suggest to you that you did not go to your parents' place that night.'

'I did.'

Woolfe continued to press him about the story sounding unbelievable, but Denyer stubbornly stuck to it. At 11.25 pm, Rod Wilson suspended the interview for a coffee break. Denyer asked for white with two and then yawned towards the camera as Wilson left the interview room.

Over an hour later, the taped interview started again and Rod Wilson again cautioned the suspect before requesting a sample of his blood. He explained that Denyer didn't have to give his consent, but if he refused, they would apply to a magistrate and get an order for blood. Denyer now began to look a little upset. He agreed in a quiet voice. Wilson then asked if he agreed to having his fingerprints taken and a sample of his hair taken. Denyer agreed.

The interview was suspended while a doctor was summoned to take the samples.

24

O'Loughlin

SENIOR Detective Darren O'Loughlin is a nice looking man in his early thirties. He comes from a family of police officers; both parents, brothers and uncles all serving or past-serving members. Tall but slightly built, O'Loughlin has a gentle, almost inconspicuous way about him. His deep blue eyes stare intently at whoever he is talking to and his quiet voice and ready smile have convinced more than one offender that confession is good for the soul.

At the Frankston police station, homicide detectives had spent hours interviewing Paul Denyer. Darren O'Loughlin had remained in his own office during this time, ostensibly waiting in case the detectives needed him for anything, but also because he, like every other detective working on the case, wanted to know for certain whether their suspect was indeed the killer.

During the wait for the doctor to arrive, Denyer requested a visit to the toilet and O'Loughlin accompanied him. Walking back to the interview room, Paul Denyer turned to Darren O'Loughlin and said, 'Can I ask you something?'

'Sure,' relied O'Loughlin.

'I see you're wearing a cross under your shirt. Are you a Christian?'

'Yes I am, why?'

'Sharon is but she doesn't go to church any more. Can I ask you something before I go back in there?'

'Yeah sure,' replied the detective, offering Denyer a cup of coffee. The two walked into the kitchen area next to the interview room and O'Loughlin made two coffees.

'I'd love something to eat,' Denyer said. He had been at the police station for nearly eight hours.

'No worries, I'll organise it. What do you feel like?'

The man accused of three brutal murders asked O'Loughlin for a hamburger.

'Anything else?' asked the detective.

'Can you tell me something off the record?' Denyer asked him.

'I won't know until you ask me.'

'How long do DNA tests take?'

'I don't know, I'm just helping out.'

'Have they got something to DNA because they've asked for my blood and stuff?'

'I don't really know. You should ask the homicide squad detectives.'

'When they get the blood, will the DNA match?'

'Again, I don't know Paul. You really should be asking Detective Senior Sergeant Wilson about all this.'

O'Loughlin looked at the 21-year-old man and Denyer met his gaze and said, 'Okay, I killed all three of them.'

Caught off guard, the young detective quickly said, 'Before you say anything else, I'll have to go and get Senior Sergeant Wilson.' O'Loughlin realised that this was the breakthrough they had been waiting for.

'Can't I talk to you about it?' asked the young killer. He had found a sympathetic face in the crowd of detectives and it was to Darren O'Loughlin that he wished to make his confession.

'No,' said O'Loughlin, firmly but gently. 'I'll have to go and get Mr Wilson. He's in charge of the investigation.'

'Okay.' Denyer was disappointed. 'You might as well tell him that I attacked another woman at Seaford the night that Debbie Fream was killed.'

'Okay,' said the detective, ushering Denyer back into the interview room, 'but don't say anything else until I speak to Mr Wilson.'

O'Loughlin sat the accused man down and contacted Mick Hughes, telling him about the confession. Excitement reigned. Hughes left to tell Rod Wilson. Wilson thought it best if O'Loughlin sat in on the interview since Denyer had shown a predisposition towards him and the young detective agreed.

A police photographer arrived to photograph the wounds on Denyer's hands and at 2.25 am Dr Faika Jappie, a police forensic physician, arrived to take blood and hair samples. As soon as she entered the room, Paul Denyer swung around on his chair, fixed her with a stare and said, 'I'm a killer.'

Taken aback, the doctor looked over the consent form which Denyer had signed for the samples to be taken. She confirmed his consent verbally and was intensely aware that the young man was trying to stare her down. The doctor, with twenty years experience in medicine and forensic lecturing, noticed that Denyer was nervous and tense. She saw his sweaty hands trembling as he refused a medical examination after she had taken a sample of blood and some strands of hair from his head. She also noticed the numerous lacerations on his fingers and on the backs of his hands. Her extensive experience in the examination and interpretation of injuries led her to estimate that the cuts were approximately forty-eight hours old. Some of them appeared to her to have become infected. She took her samples, gave them to Mark Woolfe and left the police station.

Mark Woolfe had noticed something strange when Dr Jappie walked into the interview room. Denyer had been calm and almost casual with the detectives but as soon as the woman had entered the room his whole expression changed. Woolfe noticed the way he looked at her. His look seemed to say to the detectives: if you weren't here, I'd tear her to shreds. The change in him for those couple of moments was frightening and Mark Woolfe gained a small insight into what his victims must have seen.

At 3.45 am Paul Denyer finally began his official video-taped confession in the presence of Rod Wilson and Darren O'Loughlin. Denyer began giving the detectives details of the crimes that up until now had only been conjecture.

25

Confessions of a Serial Killer

DETECTIVE Senior Sergeant Rod Wilson sat opposite Paul Denyer and Darren O'Loughlin sat to the side. The video camera taped the proceedings as Wilson advised Denyer of his rights for the fifth time. Denyer looked sullen.

Wilson then asked Denyer if it was true that he had told Darren O'Loughlin during the break that he was responsible for the murders of the three women. Denyer nodded and Rod Wilson asked him to describe the murder of Elizabeth Stevens in his own words. Denyer stared downwards, then at the camera, hesitating a full twenty seconds before beginning. 'I saw her get off the bus. I was walking across the road. Just something hit me straight in the head, you know, *go!* — so I ran across the road in front of all these cars and got to the other side, where I followed her around the corner.

'I walked up behind her and stuck my left hand around her head right here,' he said, indicating with his own big hand how he had grabbed Elizabeth Stevens.

'And then I dragged her into the front lawn, told her to shut up, and she just agreed to my terms. And I said, "Well, we're gonna take a walk." So we walked down on the road. A couple of cars drove past us and I held her hand to make it look like, you know, a couple, I suppose... So it wouldn't arouse any suspicion. Walked past two people on the footpath, a guy and a girl, and they just didn't take any notice.' Wilson asked if Elizabeth had screamed or cried out.

'No, I told her I'd kill her if she did,' he said. Rod Wilson nodded and Denyer added, a grin flashing across his face, 'With my fake gun.' Describing the gun for the detectives, Denyer said it was a square bit of aluminium piping with a wooden handle and a glove finger taped to the end. Inside the glove finger, ball bearings were loaded.

Denyer lit a cigarette as Darren O'Loughlin left the interview room to get a Melway Street Directory so the young man could show them the route he had taken from the bus stop to Lloyd Park with his cap-tive. Denyer showed the detectives where he had walked with Elizabeth Stevens and then he began describing her murder.

'Walked in a bit of bushland beside the main track in Lloyd Park. Sat there, you know, stood in the bushes for a while just — I can't remember, just standing there I suppose. Held the gun to the back of her neck, walked across the track over towards the other small sand hill or something. And on the other side of that hill, she asked me if she could, you know — could go to the toilet or — so to speak. So I respected her privacy. So I turned around and everything while she did it and everything. When she finished, we just walked down towards where the goal posts are and we turned right and headed towards the area where she was found. Got to that area there and I started choking her with my hands and she passed out after a while. You know, the oxygen got cut off to her head and and she just stopped. And then I pulled out the knife... and stabbed her many times in the throat.

'And she was still alive. And then she stood up and then we walked around and all that, just walked around a few steps, and then I threw her on the ground and stuck my foot over her neck.'

Rod Wilson asked Denyer why he had stood on her neck and Denyer replied casually, as if it should have been obvious, 'Oh, to finish her off.' His lack of emotion and casual manner would be consistent throughout the entire confession.

He told the detectives that Elizabeth Stevens's body had begun shaking and demonstrated her final death shudders for the benefit of the detectives and the video camera.

Denyer described dragging the body of Elizabeth Stevens to the drain where it was found. Sergeant Wilson questioned Denyer on the first part of his statement where he had said that he walked from Sharon's mother's house to his own mother's house. He said that he really had gone to his mother's house, and then he had killed Elizabeth Stevens after he saw her get off the bus on his way back to Sharon's mother's house. Denyer traced the route with his finger on the Melway. So well did he know the areas, he pointed to locations on the map with barely a glance.

'Did you know she lived in Paterson Avenue at the time?'

'No idea,' Denyer replied.

'You now know she lived in Paterson Avenue. Do you know where?' Wilson asked.

Without hesitation, Denyer gave the Websters' address and the number of their house. He didn't tell the detectives that he knew that house well. His brother's girlfriend Cheryl used to live in that same house and Denyer had spent many hours visiting Cheryl there before her family had sold it to the Websters. Oblivious to the significance of the house, Wilson pushed on with the questioning.

Denyer described and sketched the knife and its dimensions for the detectives and told them he had worn a green army jacket, black pants and shoes, a blue jumper and a blue and white baseball cap.

Wilson knew that the injuries to Elizabeth Stevens were more extensive than those Denyer had admitted to.

'When the body of Elizabeth Stevens was found, it had a number of marks on the chest area and seven stab wounds around the breast. Do you know how they came to be there?'

Denyer said that he didn't remember.

'You don't remember, what do you mean by that? Could you have done this?'

'Possibly,' the young man conceded with a slight nod of his head. Wilson wanted to establish the reason for the killing of Elizabeth Stevens. So far Denyer seemed happy enough to talk about what he did but the burning question was why.

'Can you tell me why you attacked her on that night? What led to it?'

'Just... I just had... just the feeling, that's all.'

'What sort of feeling? Can you possibly describe it – where you had this feeling?'

'Just wanted... just wanted to kill.' Denyer looked down at the table in front of him. 'Just wanted to take a life because I felt my life had been taken many times.' Denyer's quiet voice became even softer and he looked downwards.

'By whom?' asked Wilson.

'David,' Denyer murmured.

'Who is David?'

'My eldest brother.'

'When did he... do you wish to say what he... ?' Rod Wilson's voice showed a compassion for the man in front of him that he didn't feel.

'No, no.'

'Was it of a sexual nature?'

'Yeah.'

'When you were younger?'

'Mm.'

'Abused you?'

'Mm'hm.'

'And you felt cheated by that or something?'

'Yeah.'

Paul Denyer didn't want to expand upon what was obviously an uncomfortable subject for him. Wilson didn't push him further and led the questioning back to the night Elizabeth Stevens was murdered.

'Do you remember what Elizabeth Stevens was wearing?'

'Dark sweater with a hood, grey tracksuit pants. White socks with orange bands and—'

'How do you remember all that?' asked Wilson. 'Is it something you found out later in the newspapers or can you remember?'

Denyer told him that he had seen the mannequin the police had prepared to help jog the public's memory of Elizabeth Stevens and her last movements.

'So you don't really remember what she was wearing?'

'No.'

Wilson asked Denyer why he had picked Elizabeth Stevens and he was told that she was the only one who got off the bus.

'When would you say that you first started feeling this aggression when you were walking around here? When did you first feel like you had to kill?'

'Somewhere between Sharon's mum's place and my mum's place — somewhere between.'

'And did Elizabeth Stevens offer any resistance to you at any stage?'

'A little bit... when we got to the park.'

'Was she frightened, do you think?'

'She didn't cry,' Denyer said as if he admired her bravery.

'Well, did she see you take the knife out of your pocket?'

'No, she would have blanked out or something.' He told them he had choked her before he took out his knife.

Wilson asked where the knife was and Denyer told him that he dumped it at the side of a road in Langwarrin. He explained that the blade had broken off and he had dumped the pieces together. Wilson asked him if he had broken the blade off himself and Denyer explained, 'Well, it bent when I was stabbing her. The blade went zoop and then I broke the rest of it off and then carried it in my pocket 'til I got to there when I dumped 'em.'

'When you said that you were stabbing her at this location back at Lloyd Park, what were you feeling at the time? For example, were you angry?'

Denyer reflected for a moment. 'Happy, sad, angry... many things.'

Rod Wilson led the questioning around to evidence at the first crime scene. It was necessary for Paul Denyer to account for as much as possible. False confessions were not unheard of and the detectives needed to make absolutely sure that the man sitting in front of them was indeed the killer.

Wilson asked him why he moved the body from the site of the murder and Denyer told him that it was in order to destroy evidence. He explained that he thought the rain would wash away footprints and blood and that investigators would have difficulty finding the exact location of the murder. Denyer then described ripping a branch from a tree near the drain to conceal the body.

Denyer told Wilson that Elizabeth had been carrying a bag when he had taken her to the park and said that he left the bag about ten metres from her body.

Wilson took Denyer over the details of the abduction and murder once again, covering everything in minute detail. Denyer admitted that he had told Elizabeth Stevens that he would 'blow her head off' if she screamed and he also admitted telling her to kiss the end of the gun but she had refused.

Wilson asked Denyer if he had felt any sexual urges towards Elizabeth Stevens and he admitted that he had but that they had subsided immediately after he had grabbed her. He described his conversation in the bushes at Lloyd Park with the woman he was about to kill. He had asked her name and sounded indignant when he said, 'She said she was seventeen when she was eighteen.'

He went on, 'I said to her, "Do you want a fuck?" and she said, "How do you do that?" And I said, "Are you a virgin?" She said yeah and I said, "Well, I won't rape you or anything."'

Rod Wilson could only imagine the young woman's terror and he was fully aware that he was only getting one side of the story. Paul Denyer almost made it sound like a casual conversation between friends — not between a killer and his victim.

'She had her top rolled up tightly. Do you know how that came...?'

'Yeah, that happened when I was dragging her. It sort of got caught up on some blackberry bushes and pulled it all the way up.'

'But you can't remember inflicting those injuries?'

'It's possible, but I don't remember.'

Denyer described strangling Elizabeth Stevens and showed the detectives how he had pushed his thumb into her throat and made a stabbing motion as he described stabbing and slashing her throat. He told them that Elizabeth Stevens had then got to her feet.

'Are you saying that she got up after that? Did that surprise you?'
'Yeah, it did in a way. She got up and walked. And she didn't cry. She was just normal.'

'So how far... when you say she walked, how far did she actually walk?'

'Around in circles with me.'

You were holding her still?'

'Yeah, just under one arm.'

'Why were you doing that? Did you help her up? Is that what you're indicating?'

'Yeah.'

'So what happened after she walked around in circles?'

'There was a puddle of like... flooded area there. And I pushed her into there so she could wash her... you know... blood off her and all that. And then I dragged her across the water.'

'Well, when did you put your foot on her neck as you described before?'

'When she was lying on the side of the sort of flooded area with her legs in the water.'

'And why did you do that?'

'To kill her,' Denyer said matter of factly.

'So you did that and then she went into a sort of spasm, you said before, or some sort of quivering?'

'Yeah, her whole body just shook and everything... and then she stopped.'

'Did you think she was dead?'

No, she was still breathing... from her neck.'

'How did you know that?'

'I could hear it.'

'How long did that last for?'

'Five minutes.'

'Did you do anything more to her then to stop that.'

'No.'

'Did you ever strike her in any way, punch her, I mean?'

'I might have.'

Denyer told Wilson that he had first seen Elizabeth Stevens around 7.15 and the entire attack and hiding of the body had taken about half an hour. He described walking back to Sharon's mother's house and Sharon's mother had asked him where he had been. He told her that he had been to visit his mother but she hadn't been home. He explained to Wilson that he didn't have any blood on him; the rain had washed the blood from his hands, but he was drenched from being out for hours in the rain. Denyer told the detectives that he had eaten dinner — soup and a roast — and waited for Sharon to come home from work.

When Rod Wilson was satisfied that he had covered the murder of Elizabeth Stevens in as much detail as he could for the time being, going over all the details at least three times, he moved on to the murder of Debbie Fream. Denyer's knowledge of the crime scenes and the young woman's movements were something only the killer would know. The young man had displayed little emotion during the questioning which had by now entered the early hours of Sunday morning.

26

Debbie Fream's Murder

ROD Wilson had put in a long day. Called at 4 am on Saturday morning to the scene of Natalie Russell's murder, Wilson found himself, twenty-four hours later, still only in the early stages of interviewing the self-confessed killer. The combined triumph and relief at catching Denyer before he could claim any more lives well and truly made up for the gruelling pace. Darren O'Loughlin too had put in as many hours and it would probably be another twenty-four hours before any of the detectives would go home and catch some well deserved and much needed sleep.

It was now time to lead the questioning to the abduction of Roszsa Toth and the murder of Deborah Fream.

Denyer told Wilson and O'Loughlin that he had seen Mrs Toth walking near the station and he described approaching her from behind and grabbing her with his left hand around her mouth while sticking his fake gun to her head with his other hand. Denyer thought Mrs Toth was Spanish when she cried out in a language he didn't understand. She bit his finger and screamed. He showed the detectives the mark still remaining on his finger from the bite.

'I wrestled with her. She ran out on the road but no-one stopped. And I grabbed her by the hair and dragged her back towards the park and I said, "Shut up or I'll blow your fucking head off." And she said, "Si, si," in Spanish or something. And then she stood up and then went against her word and ran out on the road again... ' It seemed to detectives that Paul Denyer was indignant that the women he tried to kill either lied to him or tried to get away — almost as if they owed him some kind of loyalty.

Denyer had run away when Roszsa Toth had escaped him the second time but when Wilson asked him what he had intended doing with the middle-aged woman, he replied, 'I was just gonna drag her in the park and kill her, that's all.'

Wilson asked him if he had again felt the urge to kill and Denyer tried to articulate the feeling building up inside him.

'Yeah, like every day it was just going up, boiling up... 'til I got to that stage.' He raised his hand in front of him to simulate a temperature gauge.

Denyer described making the home-made knife that he carried during the attack. He had cut the aluminium at his old place of employment, Pro Marine in Seaford, and had carried it most of the time in his sock.

After the attack on Roszsa Toth, Denyer had jumped on a Frankston-bound train which took him from Seaford to the next station down the line, Kananook. He got off the train and crossed the overpass. Thwarted in his thirst for blood, he had gone in search of another victim and found Debbie Fream. Walking down McCulloch Avenue towards the milk bar on the corner, he had seen a woman pull up across the road in a grey Pulsar. He showed detectives on the Melway map.

'What caused you to select her at the time?' asked Wilson.

'Just that go feeling. While she was in the milk bar, I walked up to the car and checked the driver's door and it was unlocked, so I opened the door and put my hand through and unlocked the back door. I hopped in the car and crouched down behind the seat and pulled out a gun that I had. Then I looked up out of the car window and I saw her in the milk bar. I crouched down and I could hear her footsteps coming closer to the car. And then she opened the door. The interior light went on and then she hopped in the car. She didn't see me in the back. And then she closed the door, you know, the light went out and everything and it was dark. And I waited for her to start up the car so no-one could hear her scream or anything. And she put it into gear and she went to do a U-turn. And I startled her just as she was doing that turn and she kept going into the wall of the milk bar, which caused a dent on the bonnet. I told her to, you know, shut up or I'd blow her head off and all of that shit.'

Denyer told the detectives that he had held the fake gun in Deborah Fream's side. Rod Wilson asked Denyer if he had noticed anything in the car when he had hopped in. Denyer told him that he had seen the baby capsule in the back seat. Even if Debbie Fream hadn't told him, Paul Denyer would have had a pretty good idea that he was killing the mother of a young baby.

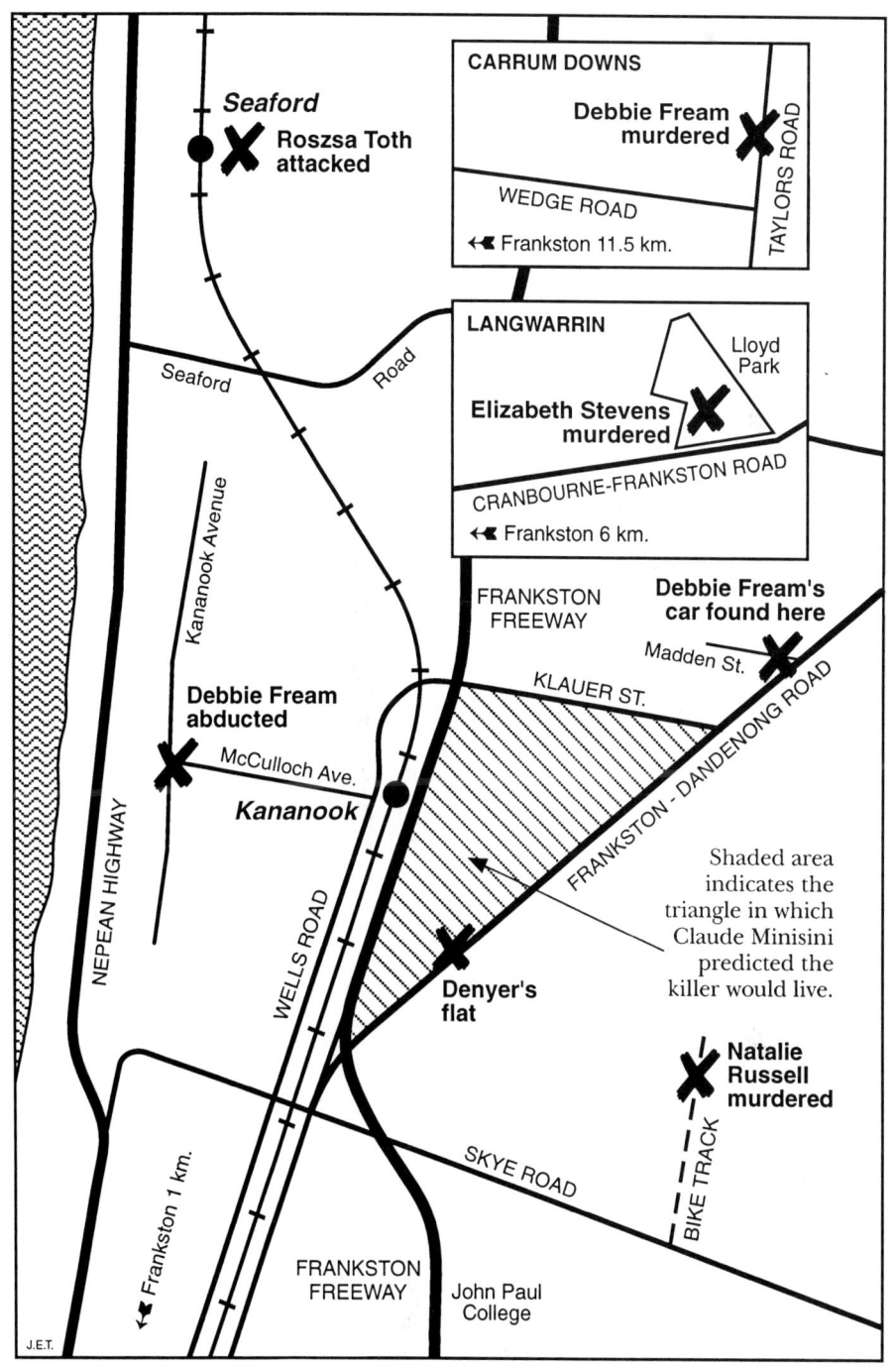

Denyer hunted and killed his victims in areas that he knew.

The mother cat Denyer slaughtered when he broke into Donna Vanes's flat.

Photo courtesy of the Victoria Police.

Denyer's death threat on the kitchen wall was written in blood.

Photo courtesy of the Victoria Police.

Sergeant Fred Barton (left) and
Sergeant Steve Lewis from
Cranbourne worked on the initial
disappearance of Elizabeth Stevens.

Lloyd Park, still largely flooded
the day after Elizabeth Stevens's
body was found.

Photo courtesy of the Victoria Police.

Police used a manequin of Elizabeth Stevens to encourage people to come forward with information.

Photo courtesy of the Victoria Police.

The toilet block opposite Seaford railway station,
where Denyer dragged Rosza Toth.

Photo courtesy of the Victoria Police.

Debbie Fream
aged 18.

The proud
expectant mum,
Debbie poses for
her cousin Sara.

Debbie bathing Jake the day before she died.

SES volunteers gather for a briefing before beginning the search for the missing mother.

Photo courtesy of the Frankston SES.

A crime scene examiner points to the breakage where the killer had ripped branches to cover the body of Debbie Fream.

Photo courtesy of the Victoria Police.

Natalie aged two and a half. Old photos of their daughter are a precious legacy for the Russell family.

Natalie Russell on school camp.

Natalie celebrating
her seventeenth
birthday.

Natalie had
blossomed into
an attractive
young woman.

An aerial view of the bike track along which Natalie Russell was murdered.

Photo courtesy of the Victoria Police.

Denyer cut this hole in the wire fence of the bike track earlier on the day he killed Natalie Russell.

Photo courtesy of the Victoria Police.

Crime scene examiners found a
broken leather strap near the
body of Natalie Russell.

Photo courtesy of the Victoria Police.

During the re-enactment, Denyer
unearthed Debbie Fream's purse
from near the bike track.

Photo courtesy of the Victoria Police.

Denyer's yellow Toyota photographed after his arrest. It had been checked twice the day he murdered Natalie Russell.

Photo courtesy of the Victoria Police.

Denyer melted the soles of his shoes to damage the tread in case he left shoe impressions at the crime scenes.

Photo courtesy of the Victoria Police.

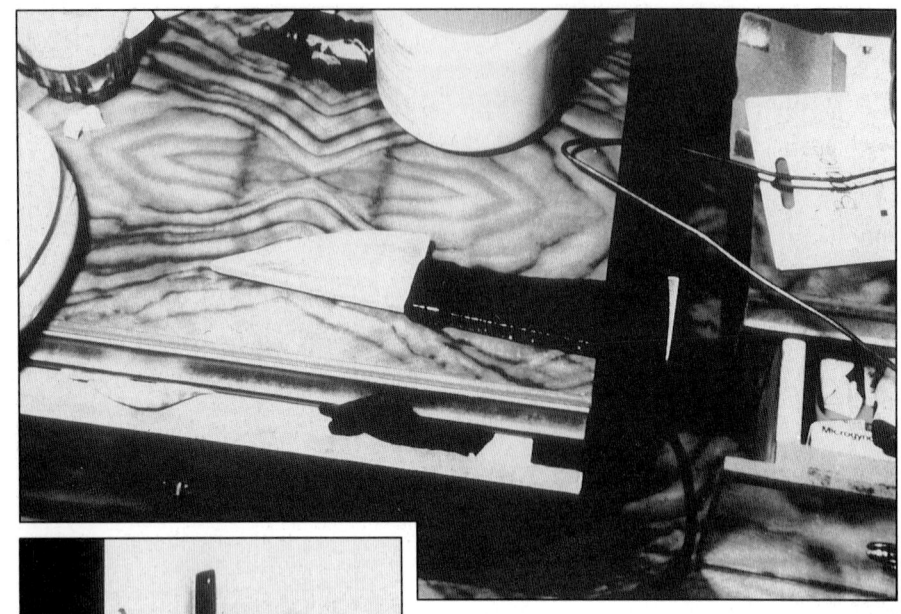

On the dressing table in the bedroom Denyer shared with Sharon Johnson, police found a replica of the home-made knife he used to kill Debbie Fream.

Photo courtesy of the Victoria Police

Hanging behind the door of Denyer's spare room, crime scene examiners found a cord with what looked like human hair caught in the knot.

Photo courtesy of Victoria Police

Sergeant Colin McKinney stands outside the door to Cell 6
in the city watch house where Denyer was initially held.

Paul Denyer aged nine.

Denyer, aged 17,
on a trip to
Queensland,
November 1989.

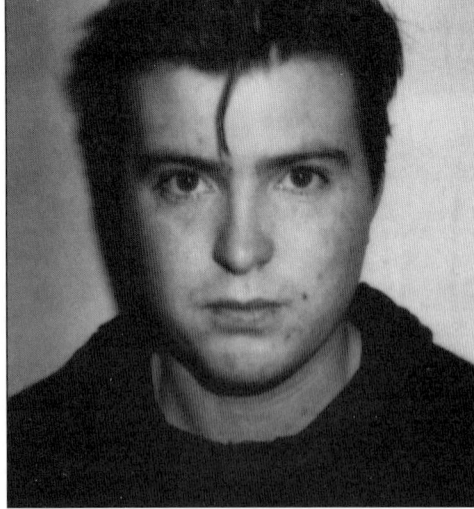

Denyer after
his arrest.

Denyer said that he had instructed Debbie Fream to drive back up Kananook Avenue — ironically right past the house she shared with Garry and their son. Denyer traced the journey on the map to Hartnett Drive in Seaford.

'I told her when we got there that if she gave any signals to anyone, I'd blow her head off, I'd decorate the car with her brains.'

Denyer was sitting upright directly behind the young mother as he directed her towards Taylors Road. Wilson asked if Denyer knew this area well.

'Yeah, I know it very well,' he replied. 'I used to sit down there in the car at night a couple of years ago and smoke marijuana.'

Denyer had directed Debbie Fream to stop the car near some trees on Taylors Road. He told the detectives that she had told him to take her money and her car and that he had told her he didn't want either. He then told her to get out of the car. Denyer had tucked the fake gun down the front of his tracksuit pants and pulled a cord from his pocket.

'I popped it over her eyes real quickly so she didn't see it... 'cause I was gonna strangle her. But I didn't want her to see the cord first. I lifted the cord up and I said, "Can you see this?" And she just put her hand up to grab it to feel it and when she did that I just yanked on it real quickly round her neck. And then I was struggling with her for about five minutes.'

'She was struggling?' asked Wilson.

'Yeah, until she started to faint a bit. And then when she was, you know, like weaker, I pulled me knife out of me sock then... and started stabbing her around the neck and the chest several... several times.'

'You strangled her?' asked O'Loughlin. 'Is that the first thing that happened?'

'As she sort of weakened and fell onto the ground, that's when I stabbed her in the throat.'

'Once?'

'Many times and once in the stomach.'

'Where was she... ?' asked O'Loughlin.

'Lying on the ground.'

'Was she dead or alive when you stabbed her in the throat?'

'Almost dead.'

'So you stabbed her a number of times. And what happened then?' asked Rod Wilson

'She started breathing out of her neck, just like Elizabeth Stevens.

I could just hear bubbling noises.'

'Did Debbie Fream put up any resistance?'

'Yeah, she put up quite a fight. And her white jumper was pulled off during that time as well. I just felt the same way I did when I killed Elizabeth Stevens.'

'What happened after you stabbed her round the throat and chest area?'

'I lifted up her top and then ploughed the knife into her gut.'

Wilson asked Denyer why and he replied that he wasn't sure.

'You lifted the top to do that?' asked O'Loughlin.

'Yeah,' Denyer affirmed.

'Do you know why you lifted her top?'

'I wanted to see how big her boobs were,' said Denyer.

'Beg your pardon?' asked O'Loughlin, momentarily taken aback by the childish statement.

'I wanted to see how big her boobs were,' he repeated.

'Was that part of the fantasy?' pressed O'Loughlin, trying to keep the hint of disgust from creeping into his voice.

'I don't know.'

'You actually recall thinking that way?'

'Sort of,' Denyer replied. 'And I saw her bare stomach so I just lunged at her with the knife.'

Denyer couldn't explain the small pinpoint stab injuries Debbie Fream had suffered to her back. He described dragging her about a metre into a group of trees and leaving her lying against a fence. He broke off two branches from the nearest tree and threw them over her body. Denyer detailed the five minute search for his knife which he had dropped in the attack. He found it and put it in his pocket.

'I took off my jumper because it had blood stains all over it. And I had blood all over here, all over my hands, all up my arms, blood all over the place. And then hopped in her car.' Denyer explained that he had adjusted the seat 'to match my height 'cause she was a lot smaller than me.'

Denyer had wiped off most of the blood using his blue jumper, tossing his into the car, and Debbie's white windcheater into the bushes.

'I hopped back in the car again and then done a U-turn and headed back down Taylors Road. I pulled up outside the New Life Christian Centre. I grabbed my jumper and wiped my prints off the steering wheel. Wiped my prints off the transmission lever or gear stick. Off the handbrake, off the door knobs on the inside. I got out of the car and just walked home.'

Wilson established the route Denyer had walked.

'Yeah, when I got back there, I took off all my clothes and washed 'em.' Denyer was home in time to telephone Sharon at work and arrange to meet her at Kananook railway station.

Incredibly, Denyer then admitted returning to the unlocked car the following morning after his girlfriend had gone to work. He told the detectives that he took the two cartons of milk and the eggs out of the car along with a packet of cigarettes and a chocolate.

'Did you think that was a bit risky?'

'At first, yeah.'

'And you took her purse?'

'It had exactly twenty-two dollars in it.'

'What happened to the money?'

'Spent it or something. Can't remember.'

Denyer told the detectives that he had gone back for the purse to find out the name of the woman he had killed. Taking the groceries home with him, he emptied the milk down the sink, threw the eggs out the back and burnt the cartons, which he saw as evidence. Denyer took the purse and buried it at the golf course along the same track where he had killed Natalie Russell. After his busy morning, Denyer told the detectives, he 'just sat back and did nothing.'

'Did at any stage Debbie Fream mention anything about her personal life to you?'

'No.'

'Why did you kill her?' Wilson asked.

'Same reason why I killed Elizabeth Stevens. I just wanted to.'

Denyer described dismantling his home-made knife and hiding the pieces in the air vent in the laundry at his flat.

'Why didn't you get rid of that? Why did you put it in the air vent?'

'Couldn't think of anywhere else to hide it.'

'Like you buried the purse... '

'Well, I thought that I might have been under surveillance so if I took it anywhere and buried it I would've been seen doing it.'

'But you might have been seen burying the purse for that same reason, wouldn't you have thought?'

'Yeah, different time of day, different method of thinking,' Denyer said cryptically.

Denyer told Wilson that he had dug the hole with his hands to bury the purse.

'How would you be able to find the spot?'

'Oh, I'll find it. I know where it is,' he replied confidently.

27

Natalie Russell's Murder

FRESHEST in the minds of the detectives interviewing Paul Denyer was the murder of year twelve student Natalie Russell less than forty-eight hours earlier. The Sunday morning sun had yet to rise, but birds were beginning to waken and sing while inside the Frankston police station, a young man began telling two tired detectives how he cut the throat of a schoolgirl.

Ironically, as the Sunday newspapers arrived on doorsteps around Melbourne, Denyer was coming to the end of his extensive statement to police. Headlines in the *Sunday Herald Sun* and *The Sunday Age* screamed, 'Killer Strikes Again' and both papers ran with stories about how police were frantically hunting for the killer of Natalie Russell, 'convinced he would strike again.' The papers would have to wait until Monday to run their 'Man, 21, In Court' headlines, bringing relief to everyone in Melbourne — especially those living in Frankston and its surrounding suburbs.

Rod Wilson began the home stretch almost forgetting that Saturday had turned into Sunday.

'The next incident occurred yesterday... sorry, it's now the day after, but on Friday. What can you tell me about that?'

Denyer again told Wilson about his car overheating and having to first stop at the reserve and then on Skye Road opposite the entrance to the bike track.

'Well, you already knew the track existed because that's where you—'

'I went up there earlier that day and cut the holes in the fences.' Denyer explained that he had cut three holes in the cyclone wire fences with a pair of pliers that he kept in the car. He had tested each hole for size by climbing through. Afterwards, he explained, he had visited his mother's de facto husband, Jim, and then gone to hunt for car parts at a local wreckers.

Denyer had driven back to Skye Road to wait for a victim.

'I sat in the car for twenty minutes 'til about quarter to three and then I saw the girl coming down the road.' Denyer explained that the girl he saw was wearing a blue school uniform and he had seen her coming out of the road where John Paul College was.

'When I saw her coming over the hill, I predicted straight away where she'd be heading 'cause she crossed the road. She crossed the road onto the golf course side. I knew exactly where she was heading.'

Strangely, Denyer denied feeling the urge to kill this time even though he had admitted cutting the holes in the fence earlier and then sitting in his car for twenty minutes waiting for a victim. He told Wilson that he had just decided to take a walk up the track. He also admitted being armed with a red-handled knife for his 'walk'. Denyer walked down the track ahead of Natalie Russell and climbed through one of the holes he had cut to wait for her.

Wilson asked him if he had any other weapons. Denyer replied, 'Oh, and the leather strap.'

'What was that? What sort of leather strap?'

'Just a thin... you would have found it at the scene — in two pieces.'

'What was that used for?' asked Wilson.

'Strangling.'

Denyer described the murder of Natalie Russell.

'I saw her walk... she was coming up the track and I saw her walk past, like, that way, and I ran out through the hole in the fence again and followed her.'

'Did she see you?'

'She turned around once and saw me. And I stuck about ten metres behind her until I got to the second hole... and just when I got to that hole, I walked up behind her and stuck my left hand around her mouth and held the knife to her throat... and that's where that cut happened.' Denyer indicated the cut on his thumb that he had earlier explained as due to sharpening a knife at home. 'I cut that on my own blade,' he admitted.

'Dragged her through the hole in the fence,' he continued.

'Was she struggling?'

'At first, but then she sort of stopped.'

'Why?'

'Because I told her I was gonna cut her throat... I said I was gonna, yeah, cut her throat. And I walked through the hole in the fence. I followed her through and I dragged her into the trees. Like she offered, she said, "Oh, you can have sex with me if you want." She goes, "You can have all my money, have sex with me," and things — just said disgusting things like that really.' Denyer shook his head to emphasise his disgust. It was the only time during the many hours of interviewing that he showed any emotion. His anger and disgust at Natalie Russell were obvious. It was equally obvious to the detectives that Denyer had no comprehension of the fact that Natalie Russell had been desperately trying to save her life. She must have known she was in the hands of the serial killer and had obviously been willing to do anything to stay alive. Denyer completely failed to see that.

'And did that upset you?' Wilson asked, surprised by his sudden outburst.

'In a way,' replied the killer, his anger quickly subsiding and his voice becoming even once again. 'And I got her to kneel down in front of me and I held the knife blade over her eye, really closely, and yeah, she had the same colour eyes as I have.'

'Why did you hold that knife so close to her eye?'

'Just so she could see the blade.'

'And why was she kneeling?'

'No, she was lying on the ground at that stage and I was lying on top of her. I wasn't lying, I was kneeling on top of her. Just holding her by the throat and with the knife next to her eye. And she struggled and then the knife cut her on the face. And she was bleeding a bit then... Yeah, and then when she got up, she started to scream a bit. And I just said, "Shut up. Shut up. Shut up. Shut up." And, "If you don't shut up, I'll kill you. If you don't do this I'll kill you, if you don't do that." And she said, "What do you want from me?" I said, "All I want you to do is shut up." And so when she was kneeling on the ground, I put the strap around her neck to strangle her and it broke in half. And then she started violently struggling for about a minute until I pushed — got her onto her back again — and pushed her head back like this and cut her throat.'

Denyer mimicked Natalie Russell's last moments as he described his attack on her. But his description of what he did to the dying schoolgirl made the detectives' stomachs turn.

'I cut a small cut at first and then she was bleeding. And then I stuck my fingers into her throat.'

'Mm,' murmured Wilson, trying to keep the shock from his face. He had to appear casual to keep the young man talking. It wasn't the time for recriminations or incredulity — they just had to remain stoic while listening to the litany of horror.

'...and grabbed her cords and I twisted them.'

'Why'd you do that?'

'My whole fingers — like, that much of my hand was inside her throat,' Denyer indicated by holding up his hand for the benefit of the detectives.

'Do you know why you did that?' repeated Wilson.

'Stop her from breathing... And then she slowly stopped. She sort of started to faint and then when she was weak, a bit weaker, I grabbed the opportunity of throwing her head back and one big large cut which sort of cut almost her whole head off. And then she slowly died.'

'Why did you want to kill her?' asked Wilson rubbing his forehead.

'Just same reason as before, just everything came back through my mind again. I kicked her before I left.'

'Why's that?'

'While she was dead, just booted her.'

'Why did you kick her after? Like she was obviously dead at that stage.'

'Make sure she was dead.'

'Kicking her, would that make sure she was dead?'

'Well, if she had've moved, I would've known.'

Denyer described walking back down the bike track and passing a young boy going the other way. The boy had looked at him as he passed.

Having satisfied his lust for blood, Denyer stuck his bloodied hands in his pockets and walked to the end of the lane. Coming out onto Skye Road, he saw something that made him stop — two uniformed police officers were walking around his car, taking down its details. Denyer told Wilson that he had merely ducked his head, turned right and walked down Skye Road towards his home.

Wilson and O'Loughlin couldn't help being struck by the carelessness of Denyer during his final murder. They remembered his account of his frantic search for the knife with which he had killed Debbie Fream and here he was telling them that not only had he left the leather strap at the scene, but he had bled at the scene too and left his car where it could be checked twice by police. Not only was there forensic evidence that could link him to the crime scene, he had parked his car on Skye Road adjacent to the bike track and sat there for almost half an hour before the killing, in full view of passing traffic, not to mention other pedestrians — many of whom had already come forward to report seeing him. Ironically, one witness who knew Paul Denyer saw him as she was driving past. She had described seeing him sitting in his car smiling to himself and then his expression had changed when he caught sight of her. The two had made eye contact as she drove past. Yet Denyer had still followed Natalie Russell down the bike track. Wilson had the distinct impression that Denyer had become cocky. He had got away with two murders and thought he could now kill in broad daylight and get away with it.

Denyer told the detectives that he had gone home to change, washed his clothes in the bath and then walked back to collect his car, by which time the police were gone. Denyer had thrown the knife in a drum in his back yard and then gone to pick up Sharon from work. That evening, he explained, he and Sharon went to her mother's and he had thrown his wet clothing into her washing machine.

Wilson asked Denyer if there was anything else he would like to talk to them about.

'Yeah, I slashed her across the face.'

'Who's that?' asked Wilson.

'The last victim.'

'What do you mean you slashed her across the face?'

'After she was dead.'

'After she was dead?'

'Yeah, I just cut her straight down this side of her face.'

'Why was that?' asked Wilson.

'Don't know,' he replied shrugging.

28

Gathering Exhibits

SERGEANT Brian Gamble had spent all day Saturday examining the bike track in a bid to find evidence at the crime scene. Around 10 pm, he was asked to examine Paul Denyer's flat. Accordingly, Gamble took his kit and drove the short distance to the flat to begin searching for evidence. At that time, the young man in custody had made no admissions of guilt, but was shaping up well as a suspect. The crime scene examiner set about looking for anything potentially incriminating.

The flat had been secured by detectives as soon as Denyer had been taken to the police station and nothing had been touched when Gamble set about his tasks. The flat had two bedrooms, a lounge room, kitchen, laundry and a bathroom with a toilet in it. Two biologists from the state forensic science laboratory joined Gamble. Looking for blood traces, the biologists found smears near the front door as well as around the taps in the bathroom.

Gamble collected three pairs of shoes from behind the front door, including the black Aerosport runners Denyer had earlier shown the detectives. He bagged and labelled all the shoes. On top of the freezer in the kitchen, he found a blue baseball cap. Picking it up and looking at the marks beneath the peak, Gamble noticed stains that could have been blood. He bagged the cap too. At 1 am, Mick Hughes drove around to the flat and took the runners and a few scrapbooks so Rod Wilson could show them to Denyer on camera.

Then Gamble entered the spare room, where clothes and rubbish covered most of the floor and an old couch. He systematically made his way around the room looking for anything of interest. He noticed the glove gun on the book case, but what caught his eye was a cord hanging on the back of the door. Gamble carefully examined the cord which was knotted at both ends. Caught in one of the knots was what appeared to be a single strand of hair. He bagged the cord.

In the suspect's messy bedroom, Gamble found a large home-made knife lying on the dressing table next to a packet of Biggies pantyhose. The knife had been cut from aluminium and wrapped with black tape around the handle.

Outside in the driveway, Gamble made a preliminary examination of the dirty yellow Toyota Corona, noting that it was in poor condition. Inside the boot, in a tool box, he noted the presence of a number of tools as well as a large wooden-handled knife and a replica plastic gun. Gamble arranged for the car to be taken to the forensic science laboratory in Macleod for a more detailed examination.

Brian Gamble spent five hours combing the flat for evidence before returning with his exhibits to the Frankston police station.

29

Anything You Haven't Told Us?

COMING to the end of Denyer's account of the three murders and the attempted abduction of Roszsa Toth, Rod Wilson asked, 'Anything you haven't told us?'

Denyer thought for a moment and then began explaining about the knife he had used to kill Elizabeth Stevens. He had bought it a while back from the Big W store at Karingal Hub.

'I walked into the store one night and went to the sporting department and I grabbed a fishing knife. And I grabbed one of the female shop assistants there in the toy department and held it to her throat and said I was gonna cut her to pieces.' Denyer couldn't remember exactly when the incident had occurred and he said he hadn't physically hurt the shop assistant and that the knife was still in its packet.

Rod Wilson asked Paul Denyer when he had first begun to 'feel the urges' to kill. Denyer told him that he had always wanted to kill and then qualified his answer and finally decided that he had wanted to kill since he was about fourteen years of age. Wilson wanted to know why it had taken Denyer so long if the urges had been with him for the last seven years.

'I don't know,' Denyer replied. 'Just waiting for the right time, waiting for that small silent alarm to trigger me off.'

'And the incident you spoke about at Karingal Hub in the Big W, was that the first time you felt you were progressing into something... ?'

'Yeah. I've been stalking women for a few years in Frankston.'

'How long do you think you have been doing that?'

'Three or four years, or since I was seventeen, I think. I've been following heaps of women around.'

'Just waiting for the opportunity?'

'Waiting for the sign,' Denyer nodded.

Rod Wilson questioned Denyer about the unsolved murders of Sarah McDiarmid and Michelle Brown. Sarah disappeared from the Kananook railway station in July 1990 and Michelle, two years later. Denyer denied knowledge of the two murders apart, he said, from what he'd heard on the news.

Rod Wilson brought up the issue of the police scanner and asked Denyer whether he had heard of his name being mentioned over a police scanner as he had previously stated. The question opened a hornet's nest and solved another crime on the books of the Frankston CIB. Denyer had told detectives, while he was still at the flat, that a friend had heard his name mentioned over the police radio scanner on Friday when his car was checked as a suspicious vehicle on Skye Road. Wilson asked who owned the scanner. The scanner, Denyer told them, belonged to a friend of Donna Vanes. It transpired that Donna Vanes was the sister of Denyer's neighbour Tricia.

'That was the girl I went to Claude Street that night.'

Wilson and O'Loughlin didn't understand what Denyer was talking about.

'She used to live there. She moved out of Claude Street because I broke into her place and killed all of her cats.'

Darren O'Loughlin, a local detective, remembered the incident.

'When did you do that?' asked Wilson.

'Earlier this year.'

'What did you do that for?'

'I went there to kill her but she wasn't home.'

'Did you prepare yourself for that?' asked O'Loughlin.

'Yeah, I had a large knife on me.'

'Where did that come from?'

'Well, I bought that for about $7.50 from Aussie Disposals in Frankston, Beach Street.'

'Was there any other preparation?'

'I had gloves,' Denyer volunteered, 'so I wouldn't leave any prints. I don't think I did leave any prints, no.'

'When did you put the gloves on?'

'Just as I walked up to the front door. I knocked on the door first to see if there was anyone there, but there was no-one there so I walked around the back and climbed through the window. Cut a hole through the fly screen and sort of wedged myself through.'

'Was the window open?'

'Yeah, wide open.'

'What did you want to kill her for? You knew her, didn't you? Isn't she—?'

'Vaguely,' interrupted Denyer.

'Tricia who lives in flat 3. Isn't it her sister? What had she done wrong? Or had she done anything wrong?'

'Didn't like her sister.'

'Trish?'

'No, didn't like Trish at all,' Denyer said shaking his head.

'So what did that have to do with Donna?'

'Well, I knew she was home by herself most of the time.'

'Donna was? Did you dislike Donna for any reason?'

'Never really liked her, no.'

Denyer and the detectives established that the cats had been killed in February and Denyer volunteered that he thought it was 28 February. It was in fact 19 February.

'And you went to Donna's flat in Claude Street to kill her?'

'Yeah.'

'And she wasn't home?'

'No, she wasn't home.'

'So you broke in and what did you do?'

'I killed her cats.'

'How many?'

'Three.'

'How did you kill her cats?'

'Stabbed 'em all.' Considering the carnage witnessed by investigators in Donna Vanes's flat, Denyer had in fact done a lot more than just stab them.

'O'Loughlin asked exactly what had happened when Denyer had first entered the flat.

'I walked slowly into the lounge room 'cause the lights were all on, just 'cause I thought somebody was there. And then I just went into a blind rage and just killed anything that was alive in the house.'

'What would have happened if Donna was there?' asked O'Loughlin, knowing the answer.

'I would've cut her throat,' Denyer said casually.

'Can you explain what happened to the cats? Where were they?'

'In the lounge room. A mother and her two kittens.'

'And what happened to the cats?'

'Well, the mother cat ran into the laundry and I chased after it. It lunged at me and I just stabbed it in the side and it died straight away.'

'And what happened to the others?'

'I slit their throats and threw 'em in the bath tub.' Denyer didn't mention disembowelling the mother cat and he didn't mention placing the picture of the model on its stomach, writing on the wall or slashing the baby clothes.

Denyer told Wilson and O'Loughlin that Donna had reported the break-in to police. 'It was on the news,' he said almost proudly. 'Everybody knew about it.'

Apart from the incident at Karingal Hub and the killing of the cats, Wilson asked Denyer if he had anything else he wished to tell them. 'No, that was about it,' Denyer replied. Rod Wilson decided to try one last time to get to the bottom of Denyer's motives for the killing spree. He asked the young man what his general attitude towards women was. 'Just don't like some of them,' Denyer explained.

'Obviously you're in love with — or, I'll assume that you're fond of Sharon.'

'Sharon's not like anyone else I know,' Denyer said earnestly, looking straight at Wilson.

'Well, you wouldn't think of hurting her?'

'Never,' replied the killer of three young women. 'No, I'd never hurt her. She's a kindred spirit.'

Responding to questions that would help explain forensic evidence, Denyer described wearing his black runners while committing each murder. He had, he explained, put them on the stove at his flat to melt the soles to prevent the shoes being used to tie him to any of the crime scenes. The pattern on his shoes could never be linked to shoe impressions at the crime scenes, because the pattern no longer existed. Although the detectives didn't consider Denyer particularly bright, they gave him credit for a degree of animal cunning.

Exhausted of questions, Rod Wilson turned to Darren O'Loughlin and asked him if he had any matters he wished to raise. O'Loughlin, who had been sitting silent for most of the lengthy interview, asked the question that was foremost in his mind.

'You mentioned David, your brother... was the cause. Is that correct?' he asked, referring to the earlier mention of sexual abuse.

'Some of it,' replied Denyer.

'Some of it,' repeated O'Loughlin. 'If that's the cause, then why have women been the victims?'

'I've only ever had two relationships and Sharon was the third. And the first two ones were older women with kids. And one of them was using me for something... yeah.'

'Can you explain why we have women victims?' O'Loughlin persisted.

'I just hate 'em.'

'I beg your pardon,' said O'Loughlin.

'I just hate 'em,' Denyer repeated.

'Those particular girls,' asked O'Loughlin, referring to Denyer's three victims, 'or women in general?'

'General.'

'You told Detective Senior Sergeant Wilson that you stabbed them in the throat. Is there any particular reason why there?'

'Well, it looked like the most vulnerable spot.'

'Did each girl get stabbed in the throat?'

'All of 'em... I saw it in a movie once and it just looked effective.'

'What movie was that?' asked O'Loughlin.

'It was called *The Stepfather*. And a guy stabbed a guy in the neck with a broken glass and, yeah, just looked effective.'

'Denyer went on to deny memory of any of the vicious marks and cuts he had inflicted on his victims, although he conceded he must have done them. O'Loughlin asked if he was in a habit of forgetting things. Denyer said he wasn't.

'How did you feel afterwards?' asked O'Loughlin, trying to get a picture of what was going through the killer's mind.

'Like the temperature gauge was coming down.'

'What do you mean?' O'Loughlin asked him.

'Well, it was going up to boiling point, then afterwards it just came down 'til it stopped at a level and then climbed up again.'

'You're referring to what type of feeling?'

'Hate, anger.'

'Is this something that you plan?'

'No, I would just go to a certain area and then pick targets around, just, you know, anyone you see walking around is... anyone, women, woman by herself. So I'd just wait for them. No it wasn't premeditated in that way.'

'Wait for the right opportunity to come along. Is that fair to say?'

'Yeah, just sort of go to the area and hope for the best.'

'Denyer discussed his weapons with the detectives. The cord he used, he told them, had come from around the waist of his tracksuit pants. It had come off and he had kept it to strangle someone with, and the fake gun, he told O'Loughlin, was on a shelf in the spare room at his flat.

Placing a scrapbook that had been taken by police from Denyer's flat on the table, Rod Wilson asked Denyer if it was his. Denyer told Wilson that it was and explained that he had been practising drawing. There was a sketch of one person pointing a gun at another. It was labelled *The Last Great Act of Defiance*. Denyer admitted drawing it. There were other pictures — a gun as well as old sketches of scrub and bushes that Denyer said he had done from sites around the Flora and Fauna Reserve where he had stopped on Friday before going to the bike track on Skye Road.

Bereft of further questions for the time being, Rod Wilson checked his watch. It was 6.05 am on Sunday morning. The interview had lasted all night. In order to prevent future possible allegations of maltreatment of the murderer, Wilson mentioned on video-tape that Denyer had been supplied with a hamburger and a few cups of coffee.

'Yeah, I was well looked after,' Denyer agreed politely.

Wilson told Denyer that he would make arrangements to go to the areas mentioned in the statement. First port of call would be where Denyer buried Debbie Fream's purse. 'Do you have any objections to that?'

'No,' replied the confessed killer.

Rod Wilson suspended the interview.

30
Re-enactment

IT was still dark at 6.40 am when Senior Constable Stephen Batten set up his video camera tripod on the footpath on Cranbourne Road. Batten turned on the bright camera light and Rod Wilson, Darren O'Loughlin and Paul Denyer stood in front of the camera waiting for Batten to tell them he was ready. Behind the scenes were a number of other officers including crime scene examiner Brian Gamble who had not long finished the examination of Denyer's flat. Gamble had joined the group to organise searches of the areas that Denyer indicated. Wilson read Denyer his rights again and the young man quietly responded that he understood. Denyer had led the detectives to the corner of McClelland Drive and Cranbourne Road to point out the location where he had tossed the knife he used to kill Elizabeth Stevens.

Can you tell us where it is?' Wilson asked, looking into the scrub adjacent to the footpath.

'Follow me,' Denyer said, and began walking down Cranbourne Road, one hand tucked behind his back. As he spoke, his breath fogged in the cold of the first day of August, while the camera view of him from behind accentuated his height and bulk.

The three men walked along the footpath and Paul Denyer's eyes scoured the scrub. He turned around to face the camera and spoke to Stephen Batten. 'Can you turn the light off for a sec? I just want to have a look in here,' he said, indicating a fallen tree. 'I'd remember it better in the dark.'

Batten obliged and cut the light, leaving the two detectives and Denyer in the dark.

'Yeah, I remember the log there.' He pointed to the tree as Batten switched the light back on. 'I can't remember exactly where; it could be here, or it could be up there,' he said, pointing further up the road.

'Can you indicate how you threw it in?' Wilson asked. Denyer said that he had thrown the knife underarm and swung his right arm imitating the movement for the benefit of the detectives.

'Actually, I saw something red in there just before,' Denyer said, bending to look in through the knee-high grass. The knife had a red handle and he wasn't aware that the police had already found it in the line search the day after Elizabeth Stevens's body had been discovered. Rod Wilson asked Darren O'Loughlin to have a look and the detective took a couple of tentative steps down the incline and bent down to inspect beneath the fallen tree. 'It's just a Coke bottle,' he reported as the other two watched on.

'Oh,' said Denyer sounding disappointed. Since the confession, he seemed to be trying to prove beyond doubt that he was the killer. After taking pains to hide forensic evidence during the murders, he was now trying his hardest to point it out to the investigators. The three men continued walking further up Cranbourne Road. Denyer kept his left hand in the pocket of his baggy blue-grey tracksuit pants, his right held to his face in concentration.

'Possibly in there,' he said, considering another patch of scrub. Rod Wilson stopped walking and stood beside him. 'I know it was in the bushes but it wasn't as far as that power pole there,' Denyer said, pointing further up Cranbourne Road. Wilson turned to the camera and told Steve Batten they would cease the interview there and go to the next location. It was 6.45 am. Just as the camera switched off, Denyer noticed another fallen log and told the detective that it could have been there so the video was switched on again and that area was filmed.

The sky was turning a steely grey when, fifteen minutes later, the camera rolled again at the corner of McCulloch and Kananook avenues. Rod Wilson again told the confessed killer that he wasn't obliged to say anything and that anything he said could be used in evidence. 'Yeah,' said Denyer. He understood the routine.

'Can you tell us what happened here?' asked Wilson.

'Well, the car was sitting over here.' Denyer pointed to the opposite corner and Batten swung the video camera around to film the empty road.

'Debbie Fream's car, we're talking about?' asked Wilson to get it straight for the record.

'The Pulsar. I was walking down this road here and saw her jump out of the car, into the milk bar here.' Denyer turned and pointed to the

milk bar on the corner and Rod Wilson took a couple of steps around
to look at the shop front.

'The car was directly across the road and I got in it. I could see her
from inside the car. I watched her come out and I crouched down
under the seat. She drove to do a U-turn down that street down there,'
he pointed diagonally across to Kananook Avenue, 'and she drove
around here.' Denyer turned to face the accountant's office next door
to the milk bar and walked over to the red brick entrance to show the
detectives where Debbie Fream had collided with the wall.

'Where did she hit?' asked Wilson standing next to him.

'Denyer bent down, scrutinised the brickwork for a few seconds and
said, 'There.' He pointed to the sixth row of bricks from the pavement,
about knee high to himself.

'Sure about that?' asked Wilson, looking closely to see if he could see
any marks.

'Positive,' said Denyer firmly. He then told Wilson that they had
driven down Kananook Avenue. That was all they needed at this
location and Wilson asked Batten to stop the tape.

At 7.19 am, the camera lights illuminated the spare room of Denyer's
flat. Cluttered with junk and second-hand furniture, Denyer picked his
way through the mess and located the glove gun he had mentioned in
his interview. From a distance, it resembled a real revolver. It was small,
black and square looking. He picked it up with his left hand, holding a
half smoked cigarette in his right. Turning the gun towards his head,
Denyer stuck the muzzle in his mouth and blew, making the rubber
glove finger pop out the other end.

Putting his cigarette in the corner of his mouth, he held the gun in
his left hand and pulled the rubber out as far as it would stretch. He let
go of the rubber finger with a snap. 'That's the way you operate it,' he
explained. 'It shoots a ball bearing.'

'Was that the weapon you used when you first approached Elizabeth
Stevens?' asked Wilson.

'Yeah, that's the one.'

'Same as the woman at the Seaford railway station?'

'Yep.'

Rod Wilson pointed to two other home-made guns lying against the
wall next to the book shelf. 'Did you use those for anything?' he asked.

'Nah, nah,' Denyer shook his head replying firmly as if the question
was stupid. He bent down to put out his cigarette in an ashtray on the
floor. He wasn't normally allowed to smoke in the flat. Sharon had

forbidden it.

Wilson turned around to face an old green checkered couch by the opposite wall. 'And this is the green jacket you wore on the night of Elizabeth Stevens?'

Darren O'Loughlin leaned over and picked it out of the pile of clothes covering most of the surface of the couch and held it up for the camera. Denyer agreed that it was the same jacket he had referred to in his earlier interview.

On a cluttered table beside him, Paul Denyer picked up a black Adidas baseball cap. He told the detectives that it was the cap he had worn on the night of Debbie Fream's murder and Roszsa Toth's attack.

'Is there anything else of any significance in here?' Wilson asked, looking around the mess. He knew that the crime scene examiners would give the room and its contents another thorough going over later, but it was important that the suspect himself point out anything of evidentiary value. It added weight to his verbal confessions.

'No, no,' he replied.

Stepping over the junk on the floor, the three men backed out of the spare room into the kitchen. It was as cluttered and untidy as the spare room; most of the cupboards were open revealing their contents. A red and white sheet hung crookedly over the kitchen window letting in little light.

Denyer pointed through the kitchen to the adjacent laundry. The roof was punctuated by single thin ventilation slats and he told the detectives that he had pushed the knife he used to kill Debbie Fream into one of the slats and then poked it further along with a bit if wire. Beneath the slats was a door leading into the back yard. 'The handle's out here,' he said, walking through the red, white and blue plastic strips hanging from the doorway. Rod Wilson followed him past a washing line full of clothes. Denyer bent down and picked up a piece of metal from the ground beneath his laundry window telling Wilson that it was the handle of the knife that he had used to kill Debbie Fream. He said he had removed the tape from the handle and flushed it down the toilet.

'The black tracksuit pants missing the cord... ?' Rod Wilson queried when they walked back past the clothes line.

'These ones,' said Denyer, unpegging a pair of pants next to where he stood. Wilson took the pants and inspected the waist. They had no cord.

'It's inside,' Denyer explained, referring to the missing cord. Before they went back inside, Wilson asked him about the knife used to kill Natalie Russell. Denyer took a couple of steps over to a metal bucket on the ground between the clothes line and an old white freezer. The knife wasn't there and Rod Wilson told him that it would have been collected by forensics.

Before leaving the tiny back yard, Wilson asked about the grey jumper Denyer had mentioned wearing during the attack on Natalie Russell. Denyer pulled it from the clothes line and handed it to the detective.

They moved back inside into the spare room again in search of the blue windcheater Denyer had worn when he killed Debbie Fream. He shuffled through piles of clothes on the floor in a vain attempt to find it in the mess.

'And that black cord,' said Wilson picking through the piles of clothes, 'where do you think that would be?'

His left hand on his hip and his right hand on his chin, Denyer thought for a second and then stepped towards the back of the spare room door. 'It was hanging here on the door handle. It's not there now. I remember seeing it yesterday, so someone's taken it.' It was the same cord Brian Gamble had collected earlier.

Rod Wilson walked towards the bedroom Paul shared with Sharon. There was a pink blanket hung across the window in place of curtains. Denyer bent to the floor and picked up the blue windcheater top he had been looking for. The tape stopped at 7.26 am.

A little over ten minutes later the camera rolled again. This time Rod Wilson, Darren O'Loughlin and Paul Denyer stood at the entrance of the bike track. After he lit a cigarette, Denyer pointed across the road to the place where he had parked his car on Friday and then led the detectives to the spot where he had buried Debbie Fream's purse. Using a pair of bolt cutters supplied by police, Denyer cut at the cyclone wire and, with his hands, twisted the wires to make a small hole. Taking up the bolt cutters again, he deftly snipped further, forming a large diamond-shaped hole. As he neared the bottom of the fence, he turned and smiled over his right shoulder to Rod Wilson: 'They're not going to charge me to fix this are they?' Denyer laughed at his own joke. The detectives didn't.

When the cutting was done, Denyer bent back the wire and stamped it down with his foot, puffing at his efforts and pushing his hair back to wipe his forehead. He then led his entourage through the fence. Walking between a couple of trees, Denyer solicitously held back the branches, telling the video camera operator to be careful.

'Just look for the softest part of the ground,' he said, standing under a tree and beginning to kick away loose dirt with his white runners. He bent over and felt the dirt with his hands, flicking away some more.

'Sure about the area?' asked Wilson.

'Positive,' Denyer replied, beginning to pant under the exertion of his shuffling feet. 'Wish I had a shovel,' he said breathlessly. Within a minute, Denyer unearthed a dirt covered black purse and held it in front of him like a trophy.

'Who does this purse belong to?' Wilson asked for the record.

'Debbie Fream,' replied the young killer, dropping it into a brown paper bag that Rod Wilson held out before him.

Denyer bent down beneath a nearby bush, flicked away a bit of dirt and picked up two plastic bank cards. Rubbing the dirt away, he explained that he had burnt them at the spot before burying them.

'Fream,' said Rod Wilson, reading the still discernible name on one of the cards. He dropped them into the bag with the purse.

Back on the main track just after 8 am, Rod Wilson, Darren O'Loughlin and Paul Denyer stood at the hole he had cut to lay in wait for Natalie Russell. He explained how he had seen her walking up Skye Road and that he had run up the track to hide through the hole, emerging when she was around ten metres further on. The men continued walking up the track and five minutes later, they stood in front of a second hole.

'What was the purpose of this hole?' asked Wilson.

'Oh, I put it there in case it was easier to kill her and drag her in there,' Denyer said, waving his arm casually through the hole. He had cut it at the same time he had cut the other hole, chosing this area because, he explained, being sheltered by overgrown trees, it was not visible from either end of the track.

As the men walked up the track towards the third hole, Rod Wilson asked, 'Were you still maintaining that distance behind her?'

'Nah, I was getting closer all the time. I walked along the grass here. Didn't make a sound.'

They stepped around puddles on the track that Denyer said weren't there Friday afternoon.

'I grabbed her here,' Denyer said when they were a couple of metres from the third hole in the fence, 'around the mouth with my left hand, held the knife to her throat, pushed her against the fence and struggled here for a second.'

'So this is the area where... ?'

'She was murdered,' finished Denyer. 'I dragged her through here.' Denyer stepped through the hole in the fence but Rod Wilson asked him to come back. The interview was over. They had what they wanted.

31

Cell 6 City Watch House

COLIN McKinney had taken promotion to sergeant when he transferred to work at the city watch house. He had been there for a year and had seen some of Victoria's worst prisoners come through, waiting for their preliminary hearings in the adjoining court rooms. The huge Gothic looking grey building adjacent to the Melbourne Magistrate's Court had been earmarked for closure by the end of 1994 but in the interim, officers and prisoners alike had to endure its squalid and archaic conditions. Having worked until eleven the night before, McKinney was well aware of the arrest of a suspect in the Frankston murders and his staff were on standby to receive him as soon as homicide detectives had finished interviewing him. When McKinney arrived for his 3 pm shift on Sunday, the prisoner, Paul Charles Denyer, had already been processed, strip-searched and allocated cell six.

Sergeant McKinney looked up at the cell monitors above the front desk and saw Denyer sitting motionless on a wooden bench inside the cell. Denyer had been classified as a separate separate, meaning that not only did he have to be separated from the main prisoners, but he also had to be held separately from those who, because of crimes against women or children, were classed as separates. In other words, he was allowed near no-one. Because of his crimes against the three innocent young women, McKinney and his fellow officers knew that if Denyer were put in with the other prisoners, he wouldn't last five minutes — such was the strange code of honour among Victoria's most hardened offenders. With this in mind, the other prisoners were not informed of Denyer's presence at the watch house, although they certainly suspected that he would end up there sooner or later.

One of his first duties at the beginning of a shift was to check on the prisoners and McKinney walked around to cell six after seeing that

Denyer's paperwork was in order. Unlocking the huge black metal gate that led into the cell block, McKinney walked down the blue stone paving to Denyer's cell. He unlocked the cell door and got his first real look at the self-confessed killer. McKinney was surprised. Denyer was still sitting quietly on the bench against the back wall of the cell. He looked up as the police officer entered. McKinney hadn't really known what to expect. What did a serial killer look like? The sergeant's first impression of Paul Denyer was one of a neatly dressed young man, overweight but clean cut, who was incredibly cool and calm considering the circumstances under which he was being held.

'You are?' asked McKinney.

'Paul Denyer,' the young man replied quietly.

'Everything okay?'

'Yeah.' Denyer remained seated while McKinney pushed the heavy door closed again. Denyer looked completely normal and completely unlike a killer. McKinney was mildly disconcerted. In his experience, it was somehow comforting when a killer looked or at least acted insane or frightening but Paul Denyer looked just like anybody else.

Not long after he checked on Denyer, McKinney received a telephone call from Sharon Johnson. She wanted to visit her boyfriend and as it was outside regular visiting hours, the sergeant contacted the homicide detectives in charge of the investigation to get their approval. It was all right with them. McKinney also decided to check with Paul Denyer before allowing the visit. When he asked the prisoner if he would like to see his girlfriend, Denyer said quietly that he would. McKinney telephoned Sharon and told her to come in to the watch house.

A little after 5 pm, Sharon Johnson rang the intercom buzzer and identified herself to Colin McKinney who could see her through the heavy metal-framed glass door. Sharon was a large, plain young woman with shoulder-length dyed blond hair. She wore no make-up and was casually dressed. To Sergeant McKinney, she looked like a woman with a mission. She didn't ask the usual questions that the sergeant had heard hundreds of times: what can I bring him? Does he need anything? She said she just wanted answers.

McKinney led her to a tiny interview enclosure. Sharon sat uncomfortably on the narrow bench and stared through the mesh to a huge black iron gate that was also meshed. She watched the sergeant open the gate and usher the other separated prisoners back into cell five. The corridor which the cells opened onto was the exercise area for the separates, while an adjoining yard housed the general prisoners.

A vague burning smell permeated the visiting area, emanating from a wick of tightly screwed toilet paper slung over a bar. The first prisoner to get a light from one of the guards each morning started the wick, which burned for hours, giving the prisoners a means of lighting their cigarettes since matches and lighters were not allowed. Not strictly allowed either, there was no way of preventing the use of the wicks unless the guards banned toilet paper.

McKinney unlocked the door of cell six and let Paul Denyer out for the first time since he had been processed. Denyer walked quickly to the black iron gate, clutched at the mesh and started to cry in a high-pitched whine as soon as he saw Sharon in the interview area across the corridor

Though he rarely observed interviews, Colin McKinney decided that this one would be worth sitting in on, so he told the prisoner that he would wait and listen from the next room, which was connected to the corridor by yet more mesh. From his vantage point, he could see both Denyer and his girlfriend. Denyer continued crying until Sharon said in a quiet but sharp voice, 'Don't cry Paul, I'm not here to listen to your blubbering, I want some answers.'

McKinney was surprised at her tone. She sounded a bit like a mother talking to a sulking child and Denyer stopped crying immediately.

'Are you all right now?' she asked. 'I want some answers.'

Denyer stood silently before his girlfriend while she continued in a business-like voice, 'I want to know, did you kill them, who you killed and where you killed them and why.'

In the adjoining room, Colin McKinney grabbed a piece of paper and began writing down what both of them were saying. He knew that Denyer had confessed to the murders to the homicide detectives, but he figured that Denyer could make further admissions to his girlfriend. He didn't want to miss anything. Sharon Johnson sounded determined to get answers.

'What about the girl Elizabeth? Did you go out to kill her or did you go to your mum's?' she demanded after Denyer had admitted to the murders.

'I went to Mum's and did it on the way home.' Denyer sounded like a child admitting to stealing lollies from the milk bar.

'What about the one in the car? Did you wait for her?' Sharon fired her questions faster than McKinney could write

'No, she went into the milk bar. I told the truth. I told them everything.'

'Did they have any evidence?' Sharon wanted corroboration. Paul had lied to her before; he could be lying again.

'My hands,' Denyer said, showing her the cuts that she had already seen.

'Was there anything at the unit?' she demanded.

'Knives.'

'Were they ours?'

'The one I put the tape around.'

'The pocket knife of yours, you chucked it near the service station?'

'Yes.'

'Why did you kill them and not rape them?' she asked.

'Anger, I got off.'

'What happened with the third one? Did you slice her throat?' Sharon wanted the details.

'Yes,' Paul admitted, starting to cry again in what Colin McKinney considered to be a self-pitying way.

'Don't start crying,' Sharon ordered. 'How did you clean your clothes?' Paul did most of their washing at her mother's.

'In the bath at home. I washed them.'

'Was anyone else involved?'

'No.'

'How come you never killed me?' she asked, the emotion at last beginning to show in her voice.

'Because I loved you, I'd never hurt you,' he told her.

'Were you going to keep killing?'

'Possibly. I need help.'

'You wanted help, didn't you?' her tone became gentle.

'Yes.'

'How come you went for two blonds and not brunettes?' Sharon had blond hair.

Denyer muttered something that Sergeant McKinney couldn't hear and then Sharon asked Paul why he did it. Denyer didn't answer. She repeated her question and still he didn't answer her.

'That's why you were late picking me up. Your car didn't break down.' Sharon was finally beginning to piece together the events and the realisation came to her that the previous Friday when Paul said his car broke down, he had actually been murdering Natalie Russell.

'Did you kill because you are afraid of dying? You wanted to see someone else die to see what it was like — didn't you?'

Paul replied, 'Yes, I've always been curious. I'm a serial killer. I've got a problem.'

McKinney watched through the mesh as Sharon told Paul that even though she didn't agree with what he had done, she still loved him. McKinney thought he heard her say something about God forgiving Paul, but he wasn't sure.

Finally, when Sharon Johnson had exhausted her list of questions, she said, 'I've got some bad news for you.'

McKinney wondered to himself what possible news could seem bad to a man already charged with three murders and probably facing a life term in prison.

I think I'm pregnant,' she said. Denyer immediately broke down and wept again. 'I'll keep it,' she assured her boyfriend who continued to cry.

When the visit was over, Colin McKinney escorted Denyer back to his cell and locked the door behind him with a strong feeling of anger towards the young man who, it seemed to him had absolutely no idea of the consequences of his actions. He walked around and led Sharon back to the office. He was curious about her. She seemed so unlike other women who came in to visit their partners. Some of the women he had seen were so distraught that they were incapable of sensible conversation. Sharon was different.

In the office, McKinney asked her if she had suspected anything and Sharon told him that she had questioned Paul when Donna Vane's cats had been slaughtered. Paul denied killing them but she had been suspicious enough to ask. Sharon told McKinney that she and Paul had often discussed the murders and that after each, she had asked him what he had been doing on the night. Every time the murders were featured on the television, the two had discussed them. After Debbie Fream went missing, Sharon said that Paul's face had been covered in scratches and that when she had come home from work, he had been sitting in a lounge room chair with a piece of coat hanger wire. Paul told her that he had tried to kill himself by scratching at his face. McKinney asked if she thought that was strange and Sharon merely shrugged.

As Sharon left the watch house, McKinney was aware of feeling a certain anger towards the young woman too. Even if she didn't know that her boyfriend was the killer, she had plenty of occasions to make an educated guess: Paul Denyer walking the streets of Langwarrin the night that Elizabeth Stevens was murdered, scratched after Debbie Fream went missing and cut after Natalie Russell's murder, his car 'broken down' on the days of the second and third murders and his frequent talking about the murders. But perhaps the wisdom of hindsight was too much to ask.

When McKinney left work that night, he couldn't stop thinking about Paul Denyer. He saw hundreds of hardened criminals through his work at the watch house, but Denyer was different. He was so calm and unaffected by his situation. He didn't seem to care about being locked up. He showed no signs of remorse or sorrow — the only emotion he had shown was during Sharon's visit and even then, it seemed that he was more sorry for himself.

32

Sharon

WHEN Paul Denyer was taken into custody from his flat on Saturday afternoon, Sharon Johnson had been escorted to the police station too. Detectives didn't know whether she knew about the murderous habits of her de facto or indeed whether she was even an accomplice.

When she walked out to her letter box late that Saturday afternoon and met the police officers, she didn't really understand what was happening. She and Paul had spent the morning shopping and looking for car parts; Paul had dropped her at the hairdressers for an appointment. When they had arrived home, there had been the detective's card wedged in their front door. Sharon had telephoned herself, and the detective she spoke to said that he would be around shortly.

Sharon Johnson had no idea that the detectives had been waiting for her call, that Paul's car registration had been taken at the entrance to the bike track on Skye Road around the time that Natalie Russell had been murdered and that Paul was a prime suspect in her murder. Sitting in an interview room giving an official statement to two female police officers was daunting. They began asking her about Paul and she explained how they had met at Safeway.

Answering questions about Paul's car, she told the officers that she didn't drive and Paul was the only one who ever drove his car. It was unregistered and had no number plates although Paul had a permit to drive it for twenty-eight days before it had to be registered.

Sharon explained the previous day's activities telling the officers that Paul had driven her to work and they had spoken briefly on the telephone around 9.30 am. She told them Paul picked up her pay cheque in the late afternoon from her second job and phoned her from there. He had explained that he would be a bit late picking her up because his car had overheated and he had to fix it. Sharon hadn't pressed him for details and the conversation had been brief.

Paul picked her up from work at 5.20 pm. Sharon got into the car and as Paul handed her the money from her pay cheque, she noticed that he had lots of cuts on both his hands and a deeper one on the middle finger of his left hand. Instead of inquiring about the cuts, Sharon asked him what happened to the car and Paul explained about the hose coming loose.

Sharon told the officers that she and Paul stopped at McDonalds to get something to eat and then drove to their flat so she could change out of her work clothes and pick up their dirty washing to take to her mother's.

While they visited, Paul did the washing in Sharon's mother's washing machine.

Bringing her narrative up to date, Sharon described the morning she had just spent with her boyfriend. She had slept until 10.30 am. Paul hadn't been home when she awoke but he arrived shortly after with the newspapers.

At 1 pm, they went to Harvey's Wreckers in Langwarrin to look for a speedo cable for Paul's car. Driving to Langwarrin, Sharon again noticed the cuts on Paul's hands and this time she asked him how they had happened. Paul told her he cut himself on the fan on his car when he had reached in to adjust some cables. At the wreckers, while Sharon looked on, Paul had reached in to get a speedo cable and cut himself again.

Sharon told the officers that Paul had been to visit a couple of wreckers either Thursday or Friday — she couldn't remember.

Sharon explained that for the last three weeks she had worked two jobs and that before Paul bought the car, he would catch the train to Moorabbin station every evening and meet her after work. They would both catch the train back to Kananook together. Paul had, she recalled, only missed one night, but although she couldn't recall which night it was, she did remember Paul ringing her at work and saying that he had missed the train and he would meet her at Kananook station.

Sharon told the officers that when she had arrived at the Kananook railway station, Paul had been waiting for her and next to him stood two police officers.

When I walked up to Paul, one of the policemen started talking to me. He asked if Paul was my boyfriend. I said he was. The policeman said I was lucky to have someone to meet me at the station.'

As they walked down the ramp, Sharon had asked Paul what was

going on and he told her that the police had been looking for some
Maoris who had been causing trouble at the station. Sharon told the
officers that she thought it must have been a Thursday night because
she remembered telling Paul that the police should have checked the
station on a Friday because that was when the Maoris hang around.
Having little else to add, Sharon completed and signed her statement.
Two days later, Sharon Johnson returned to the Frankston police
station to give a further statement. She told the officer taking her
statement that she had been confused, tired and upset when she had
spoken to police on Saturday. She explained that she had now begun to
think more clearly and had remembered things that she couldn't think
of on Saturday. The fact that Paul had now confessed to the killings
made her connect events in the last couple of months.

'I remember telling the police about the night Paul met me at
Kananook railway station. I can't remember the date but I know it was
a Thursday. When I got off the train — I'm not quite sure if it was the
same night we saw the police there — I met Paul on the platform. Paul
always used to meet me on the platform. I walked up to Paul and
straight away, I saw the scratches on his face. The scratches were
everywhere, I think mainly on the right hand side of his face. They
were extremely fresh as if he had just cut himself. There wasn't just like
two or three, there were heaps of marks and scratches. There were
some going down his face. They weren't all going down his face, they
were all over the place. There was a big circular red spot in his ear. It
was like a cut or something, just red like blood. It looked deep and I
think it was either just on the edge of his ear or just inside. There were
quite a few scratches on his forehead. His hair covered them but when
I moved his hair back, that's when I saw them.'

Sharon explained that they 'looked all bloody.' She had asked Paul
what had happened. 'Paul said that he must have got them from Trish's
clothes line because there was some wire hanging down. Trish lives in
unit three and her clothes line is right at the back of the block of units.
He said when he was walking around the back of the units, he had got
caught on the wire. Then he said when he walked back around he got
caught on the wire again. I said to him that I couldn't believe that he
would get caught by the same wire twice and that he must be lying.'
Paul denied lying but Sharon still hadn't believed him. She told the
officers that the scratches hadn't looked like they had been made by
wire. There had been too many of them.

'I kept on his back about it and told him to tell the truth. I thought he had been in a fight or something like that and didn't want to tell me about it. I kept whingeing at him about how he got the scratches but he just kept saying the same thing. Paul started to get annoyed with me so I eased off asking him questions.'

Sharon explained that she continued asking Paul about the scratches that night and the following day. That evening, they both had dinner at Sharon's mother's house and her mother also asked Paul about the scratches. Paul told her mother that he had scratched himself on a coat hanger on the clothes line. Sharon had confronted him about what she considered to be a lie, since he had changed his story, and kept up her tirade until her mother had given her a look to make her ease off. On the Saturday morning, Sharon had telephoned her work to tell them she was feeling sick and took the morning off. Paul's brother Steve had called around and he too had asked her about the scratches. Sharon told Steven the story about the clothes line and added that she didn't believe Paul. She said Steve didn't believe his brother either.

When we said this, Paul was hanging the washing on the line and he was just blocking us out. Steven asked him then if he had been in a fight. Paul just said it was the wire. I noticed a coat hanger then that had been undone and twisted around the line so that a piece of wire was hanging down. I'd never noticed it before. When I saw that, I eased off a bit because I thought maybe he was telling the truth.'

Nonetheless, Sharon continued questioning throughout the following week and by the end of it Paul was really annoyed with her. Sharon explained to the officers, 'At the start of our relationship about eighteen months ago, Paul used to lie quite frequently. Because of that, I always doubted what he said and I liked him to prove what he was saying.

The officers asked Sharon if Paul had ever been violent towards her. 'In about May this year,' she replied, 'Paul was working at Pro Marine in Seaford as a general hand. During that time, we had a huge argument. I don't remember the day or what we were arguing about. One night we just started arguing and it went on for hours. I hit Paul, but I can't remember where, then he hit me back. We hit each other a few times and then Paul started really getting angry and he put both his hands around my throat. He squeezed really hard and I couldn't breathe. He kept doing it until he could hear that I was choking and then he just let go. I tried to talk but I couldn't. My neck really hurt and I can remember it hurt for about two weeks after that. I ran into the bathroom and locked myself in. I was terrified. Paul came to the door and was very apologetic. He didn't do it again.'

Sharon told the officers she had noticed another scratch on Paul's face when he had met her after work on Friday afternoon. He had told her he got it while fixing his car. Adjusting the heater control as Paul drove, Sharon also noticed a knife on the dashboard. It was a long knife with tape around the handle and Sharon vaguely remembered seeing the knife months earlier while washing the dishes. Paul told her that he'd used the knife to fix his car. The knife was burnt on the end and Sharon was angry that Paul had ruined it. She told him to throw it out because they couldn't use it any more.

Sharon repeated how they had gone to her mother's house for dinner and she added that Paul had complained of feeling ill. She didn't know if he had actually vomited, but he had felt sick all night. On the way to the wreckers in the morning before the police arrived, Paul and Sharon had driven down Skye Road and seen all the police cars near the entrance to the bike track. The police were pulling over some cars and questioning occupants. Paul had commented that the girl could have been found on the bike track.

Sharon also recalled driving up Taylors Road a couple of weeks earlier on the way to a friend's place. Paul had mentioned Debbie Fream by name, telling Sharon that this was where she had been found. In hindsight, Sharon wondered that they had taken Taylors Road since they didn't usually drive that way to visit the friend.   Sharon told the officers about visiting Paul the previous day in the city watch house.

'I started talking to Paul about the murders he'd been charged with. I assumed the policemen at the watch house could hear what we were talking about. Paul told me about the knives he used to kill the girls, how he got Debbie Fream and also the first girl. I asked him a lot of questions and he answered everything. He told me when he killed the first girl, he was on his way back from his mum's. He said he cut her throat with a pocket knife. I asked him if he threw the knife near the petrol station in the grass and he said he did. He said he told the police where that knife was. That was all he said about that first one.

'He started talking about the next girl. I asked him what he was doing up there and he said he was wandering around up there and he saw Debbie go into Food Plus. While she was in there, he got in the car. With the third girl, he said he was driving and saw her crossing the road. He didn't say which road. He then just said that he killed her. He said it was a spur of the moment thing. I didn't go into details. He mentioned the knives he used. They were the ones he made at Pro

Marine and the one I saw in the car. He said he did it because of his family. I know his family don't take any interest in him and they think he's a liar. They only come to see him when they want something. Paul was mad about his dad because he never paid any interest whatsoever. Paul also thought that his dad's children from his current marriage get everything they want.'

Sharon mentioned in her second official statement that earlier in the day two police officers had come around to her flat and taken, amongst other things, some video cassettes. She said Paul liked dramas, thrillers or 'anything with cops in it,' and that the last video they had hired was about a man who strangled women. 'I didn't like that video. Paul said he didn't like it either.'

Asked what else Paul liked to watch on television, Sharon told the officers that he liked *Australia's Most Wanted*, *Cops* and *Hard Copy*. Programs like *Inside Edition* and *The Extraordinary* were also favourites. Sharon said she had never seen Paul read a book — because, he told her, he couldn't concentrate for long enough. However, he did like to draw — mostly scenery, but she had seen him draw a couple of guns.

When asked about the glove gun that Denyer had used to threaten his victims, Sharon admitted that she had seen it before, indeed Paul had shown her how it worked and a couple of times when they had gone out had carried it with him. Sharon had told him he was stupid to carry it. Apparently, Paul had replied that it looked like a gun and someone wouldn't know in the dark if it wasn't. He had said that it was just a bluff.

Sharon remembered Paul carrying a pocket knife which he claimed was for protection. The knife had gadgets on it and Sharon remembered them both looking for it about a month ago to use the corkscrew but they couldn't find it.

Sharon had no more to say. She signed her written statement and left the Frankston police station.

Sharon Johnson was one of three girls in her family. Her parents had separated when she was only a baby. Sharon was living with her mother when she met Paul Denyer at the Safeway store at Karingal Hub where he worked as a shop assistant two years before. A couple of months later, Sharon and Paul began a relationship and Paul moved into Sharon's mother's house. Not long after, the couple moved out to the flat which they now shared on the Frankston-Dandenong Road.

At nineteen years of age, Sharon was working two jobs to support herself and Paul, who had been unemployed for the last couple of months. She would finish her job as a tele-marketer for a charity in the early afternoon and go straight to her next job where she worked into the early evening.

When Sharon began working for the charitable organisation a number of fellow workers thought she was a bit strange. She dressed like someone much older, favouring long cardigans and dark floral dresses, and spoke mostly about Paul and work as if she had few other interests. One of Sharon's co-workers, Lorna Stark, remembers her as being usually calm except for one day when her boyfriend Paul couldn't be found. Sharon had tried phoning him. He should have been home but he wasn't. She grew increasingly frantic, phoning Paul's family as well as her own to try to track him down. When he finally returned home and answered the phone, fellow workers were aware of a loud argument between the two. Sharon always wanted to know where he was and when she didn't, everybody knew about it.

Many at the charity felt uncomfortable with Paul Denyer from the moment he accompanied Sharon to her initial job interview. He waited outside the manager's office while Sharon was interviewed and when she was called back for a second interview, Paul actually went into the office with her.

Often he would pick her up from work and would either wait in the car or come inside and wait by her desk. Sometimes he would play on the office computers, occasionally exchanging small talk with the women in the office. Lorna Stark recalls a number of occasions when she walked to her car after work and waved to Paul as he sat in his car waiting for Sharon. He never waved back, even though they had spoken in the office many times. He would just stare at her in a way that made her feel really uncomfortable, giving no acknowledgement that they had ever met.

One day, after Lorna had read an article in the paper about domestic violence, she spoke strongly about the subject. When Sharon remarked casually that Paul had once tried to strangle her, Lorna asked bluntly why she was still with him. Sharon had shrugged and said that they sometimes fought and that on that occasion, she had made him angry. Other times the women in the office discussed the murders in Frankston. Not long after Elizabeth Stevens's murder, Sharon told a co-worker that Elizabeth Stevens had noughts and crosses carved into her chest. The co-worker was surprised. She had read nothing about noughts and crosses in the paper and asked Sharon how she knew. She explained that Paul had a friend who was a police officer and he had found out through the friend. Sharon also discussed a possible move to another flat in Frankston. Co-workers spoke of how dangerous it was to live in Frankston at the time but Sharon had replied rather strangely that the murderer was a taxi driver and she didn't catch taxis. Although Sharon was happy and friendly at work, with Paul, it seemed, it was a different matter. Fellow workers couldn't fail to notice the arguments they had over the phone. They felt she totally dominated him in every way.

Another woman at the office took an instant dislike to Sharon and her boyfriend. It was her job to show Sharon the ropes of the computer and the tele-marketing side of the job. But she would avoid any excess contact with the young woman. She even told other workers that she was scared of Paul Denyer. So great was her feeling of unease, that she quit her job when she knew that Sharon was returning to work after Paul's arrest. When Sharon's trial period was up, the charity let her go and the woman returned to her old job. She was the only one at the office who wasn't surprised when Paul was arrested.

When Sharon did return to work a couple of weeks after Paul's arrest, she spoke to Lorna Stark. 'I suppose you know what happened?' she said. Lorna looked at Sharon sympathetically. The young woman had dyed her blond hair black which made her look different. Lorna told her that she had heard that Paul had been arrested and said soothingly that Sharon could now pick up the pieces and get on with her life. To Lorna's surprise, Sharon said happily that she was sticking by Paul and that there were reasons for what he had done.

'Sharon, there are no reasons for what he did. He didn't kill one person in anger, he killed three women in cold blood.' Lorna couldn't fathom Sharon's reasoning.

But there are reasons,' Sharon insisted, 'you don't understand. It will all come out soon. I love him and I am not going to leave him because of what he's done.' That was the end of the conversation. As far as Lorna was concerned, if Sharon could love a man who killed three women, she wanted nothing to do with her.

Lorna had been off work with the flu and had left work early on the day that Natalie Russell had been murdered but fellow workers later told her that Paul had come in to pick Sharon up and had seemed unusually happy and animated. He had waited while Sharon finished off some work and played on the computer.

33
Flowers

THREE weeks before she died, Natalie Russell was talking with a friend, Karen. 'When I die,' she said, 'I don't want to die in my sleep, I want to go out with a bang.' In one of life's ironies, Natalie Russell got her wish. Her funeral made national headlines and was attended by over a thousand people.

As Carmel Russell left her home in Forest Drive to go to her daughter's funeral, she took one last look around the lounge room. It looked like a florist shop there were so many flowers. She reflected sadly that when a clairvoyant had told her just a few weeks ago that she would soon be surrounded by flowers, she had thought it meant she would receive a couple of bunches for her birthday. Just last week, when her eldest daughter Lisa had sent her a bunch of flowers, Natalie had told her that the prediction had come true. They had laughed about it.

At the John Paul College hall, hundreds of bunches of flowers surrounded the makeshift altar in the hall as a thousand people, many of them fellow students in the light blue John Paul College uniform, took their seats. Quiet music played as they waited for the service to begin.

Constable Angela Butts, who had stayed with the Russell family on the night Natalie was murdered, was there. She wanted to show the Russell family that for her, it wasn't just a job. She cared. With so many people milling around the giant hall at John Paul College, Angela Butts wasn't even sure whether Carmel Russell would remember her or even notice that she was there. However, as soon as the policewoman appeared, Mrs Russell walked over to her and gave her a hug. Invited to sit near the family, Angela Butts was initially reluctant. Siting nearby was a high-ranking police officer in full dress uniform. 'If I cry,' she told Carmel, 'I don't want him to think that I'm weak.' Angela Butts need not have worried. Halfway through the service she looked over at the police officer and saw the tears running down his cheeks.

Walking in two lines, all the year twelve students filed into the hall. Two friends of Natalie's were carrying a huge red cross which they placed on top of her small oak coffin. Many heads were bowed with the incredible sadness of it all. Eight priests followed the procession of students and the congregation sang *God Gives His People Strength*. John Paul College principal Liam Davison welcomed the gathering and offered his sympathy to the Russell family. Then Fr John Rogan began the service. In the centre of the hall, the polished floor gleamed, lined with the markings of a basketball court. Natalie's coffin rested on a trolley standing on a red rug on the area in which she used to play netball.

Fr Rogan called upon four students to lay a white cloth over the coffin and another four brought forward a t-shirt, a poster, one of Natalie's favourite childhood toys and her netball skirt. The symbols of her life were placed on the floor in front of her coffin.

In his homily, Fr Rogan told the congregation, 'In truth, we have been faced with rampant evil and its effects on our very doorstep and we feel shock, fear and anger and the weight of great sorrow. Natalie left school last Friday afternoon with all the expectations of a normal seventeen-year-old, all the hopes and probings of one who loved life. In her own way, she influenced so many of her friends. One who loved her netball, her music, she took on the demands of the VCE, and questioned with real energy the values of the society in which she lived. All of this was part of her unique and particular story.' Fr Rogan told the congregation that everybody's story deserved to be told and that death was much easier to cope with after a long and full life. 'Natalie's death,' he said, 'had come in the first flush of her youth, an abrupt, painful and cruel end.' The priest spoke about God's love and the freedom of will that could sometimes lead to such evil.

'Why has this happened? Why does such a dreadful thing happen to a good and innocent young woman?' he asked, before assuring the congregation that it was not God's will. 'God suffers with us today,' he said, bowing his head slightly. Fr Rogan told everyone to take comfort in God and He would lead Natalie to her eternal place with Him.

The priest stepped away from the pulpit and Bernadette Naughton, Natalie's aunt, took his place. Her voice was soft with emotion. She had written a eulogy, painstakingly trying to capture the essence of her niece.

Natalie was a loving daughter and sister, she loved animals and had a great sense of humour. Making the congregation laugh, Miss Naughton repeated some of the nicknames that Natalie had given to staff at John Paul College, as well as, like so many other young people, referring to her parents as 'the olds'. Bernadette spoke of the 'Joyce' video that Natalie had made with her friend Sally. Everyone who had seen it smiled at the memory of Natalie dressed in a navy tracksuit playing a failed Nutri System customer. She had stuffed a pillow up her top and filled the legs of her pants with padding. She played the character straight while Sally giggled behind the camera. 'Joyce' went out the front gate and walked around the neighbourhood shouting 'Hi' to boys riding past on bikes. She tumbled around at a local park, swinging on the monkey bars and sliding down a yellow winding slide head first.

'Natalie has touched each of us in her own special way,' Bernadette Naughton said. 'Her passion for life, and her comic appreciation of it will bring a warmth to our precious memories of her. Natalie has left the world a better place,' she said, before stepping away from the pulpit.

Sitting through the service, Carmel Russell thought about Natalie's last years on earth. Her treasured daughter had blossomed into a confident young woman. Something Natalie's boyfriend David had repeated to Carmel came to her mind. Two days before she died, Natalie spoke to David on the telephone. 'I've got ace parents,' she had told him. 'They trust me. I must be the happiest girl in the world.' Carmel knew that her daughter died having known the utter joy of being young, loved and appreciated. It was a comfort to the grieving mother.

Carmel thought of something else that David had told her. A couple of weeks earlier, Natalie had visited David at his flat. Sitting in an armchair in his lounge room, she had suddenly burst into tears. Crying and shaking uncontrollably, Natalie had later been at a loss to explain her tears. She said she didn't know why she was crying. There was no reason. Now, Carmel wondered whether somehow Natalie knew that she would never live long enough to enjoy her life, never grow up, never become a journalist, never have children. Carmel wondered.

Next to speak was Natalie's sister Janine. On the verge of tears, Janine spoke haltingly about her sister. 'We will never forget you. We love you and we are going to miss you.' But somehow, mere words could not express the sheer and total loss they all felt.

At the end of the service, Fr Rogan circled the coffin sprinkling it with holy water. Another priest swung the brass incense holder; its smoke rose upwards in thin wisps as the congregation sang *Come to Her Aid O Saints on High,* to the tune of *Amazing Grace.*

The white cloth was removed from the coffin and folded carefully by one of the priests as six men approached to carry the coffin out of the hall. *Pictures of You* — Natalie's favourite song by The Cure — played as the funeral procession moved slowly from the church followed by the family, all leaning on each other for support. Moving through the foyer, the procession passed a display of enlarged pictures of Natalie Russell from when she was little to more recent shots, the photographs were surrounded by bunches of beautiful flowers.

Outside the hall, Carmel Russell looked around at the huge crowd and she knew how much her daughter was loved. As the family drove slowly through the guard of honour formed by hundreds of students along Skye road, a police escort in front of them, Carmel said aloud, 'Look Nat, they don't even do this for royalty. You got your wish, you went out with a bang.'

34

On Trial

Hi everybody,

I just got your letters and card. Thank you dearly for them because your understanding makes me feel a lot better.

Well I guess it's another day over and done with and I still probably have another 20 years or more to go. That's just an estimate.

I got a lot of work done today in the tailor shop till we ran out of canvas. Oh well, you can get that anywhere.

I remember now, that I rang you shortly before I was arrested. Could you tell that there was something wrong by the sound of my voice? Some people have said to me that I sounded like a stranger before. Well that was the old me. I know that I can't turn back time but the only thing to do is to say 'what now' instead of 'what if'. My only mistake in life was I couldn't trust anyone with the truth of my past. It still hurts now to think of that. Mum has probably told you all about who it was.

But people seemed so mean and I found it very hard to talk to my brothers. The day before the second incident, I was at Richard's place and trying to talk to Steve and Richard. They didn't believe me when I told them about the flashbacks I was having about David. They just accused Sharon and her mother of putting that into my head.

I kept telling them that whole afternoon I was having these images about the abuse even before I met Sharon.

So I left their place feeling awkward and very upset as I walked to the bottle shop. I bought alcohol and went home to get drunk. After drinking for about one hour I went out and the rest is history. I don't remember much after that. It was things like this and the other problems I was having that led me to these horrific acts. Could you please do me a big favour, not to tell anyone about what I have just said till after I am convicted because it's supposed to be classified information. But I know I can trust you not to say anything to anyone because the chances of the media coming into it is one hundred per cent.

Well I hope Tricia finds a job soon because I know how I felt not to have a job. To me that is, it takes away your pride and self-worthiness and it makes you feel useless to the world and your partner. That's how I felt at the time watching my hardworking fiance Sharon go to work every morning at 6.30 am and them waiting for her to come home at 9.00 pm. But at least I'm happy now that I'm working and that Sharon doesn't have to support me any more. So good luck Trish.

Before I came to prison, I never realised there are compassionate people on this earth. Everyone looked so mean and unwilling to help me or anyone. I went to Steve and Richard one day discussing my abuse and they seemed like they didn't want to know. Sharon tried to do what she could for me but with the pressures from my family, I guess she gave up a bit.

Well Richard and Steve are not talking to me and Dad has been very helpful. Sharon and her mum or sister come to visit every Tuesday and Wednesday for an hour. We pray together for everyone that I have hurt and sometimes I feel better about myself. I know I will be in here for many years to come and I know that my beloved Sharon will be standing by me. Our love can never be imprisoned and these bars can't keep it out.

Well what I want for the future is to try and put back what I have taken away. I know that it will probably never be done but I will try my best to help others.

I'm only going to better myself while in here and I am putting what happened behind me.

So I have two more days in court in December some time and there will be a bit of shit going round but eventually it will die down.

I have met a few other wrong doers in here and none of them are what the media have described. They just want the public to believe other things and whatever they make up.

Well I will close at this and if you want to you can write to me in here because I would like to keep in contact.

With more time, I can provide (whoever is interested) with the answers to the questions that are bouncing around in all of your minds.

God bless
Love always
Paul xxxxx

On Wednesday 15 December 1993, five months after his arrest, Paul Denyer fronted court, pleading guilty to all three murders as well as to the abduction of Roszsa Toth. Initially, in relation to Roszsa Toth's abduction, Denyer had been charged with attempted murder, but he had refused to plead guilty. He would however plead to the lesser charge of abducting her. It seemed strange to those involved with the case, because Denyer admitted in his police interview that he had intended to kill her only she got away before he had the chance.

Carmel Russell did not go to the trial itself, though she intended to be there for the sentencing. Her daughters Janine and Lisa wanted to attend so they went with Carmel's sister, Bernadette Naughton. After they left Frankston for the Supreme Court, homicide detective Mark Woolfe telephoned the Russell house to see if any of them were going to the trial. When Carmel explained that the girls were already on their way, Woolfe told her that he would try to protect them from the media.

When they arrived at the Supreme Court Janine, Lisa and Bernadette climbed the stairs to the visitors gallery. The seats were hard and uncomfortable and, even though it was summer, the three women shivered in the cold of the old building. Soon after they were seated, Janine felt a tap on her shoulder. It was Mark Woolfe. 'You shouldn't have to sit here,' he told her. 'Come downstairs, I'll organise a special seat for you.' He also gently told the women to be prepared because some of the evidence would be disturbing. It didn't matter, because Janine had such a strong feeling of unreality that afterwards she was unable to recall any of the graphic details.

Downstairs in the main court room, Janine, Lisa and Bernadette waited for Paul Denyer to be brought in. It was a moment filled with tension; Janine had never laid eyes on the man who had taken her youngest sister's life. They watched intently as Paul Denyer was brought into the court by two prison officers. Bernadette Naughton was surprised. Paul Denyer was a big man with a boyish face. A chilling thought occurred to her; if she met him on the street, she wouldn't have hesitated to ask him for directions. He looked like any ordinary person.

During the hearing, Janine's older sister Lisa left the court room for a break. As she walked past Paul Denyer in the dock, he stared at her, his eyes following her as she left. She stared right back at him. Prosecutor Nigel Parkinson presented the evidence in order: Elizabeth, the abduction, Debbie and finally Natalie. By the time the evidence got around to Debbie Fream, Bernadette Naughton was reaching for a second tissue. Opening her bag for one, she was vaguely concerned that the police might think she was reaching for a gun. Bags hadn't been checked at the door and it occurred to her that it would have been easy for someone to have brought a gun into the court. By the time the evidence came to Natalie, Bernadette was sobbing uncontrollably. She was so distressed that she had to leave the court room to try to compose herself.

Paul and Rita Webster attended the trial as well. It wasn't a pleasant way to spend their wedding anniversary and the irony didn't escape them. Liz had been murdered four days before Paul's birthday and afterwards, when they were going through her things, he had found a present wrapped up waiting for his birthday. She never got to give it to him. Now their wedding anniversary was to be tainted in the same way. They too had initially sat upstairs and then moved downstairs to be closer to the proceedings. Rita Webster had watched closely as Denyer was brought in. As soon as she saw his face, she drew in a sharp breath. She recognised him. Unsure exactly where, Rita Webster knew that she had seen Denyer somewhere before. That she could have walked past him or shopped at the same places was a frightening feeling. Paul Webster sat and stared at the young man in the dock and fantasised about what he would do to him if only he could bridge the couple of metres separating them.

A clinical psychologist, Ian Joblin, had examined Denyer for a number of hours in prison. In his view, Denyer appeared to be without remorse and even enjoyed telling about his crimes, seemingly getting a vicarious pleasure recounting his atrocities. Denyer had listed a number of factors in his life that he claimed had contributed to his murder spree: his hard upbringing, his brother David's alleged sexual abuse of him and his chronic unemployment. These apparent triggers didn't satisfy the psychologist. Thousands of people lived under similar conditions to Paul Denyer; few of them became serial killers. Joblin's profession was to examine adult offenders and in his years as a clinical psychologist he had interviewed many, but none like Denyer. Denyer's psychology was totally different.

Joblin told the court that Paul Denyer was a rare breed of serial killer committing his murders at random with no motive — making Denyer the most dangerous type of criminal known to our society. The psychologist said that Denyer had a cruel and demeaning nature and had exhibited aggressive behaviour since childhood; he seemed amused by the suffering that he had inflicted. Joblin told the court that Denyer was a sadist whose pleasure and satisfaction after each murder dissipated quickly so that he would again feel the desire to kill. The psychologist concluded by telling the court that there was no effective treatment for Denyer's sadistic personality. Justice Vincent asked if his behaviour was driven. In Joblin's view, it was.

When all the evidence had been heard, prosecutor Nigel Parkinson told Justice Vincent that Denyer should be given a life sentence with no minimum term for the despicable murders he had committed. He said that Denyer hated women and was a danger to the community. 'He is sadistic, he's a killer, he's not insane. He has a gross or severe personality disorder. The prognosis is poor.' The prosecutor went on to tell the court of the far-reaching consequences of Denyer's murders on the community. 'It may be that the lifestyles of many thousands of women have changed forever, and for them, Melbourne will never be the same place it was before.'

Despite all the evidence Sean Cash, appearing for Paul Denyer, urged Justice Vincent to impose a minimum sentence that wasn't inordinately long. Cash stressed how Denyer had pleaded guilty and saved the victims' families the ordeal of giving evidence. Denyer was a young man, he said, and should be given the chance to rehabilitate himself. With most of the court room overtly hostile to the young killer, Cash's words sounded hollow. Many shook their head in disbelief when the lawyer said that not only was the case sad for the families, but it was sad for Denyer too. 'It is fair to say he'd give anything as he sits there now to be normal. He doesn't only deserve punishment, he needs understanding and compassion and a chance to rehabilitate.' There was more than one person in the court room who thought the killer deserved nothing more than a hangman's rope. Janine's anger was welling up inside her as she sat for an hour listening to Denyer's lawyer describe his hard childhood and the allegations of sexual abuse. Cash told the court that Denyer wanted to rehabilitate himself, marry Sharon and perhaps write a book. Janine would later describe listening to that part of the trial as the hardest thing she ever had to do. Here was the murderer of her sister having his lawyer list his hopes and dreams for the future. Janine's baby sister had no future. She wanted to scream and shout but the families were all unable to voice how they felt. The only comfort Janine allowed herself was to periodically clear her throat loudly in an attempt to remind the killer and the lawyer that she was there.

Sean Cash finished his plea for a minimum sentence by saying again that Denyer had the support of his girlfriend whom he wanted to marry and that he had also found God. Justice Vincent quickly looked up from the bench and reminded the barrister that Denyer had dumped Debbie Fream's car right outside a Christian centre after he stabbed her to death. The point was not lost on the onlookers.

Justice Vincent held the sentencing over until the following Monday. After the hearing was over, Nigel Parkinson approached Bernadette, Lisa and Janine. He apologised for the evidence that had to be given in court. Bernadette knew he must have heard her sobs, but she also understood that the evidence would help keep Denyer behind bars forever and she told the prosecutor that he was doing a good job.

Janine had to fly back to Sydney on the weekend and was unable to attend the end of the trial on Monday 20 December, but her aunt Bernadette did and so did Carmel Russell. Over the weekend, Bernadette Naughton had done a lot of thinking. Hearing the evidence had upset her terribly. It was the first time since Natalie died that her emotions had run unchecked. In the days following the murder of her niece, Bernadette had been immersed in the many things that had to be done. She had to be strong for the family, helping to organise the funeral and write the eulogy. There were cards and letters to be answered and people to comfort. Bernadette was a nurse and the practical side of her nature came to the fore in the aftermath of the tragedy. During the trial was her time to truly grieve for her lost niece. One comfort over the weekend was the fact that Judge Vincent seemed such a compassionate man. Bernadette thought that he had kind eyes. During the Wednesday hearing, he took pains to describe things in layman's terms for the benefit of the families and Bernadette thought that he looked truly disturbed by the evidence. Speaking to a friend over the weekend, she had said with confidence, 'That judge will give us justice.'

On Monday morning, Justice Frank Vincent sat up on the bench and began by sentencing Denyer to life terms for each of the murders and an additional eight years for the abduction of Roszsa Toth. The sentences, he said, would run concurrently.

'The only question which remains,' said the judge after sentencing, 'is whether a period of imprisonment should be fixed after which you would become eligible for parole. Your counsel when presenting submissions on this aspect, emphasised your youth and the dreadful prospect which you would face if this were not done. He pointed to the views expressed by the High Court in *R*. v. *Bugmy* (1990) as to the care which a sentencing judge must take in predicting an offender's prospects for rehabilitation. He submitted, quite correctly, that we cannot know whether in 25, 30 or at some time beyond 30 years, the fires of your aberrant desires may have been long quenched or whether our understanding of such matters may have progressed to the extent that some solution to the problem which you pose may have been found.

'Unfortunately, I must sentence you now and I cannot abrogate my responsibility to some distant parole board. Recognising the importance of rehabilitation as a sentencing consideration, there are very occasionally situations in which that factor must be subordinated within the confines of a proportionate sentence to the need to protect the public against the truly dangerous. The evidence before this court is tragically clear on that aspect. You do constitute such a danger, and at our present state of knowledge, apart from separating you from society, there is nothing that can be done about it. Any non-parole period which I fix would have to be very long in any event and calculated without reference to the potential risk which you could then pose. Perhaps there will come a day when you will be able to walk among the ordinary people of our community. Whether you will ever do so must await the passage of years and the decision of the executive government of the time.

'I do not consider that it would be appropriate to fix a non-parole period in your case.'

Emotion was evident in Justice Vincent's voice as he concluded, 'The apprehension you have caused to thousands of women in the community will be felt for a long time. For many, you are the fear that quickens their step as they walk home, or causes a parent to look anxiously at the clock when a child is late.'

After the sentencing, Paul Denyer's lawyer told the court that his client wished to make a statement. There was an immediate barrage of booing from the onlookers in the court. Bernadette Naughton stood up in the crowded court room and said, 'Let him speak if he chooses, it is his right.' She looked at Justice Vincent who, after deliberating for a moment, nodded in agreement.

From the dock, Paul Denyer turned to the families of his victims and said, 'I'm truly sorry for what's happened. I'll do my sentence and I will become a better person and I will not re-offend. That's my promise to God and to the people of Melbourne.'

Overcome with anger, one of the other relatives stood and said, 'May God forgive you because I never will.' Carmel Russell shook her head and said quietly, 'No, no, no.' She thought to herself, 'Your Christmas present to us was taking Natalie; this is our Christmas present to you.' After Denyer was sentenced never to be released, Justice Vincent turned to the court guards and said, 'You may remove the prisoner from the dock.' The reality hit Bernadette Naughton. Up until that point, Denyer had been referred to in court as 'the accused' — now he was officially 'the prisoner'. Natalie Russell's aunt knew well the premise: innocent until proven guilty. Even though Paul Denyer had confessed, he had now officially been found guilty. It was a huge relief.

The following day, the front cover of the *Herald Sun* featured a large picture of Sharon Johnson wearing a long blond wig under the banner, 'I Love Him'. She said in an interview on *Real Life*, 'I still love him. I'll stand by him a hundred per cent, not for what he has done, but I stand by him for the person he is.'

Pentridge Prison   *Monday 27 December 1993*

Hi again. I hope you all had a good Christmas and by the time you get this it will probably be New Years, so happy New Year too.

Christmas was alright considering the environment I'm in. We ate quite well. I can say that much anyway. We had the Salvation Army and other fellowship groups bringing in small gifts. What was missing though was Sharon but I guess this feeling will get easier as the years go on.

So no doubt you have heard the outcome of the trial. Well it's justice for those people who are hurt and that's what's more important. I had my say in court too. I got to say that I'm sorry and promise to better myself. I don't know if they would have printed that in the paper up there, but that's straight from the horse's mouth. The media always blow things out of proportion just to sell papers.

Well you wanted to know how much of it was true. To be certainly honest with you, I didn't read any articles but my guess is that only ten per cent of it would be true. The Herald Sun are well known for that.

I don't know if you saw Sharon on TV. She was on 'Real Life' just telling the people what I'm really like and how I just went off the path of life. I saw it that night and I was amazed at how little true feelings of mine they said. Sharon was well disguised though and she hasn't had anyone approaching her. She meant every word of it too. Well I won't say too much because I don't know if you saw it. But my guess is the publicity was increased more up where you are.

My day in court went quite smooth. I wore my black suit and red tie that

Sharon brought in for me. But never seen on TV either.

I had a little bit of shit from other prisoners lately. But most of them are stupid and don't understand the in between the lines on the case. Most just chastise me to escape their own problems and charges. It will all die down soon enough.

But I'm doing fine myself. I've completed about 400 pages in my journal and diary. I write about anything I think of, my hobbies, days in court, religion and anything. I've estimated about 7000 pages would be done by the time I'm released.

I'm changing my name too. I don't know what it will be as yet but after the publicity is gone, I will see legal aid and get it done.

I haven't done much today, just watch some TV and made my phone calls to Sharon. She's coping quite well in fact.

Anyway, I will close at this for now but I will write again soon.

PS, I like the sound of Jason's new car. I don't know about anyone else but a HQ Holden will do me fine.

Anyway, write to you soon.
Happy New Year
Paul Denyer xxxxx

35

The Appeal

ON New Year's Eve 1993, Denyer's solicitor lodged an appeal against
the severity of Denyer's sentence on two grounds:

1. That in relation to counts 1, 2, 3 and 4 on the presentment the
   sentence on each count was manifestly excessive.
2. That in relation to each of counts 1, 3 and 4, the sentencing
   judge wrongly exercised his discretion in failing to fix a minimum
   term of imprisonment being a term of imprisonment less than
   life imprisonment.

Soon after, Melbourne barrister Dyson Hore-Lacy was approached to
represent Paul Denyer in an appeal to the Full Court of the Supreme
Court against the severity of Denyer's sentence. As far as Hore-Lacy
was concerned, barristers had a duty to appear for anyone who
requested their services and everybody had the right to receive the best
representation they could. Denyer was no exception. Preparing the
appeal in his spacious but cluttered seventh floor office a short walk
from the County Court, Hore-Lacy read through the brief and the
summary documents prepared by the Crown Prosecutor. It soon
became obvious to the experienced barrister that the appeal was based
on a narrow legal principle: should Denyer have received a minimum
sentence?

At his huge polished wooden desk surrounded by weighty, bound
legal volumes, Hore-Lacy prepared the defence appeal, noting cases
which set a precedent as far as minimum sentences were concerned.
He saw the importance of a minimum sentence for every offender in
terms of potential rehabilitation. In spite of the crimes, it was a legal
principle requiring a somewhat clinical approach and it was under the
simple premise that fair legal representation was the cornerstone of
democracy, that Hore-Lacy went to work on the appeal.

Partly as a courtesy, Dyson Hore-Lacy made a visit to Denyer in Pentridge. Meeting the prisoner for the first time, Hore-Lacy thought he seemed like an average, quietly spoken person, but then again, he figured, dress most murderers in a suit and put them in a room full of accountants and you'd never know which were the murderers. Denyer was no exception, which was almost chilling considering what he'd done.

When the case finally came before the Full Court of the Supreme Court in July 1994, section 11 of the *Sentencing Act (1991)* came under scrutiny by the three presiding judges, William Crockett, Alex Southwell and Chief Justice John Phillips. Section 11 reads:

> If a court sentences an offender to be imprisoned in respect of an offence for —
> a) the term of his or her natural life; or
> b) a term of 24 months or more — the court must, as part of the sentence, fix a period during which the offender is not eligible to be released on parole unless it considers that the nature or the past history of the offender make the fixing of such a period inappropriate.

The defence application contended that the judge had erred when he had said, 'Unfortunately, I must sentence you now and I cannot abrogate my responsibility to some distant Parole Board.' The defence felt that the statement was indicative of the intrusion of an irrelevant circumstance into the judge's considerations.

The defence also objected to Justice Vincent's wording when he had said, 'Whether you will ever do so [walk among the ordinary people of our community] must await the passage of years and the decision of the executive government at the time.'

Justice John Phillips upheld the defence submission that Justice Vincent had erred when he said he couldn't abrogate his responsibility to some distant parole board. 'In my opinion,' Phillips told the court, 'in the exercise of the discretion, no such abrogation arose.' It was then that section 11 became relevant. A non-parole period *must* be set unless the nature of the offence or the past history of the offender make the fixing of such a period inappropriate. Although Paul Denyer's crimes were abhorrent, he had no past criminal history. However, Phillips upheld the original sentence in his refusal to grant a non-parole period. In his summing up, Phillips wrote:

THE NATURE OF THE OFFENCES:

Three murders and one kidnapping of women were committed over some six weeks. The murderous attacks were pressed home with almost unbelievable savagery. There were elements of preparation, planning and subsequent concealment involved. The applicant well knew what he was doing. It was conceded, both before the sentencing judge and before this court, that life sentences were appropriate on the murder counts.

THE PAST HISTORY OF THE OFFENDER:

For years prior to these offences, the applicant had harboured thoughts of killing and had carried out stalking of women. According to undisputed expert evidence before the sentencing judge, for a number of years, the applicant had an entrenched sadistic personality disorder for which no effective treatment was presently or prospectively available. The applicant had a hatred for all females except his (de facto) wife and mother and finds the infliction of injury, suffering and death intensely gratifying and pleasurable.

In the light of the above summary, it might be said that, on its face, the case of the applicant called for the discretion vested by section 11 to be exercised adversely to him. But there are other considerations. The relevant authorities show that minimum terms of imprisonment are to be viewed, in appropriate cases, as benefits to prisoners and conducive of rehabilitation as well as being sentences which, according to the dictates of justice, must be served.

The matter of rehabilitation can present in a very great variety of circumstances. It may fall to be considered in relation to offences committed by a youthful person being led astray or by reason of transient pressures or conditions. It may fall to be considered in relation to offences committed by an apparently incorrigible criminal. In the case of the applicant, it falls to be considered in the light of the undisputed expert evidence to which I have earlier made reference. Although, as the learned judge noted, the possibility of some alleviation of the applicant's mental condition in the future cannot be completely dismissed, in my opinion, this expert evidence reveals the applicant's prospects of rehabilitation to be theoretical rather than real.

Notwithstanding that I am prepared to find error in His Honour's reasons for sentence, I have come to conclude, after consideration of the relevant criteria, that the case of the applicant is one where it is inappropriate that a non-parole period be fixed. Accordingly, I would dismiss the appeal on the grounds that I do not think a different sentence should have been passed.

It was Justice William Crockett's view, however, that the application rested with the sentencing judge's refusal to set a minimum sentence, thereby withholding from the prisoner the benefits of such a minimum sentence. Was the sentencing judge obliged to set a minimum sentence? Justice Crockett summarised the attacks in his findings:

> The nature and extent of the wounds can only allow each attack to be described as one of scarcely credible cruelty and barbarity... The foregoing events are sufficient to suggest strongly that there must have been something in the applicant's mental condition that was seriously amiss. And so there was. The evidence of a psychiatrist and of a psychologist was that the applicant suffered from what is termed a 'sadistic personality disorder'. A sufferer of such a condition possesses 'a narcisstic personality with features of self-idealisation.' It was said that the applicant obtained immense gratification from the humiliation, mutilation and killing of others. There is much more in the evidence descriptive of the applicant's psychological condition of the symptoms of that condition. Elaboration of them is not necessary.

Crockett went on to say that Paul Denyer had been stalking women since he was fourteen and that he had freely admitted that he would have continued his 'regime of homicidal attacks upon women.' Crockett then moved in his deliberations to the wording of the original sentencing judge, Justice Vincent. The crucial wording of the *Sentencing Act* regarding the obligation by a sentencing judge to fix a non-parole period when an offender is given a life sentence came under scrutiny. Referring to Paul Denyer, Justice Crockett said:

> His past history was unremarkable. He had been free from previous trouble but for a trifling indiscretion dealt with in the Children's Court nine years ago. Guilt of the crime of murder, of itself, is not sufficient to require the sentencer to abstain from fixing a non-parole period. We were told of a number of cases where such a period was fixed where murder was the offence and the circumstances of its commission were every bit as sickening as those in the present case. Moreover, perpetrators of multiple killings have not been denied the benefit of an order fixing a non-parole period.

Indeed, it might be thought that a refusal to fix a period that rests solely upon a finding that there is now, and there may be for the rest of the applicant's life, a risk of danger to the community were he to be granted his liberty at any time in his lifetime, was a refusal which the section did not empower the judge to make. It may be said that the suffering of a mental condition that makes the applicant a danger to society has nothing to do with the nature of the offence or the applicant's past history.

Crockett argued that if no non-parole period was set and the average life expectancy was around seventy years, then Denyer's effective sentence was one of around fifty years, perhaps longer. Denyer, he argued, would be devoid of any incentive to rehabilitate himself. Crockett also argued that if, hypothetically, a forty-year-old man had committed the same crimes, he would only serve thirty years if he lived to the average age of seventy. That, said the judge, would be a substantial difference in penalties: 'The length of the sentence served and, thus, the measure of the punishment inflicted is dependent upon the pure chance of the offender's age.' To the family members listening, it seemed that the judge was saying that no-one should get more than thirty years, no matter what crimes they committed.

With the exception of Stanley Taylor, the man convicted of the Russell Street bombing, the judge told the court, no-one had ever been refused a non-parole period. Taylor was fifty- one years old and had a lengthy record of serious crimes of violence.

While Crockett conceded that Denyer would be an undeniable danger to the community if free, he ruled in favour of a minimum sentence: 'The need to protect the public from an offender's depredation does not permit his incarceration beyond what is an appropriate sentence having regard to his moral culpability. The sentence cannot be allowed to act as one of preventative detention.' Justice Crockett then discussed the possibility that Paul Denyer might one day be cured of his murderous impulses and it would then be the responsibility of some future parole board to decide whether he was released. Justice Crockett concluded that he was of the opinion that 'neither the nature of the offences nor the past history of the offender entitled the court to conclude there would never be a prospect of rehabilitation. Consequently, it was the duty of the judge to have fixed a non-parole period. Error having been disclosed, the order refusing to fix a non-parole period should be set aside. In lieu, I would fix a non-parole period of thirty years.'

When the third judge, Alex Southwell, agreed with Justice Crockett, Denyer was granted a thirty year non-parole period on a majority verdict on Friday 29 July 1994 — one day before the anniversary of the day he killed Natalie Russell.

As far as Dyson Hore-Lacy was concerned, the community didn't lose by the decision. Denyer's minimum term was the highest non-parole period ever imposed in Victoria, equal only to that of Burwood triple murderer, Ashley Couston. It was three years longer than that imposed on Hoddle Street killer Julian Knight, who had received a twenty-seven year minimum. Hore-Lacy also knew that if the prognosis of Paul Denyer's condition didn't change, he would never be released. Future parole boards would have full access to Denyer's file and if there was no cure for his condition and if he continued to be a danger to the community, he would remain in prison forever. His sentence hadn't been reduced; he would simply now have the same opportunity as almost anybody else to be released on parole, if suitable, after serving the minimum term which the majority of the Full Court believed was appropriate in the circumstances. Hore-Lacy was also aware that with the incredible advances in medical technology, it was impossible to predict what treatments would be available in thirty years.

36

How Long is Life?

WITH the granting of the minimum sentence, Paul Denyer was once again the focus of media attention. Paul Webster was interviewed for the evening news voicing his outrage at the thirty year sentence. 'That's ten years per life,' he said. 'It's unbelievable.'

Natalie Russell's mother Carmel was photographed in full colour for the Friday edition of the *Herald Sun* under the banner: 'Lament for a life taken.' She told journalists that she still, a year later, walked into her murdered daughter's bedroom every morning and said, 'Morning Nat.' Pain was still visible in the mother's eyes.

Especially painful for the Russell family was the Supreme Court decision coming on the eve of the anniversary of Natalie's murder. Carmel Russell spoke poignantly about the family's plans to visit Natalie's grave and to walk along the bike track and place flowers at the site where Natalie was murdered. The last thing the Russell family needed was to hear that their daughter's killer had been granted a minimum sentence. Now the media followed them and the pain began all over again.

Carmel Russell voiced the community's concern. 'He cannot get out because he's going to do it again and people will say, Oh, he shouldn't have been let out.'

Debbie Fream's grandfather, William Fream, told the press that 'A person who can do that sort of thing forfeits the right to live in our sort of society at all. They're not human and the fact that he will get out in thirty years, or probably less with good behaviour, it frightens me.'

Also speaking out strongly against the reduced term was the president of VOCAL — Victims of Crime Assistance League — Ms Tricia Rhodes. She asked publicly what an offender had to do to stay in prison forever. 'The judgement by two out of three judges of the

Supreme Court ignores the death and mutilation of three innocent young women,' she said. 'It ignores the pain and suffering that their families go through to this day and will continue to go through and, just as important, it ignores the feeling of the community.'

The media made much of the hundred thousand signatures, collected since the murders began, to bring back the death penalty for Denyer. The *Herald Sun* even set up a line where readers could register their vote that 'life meant life.'

Radio broadcaster Neil Mitchell had followed the Frankston murders from the beginning on his radio program on 3AW. Mitchell had spent his formative years in Rosebud where his father was a teacher so he knew the Frankston and Peninsula area well from his childhood. Before Denyer was apprehended, Mitchell had devoted a lot of air play to the reaction of the community. Indeed, the listening audience on the Peninsula had increased by sixty per cent with people following the latest news of the murders. The fear was palpable and the only case that Mitchell could compare it to was the reaction to the so-called 'Mr Cruel' abductions and the murder of Karmein Chan.

The first strong wave of public feeling had come after Debbie Fream's body was found. Because reports filtered through that her car had been sighted after her abduction with its lights flashing, it was obvious that she had been kidnapped and then murdered. Her ordeal must have been terrifying. The nature of the victims had a lot do with the community fear and empathy; they could have been anybody's sister, daughter or wife. Mitchell said, 'There are some murders, because of the entirely innocent nature of the victims, that just grab you.' Mitchell wouldn't let it rest.

Devoting much of his program's time to debates on the use of capsicum spray, personal alarms and self defence methods, Mitchell called upon experts to offer the public advice on personal security. Then Denyer was caught.

Speaking off the record with police officers, Mitchell had been privy to some of the worst details of the murders and Denyer's subsequent confessions, and he had decided to follow the case publicly to the finish. When, on behalf of Carmel and Brian Russell, Bernadette Naughton contacted Neil Mitchell a week after Natalie's murder, he invited them to come on his program. 'They really impressed me,' he said later, 'I was in tears on air.' Mitchell has a daughter and as a parent he felt their pain.

Once the disgust with the granting of the minimum term was voiced on air, the public took over. One caller said, 'We've got to appeal. We've got to make them listen.' Mitchell agreed and encouraged people to write to the Director of Public Prosecutions to voice their concern. Using Premier Jeff Kennett's weekly spot on the program to discuss the issue, Mitchell spoke of the crimes and the subsequent sentencing. Kennett himself wondered on air what one had to do to get the maximum sentence.

During Jeff Kennett's interview, Bernadette Naughton rang the station and was put through to the premier. She told him that the Russell family wanted justice and the premier agreed that Denyer should never be released. It was the beginning of the ground swell of support to lobby the Director of Public Prosecutions to appeal the minimum sentence. Initially sceptical that public opinion would have any effect on the DPP, Neil Mitchell nonetheless encouraged the appeal. He had appealed to the DPP before on other cases, but to no avail. Lawyers and police he spoke to said he didn't have a chance of success, but to Mitchell, some things were worth fighting for, even if it was just to send the DPP a strong message. He figured that the DPP needed to listen to the public feeling and represent the people.

The only thing that concerned Neil Mitchell during the whole process was the element of a 'lynch-mob' mentality that was apparent in some of the callers. Every time someone phoned in to support the death penalty, he would argue strongly against them. In Mitchell's opinion, if ever there was a case that deserved the full punishment of the law, it was this one and that was exactly what he was fighting for — not the death penalty.

Bernadette Naughton made contact with Sara Smith, Debbie Fream's cousin, as well as Elizabeth Stevens's uncle, Paul Webster. Together, they organised petitions and hit the streets to gain support. At first, Bernadette was reluctant to walk the streets for signatures. Angry that she was being forced by circumstances to do what the legal system should have done, she nonetheless pushed on with the effort. She found that those most willing to sign petitions were young mothers with babies in prams. Perhaps they figured that if Denyer was released, their own babies might one day be his victims. When Bernadette approached one young man, he asked her if she was collecting money for something. She replied, 'No, I want your signature. It is much more valuable to me than money.'

On Wednesday 10 August 1994, a public meeting was held at the Pines Forest Community Centre hosted by Phil Wild, a member of the group PALS — People Against Lenient Sentences. The small hall was filled to capacity with nearly two hundred people braving the winter chill, each with their own personal reasons for coming. Phil Wild informed the crowd that Natalie Russell's mother was in the audience as were Paul and Rita Webster and Debbie Fream's cousin Sara Smith. One middle-aged woman stood and told the assembly that she lived in the same street as Debbie Fream. 'We just feel very sad that this happened in our community,' she said, and went on, her quiet voice rising in indignation, to ask if public money funded Denyer's recent appeal to have a minimum sentence declared. Other voices joined hers in outrage.

A middle-aged man stood up and introduced himself as a member of the Crime Victims Support Association. His daughter, he said, had been murdered and her killer had appealed his sentence but to no avail. 'Why can't victims appeal against sentences too?' asked the man. And then people shouted in agreement when a tall, young, denim-clad man at the back of the hall stood up and shouted, 'Death! Death!' The meeting had run exactly twelve minutes and already there were echoes of a lynch mob — such was the feeling and emotion brought on by such a killer in their community.

Phil Wild brought the meeting to order by repeating that since Australia had no death penalty, legal execution wasn't an option in Denyer's case. But he did point out that Denyer's original life sentence served justice better than the recent thirty year minimum handed down. Quoting Justice Crockett in his finding that Denyer should not be made to serve longer than he deserved, Wild told the assembly that he believed the original life sentence was no longer than the killer deserved. The crowd cheered its collective approval.

Three television cameras and their bright lights circled the assembly, catching on film the impassioned pleas from the members of the Frankston community. A nineteen-year-old woman spoke passionately about how she had known two of Denyer's victims and of how her greatest concern was that when her own children were teenagers and Denyer was released, she would face the panic that her own mother had experienced during Denyer's killing spree.

The views of the assemblage went from the reasonable to the ridiculous. One man suggested publishing names and addresses of all judges so that people could write to them to voice their outrage at lenient sentences. A woman challenged nobody in particular to 'give Denyer to us' — he wouldn't have lasted five minutes. Another man cried, 'the bastard should be hung!' to a chorus of approval. Ironically the voice of reason came from the families of the murder victims themselves. Sara Smith quietly told the crowd, 'They can't let Denyer out ever. I lived through that terror with my family,' but she stressed that the danger was that 'in thirty years, nobody will remember the terror.'

Paul Webster called upon the two dissenting Supreme Court judges to resign because they were out of touch with public opinion.

Finally, Carmel Russell stood and thanked everybody for coming. 'We felt happy when we knew he had life,' she said in a soft voice. 'Life is life.'

On Monday 15 August 1994, Director of Public Prosecutions Bernard Bongiorno announced that he had decided to make an application to the High Court for special leave to appeal the granting of the thirty year minimum sentence.

Among others, Neil Mitchell was surprised. He had never believed that the DPP would appeal the minimum sentence, and he saw the turnaround as a victory. But the victory would always be a hollow one. It wouldn't bring the girls back. The relatives of the murdered women saw the appeal as a way to continue to fight for justice. They would put all their strength into the appeal and into continuing to get public feeling on their side — the side of justice.

One of the ironies of the Full Court's decision to grant Paul Denyer a minimum sentence was that other vicious killers used the precedent to further their own attempts to be granted minimum sentences. If his crimes were the worst the state had ever seen, they figured, their own crimes should make a minimum sentence more easily attainable. Raymond Edmunds, the man convicted of murdering Abina Madill and Gary Heywood in Shepparton in 1966 as well as of three rapes and two attempted rapes, sought a minimum term under the *Sentencing Act*. His lawyer argued that Edmunds 'was no Denyer.' In this case, the Full Court refused to grant his appeal.

37

Paul Charles Denyer

ON 16 June 1826, a farmer called Fredrick Fisher disappeared walking home from the local pub on the outskirts of Campbelltown. On a moonlit night a couple of months later another local, John Farley, was driving his empty dray back from Sydney. Farley passed Fisher's property and to his surprise, recognised his friend Fisher sitting on the farm gate. Farley called out to him but, as legend had it, Fisher didn't reply. Instead, he seemed to glide across the moonlit paddock in the direction of an adjoining farm belonging to George Worrall. Worrall was later hanged for Fisher's murder and Fisher's Ghost entered the annals of Campbelltown folklore. It was in Campbelltown that Paul Denyer's parents, Anthony and Maureen, settled after migrating from the United Kingdom.

They came to Australia as ten pound migrants in 1965, and stayed for a short time in Adelaide before moving their growing family to Campbelltown. When the children were older the family moved to Melbourne.

Maureen and Anthony Denyer's first child David was born in 1963, about a year and a half before the couple migrated to Australia. Five others followed: Steve in 1971, Paul in 1972, Richard in 1974 and twins Anthony and Natalie in 1976.

When Paul was a baby, his mother Maureen recalls him rolling off a bench and knocking his head. Occasionally, his childhood misdeeds were flippantly attributed to the knock on the head.

At kindergarten Paul Denyer didn't mix too easily but by the time he started school, his social skills with other children had improved. Academically, he struggled through school right from the beginning. Taller than the other children his age and with a propensity towards being overweight, Paul became known as a bit of a trouble maker. Most of his primary teachers agreed that he was hard to motivate and that if he had applied himself, he could have done much better.

Just as Paul began to finally settle, his father accepted a job offer in Melbourne and the family uprooted to a rented house in Mulgrave and Paul was enrolled in Northvale Primary School.

By the time he got to grade six, Paul was overweight and much taller than most of his class mates. Even so, he tended to disappear into the background in his final year of primary school, a fact that his grade six teacher attributes to the dynamics of the group. There were a number of troublesome boys in the class and Paul never got to assert himself.

However, one incident that his grade six teacher has never forgotten was when Paul Denyer nearly killed one of his class mates. The children were all returning from a physical education lesson and one boy ran back before the others. He was standing by the door chewing on the blunt end of a pen. As Paul Denyer walked through the doorway, the boy made a derogatory comment to him and in the blink of an eye, Paul lifted his hand and viciously slapped the boy across the face, hitting the pen and shoving it deeply into the boy's mouth. Lodged in the boy's throat, the pen had missed his windpipe by only a few millimetres. An ambulance was called and the boy was rushed to hospital. Paul Denyer was unemotional and unrepentant. Later, when the shaken teacher tried to discuss the incident with him, Paul merely shrugged. He wouldn't explain why he did it and he wasn't sorry.

Apart from that one visible loss of control, Paul was basically a quiet student. He struggled academically and his teacher would often sit by him and help him with his work. He didn't really seem interested in academic achievement, a fact his teacher put down to a self-esteem problem. Paul was isolated from the group and had no friends; other children tended to keep away from him. So great was his ability to fade into the background, Paul's grade six teacher says that if it weren't for that violent incident and his large size, she might hardly have remembered him. He was so quiet and well behaved that the incident with the pen stood out, as did his complete lack of emotion with everything he did.

While Paul Denyer may have faded into the background at school, at home was another matter. His family noticed a number of strange events occurring around the house. When Natalie Denyer was seven, her brother David had given her two big 'care bears'. One day she went into her room to find the two bears had their throats cut and most of the stuffing pulled out. When confronted with the mutilated toys, Paul merely smirked at accusations that he had done it. It was the same as his reaction to the pen incident at school—no emotion, no feeling. Another time, Natalie found her favourite Agro toy buried in the back yard.

When he was ten, his brother found the family's kitten hanging dead in a tree. It's throat had been cut. Paul said that somebody in the neighbourhood musn't like them, but when his brother demanded to see his pocket knife, it was smeared with cat fur and blood.

Four days before his thirteenth birthday, Paul Denyer was charged with the theft of a motor vehicle and cautioned as a juvenile. Two months later, he was charged with theft and wilful damage and making a false report to the fire brigade. In September 1987, aged fifteen, Denyer was charged with assault; he had made another boy masturbate in front of some other children.

When the family moved to Long Street, Langwarrin in 1987, Maureen and her husband had separated, David had left home and Paul had dropped out of school and was walking around the streets most evenings. His family thought little of his nocturnal wanderings; they had no inkling of his urges to kill. He was still overweight and they figured that the exercise would do him good. It wasn't long before he began what was to become four years of stalking women and mapping out plans for his eventual murders.

Denyer was once caught looking through the window at Melissa, his brother Steve's girlfriend, as she undressed. Fumbling with the buckle of her jeans, Melissa noticed a figure at her window. Hurrying over, she flung it open and saw Paul staring at her transfixed.

'Paul, Paul,' she said, waving her hand in front of his face a number of times before his eyes lost the glazed look that she had never seen before. 'What are you doing?' she yelled at him. He came to his senses and ran away. When she told Steve what his brother had done, he angrily confronted Paul and told him what he would do if he ever caught him looking at Melissa again. Paul never did, he simply took his strange habits elsewhere leaving the family oblivious to his increasingly bizarre behaviour.

Paul spent a lot of time with Steve and Richard because he didn't really have any friends of his own. The brothers were all close and Richard and Steve never minded Paul tagging along. They felt they had to look out for him because he was socially inept, although around his brothers he was good company, known for his jokes and his happy disposition. In fact, the Denyer clan never really needed anyone else. Although Steve and Richard were very popular, they were just as happy to hang out together; the family was big enough to be an instant crowd. Steve's girlfriend Melissa fit right in and they would all sit around watching videos — usually comedies but sometimes horror movies — or listening to music. Occasionally, they would all take off and drive down to Taylors Road in Carrum Downs and smoke marijuana. Maureen Denyer never approved of the kids smoking dope and consequently, the teenagers took off to find other places. Taylors Road was a favourite place because it was so isolated and the chances of getting caught were slim. When Paul smoked the drug he became mellow and happy. He loved listening to Creedence music and Melissa was trying to teach him the basics of guitar. He wasn't very good but the family would listen to him and encourage his hobby.

Maureen Denyer struggled to keep a comfortable home for her children. Now a single mother, she worked as a cleaner and then came home, cleaned, shopped and put food on the table. Every evening, the family would sit around the table and eat fresh bread with the simple but well cooked meals that she prepared. Afterwards, Maureen would be on her hands and knees scrubbing the floors and keeping the house spotlessly clean.

The Denyer family had no idea of the homicidal thoughts that occupied Paul's mind though they did notice that he daydreamed a lot. He would stare into space with a blank look on his face and sometimes laugh for no reason, but the aberrations were slight and, to his family, Paul was normal and happy.

Paul's oldest brother David had gone to the United Kingdom for a holiday in 1989. Staying with his uncle Tom and his aunt Julie, David soon began a relationship with his aunt whom he married the following year after she divorced Tom. Bringing Julie and her two children home to Australia in May 1990 was a big mistake. At the airport when Maureen collected them, David announced that she was to acknowledge Julie's children — her niece and nephew — as her grandchildren. It wasn't a good start. Maureen was embarrassed about what David had done; it was her brother's wife who David had stolen.

Despite Maureen's discomfort, the Denyers tried to make David and Julie and her children feel welcome. David was adored by his brothers and sister. Being the eldest, he had become something of a substitute father after his parents' divorce and they all looked up to him. He was smooth and charming. But Julie didn't try to fit in and it wasn't long before trouble began.

Steve drove David around looking for furniture, lending him money to buy mattresses for the children's beds and, on occasions, letting him use his car. David crashed the car and didn't offer to pay for the damage and he didn't offer to pay Steve back for the beds. A couple of weeks after David and Julie arrived in Melbourne, Julie sent Maureen a letter:

Maureen,

This will be the last time you ever hear from Dave and myself, but before we go off completely I would like to let you know how we feel. I was willing to make things work with you. I had a chat to you on the phone before we left England. I could see from that phone call you were not interested in trying, but still I gave you a chance. From the time we all met at the airport, you ignored not only myself, but my children. I can handle you not talking to me as you are not the sort of person I would like to associate with anyway. But for David's sake, I was willing to give you a go. So now you have made it quite plain you do not wish to be grandmother to my children, not even for your own son's sake. Just shows us how much you think of your son. As far as seeing your new grandchild goes, you can forget it, he or she will not even be told about you, our baby deserves better than you can ever give. I think you fall into the same category as David's father. I find the family greatly lacking in grey matter between the ears. Tom's the best one out of the lot of you, he just needs to stand on his own feet. David's brothers and sister are all very nice and thank God have minds of their own. They know the way we feel about you so its up to them if they wish to come to see us. But they will always be welcome in our home, you will never be. I will close now, I think I have said everything I wanted to say to you, Maureen. At least I can never be accused of being two faced. I have always told your dear mother what I thought and now I am letting you know too.

Thanks for nothing,

Julie

The next thing they knew, David and Julie had taken out restraining orders on the whole family except the twins who were only in their early teens. Puzzled by the court orders, Steve and Melissa drove around to David's house. They knew that David was having problems with Maureen, but they couldn't understand why David would issue court orders against his brothers as well. Steve wanted to sort out the trouble that had begun and he wanted to know why David was distancing himself from the family. His brother wasn't home, so Steve and Melissa waited for a while in their car until he returned. Melissa remained in the car while Steve went to the door to speak to David.

Ten minutes later, he returned to the car and they left. Melissa had never seen Steve so upset. He had tried to ask David about the court orders, but David refused to discuss the matter and threatened to call the police.

Steve Denyer couldn't understand why his brother did what he did and he never saw the money for his wrecked car or the money he lent David for the beds.

Later, after Paul's arrest, David told the police how Paul had followed him and had once threatened Julie when he ran into her while she was shopping at Frankston. While the media made much out of this incident, Richard Denyer's girlfriend, who was with Paul at the time, witnessed his outburst to Julie and claimed that Paul's anger was proportionate to what David had done and the grief he had caused. Indeed, the whole family was angry with him. David took the incident even further, telling a current affairs program via satellite from the United Kingdom that Julie might have been one of Paul's victims had they remained in Australia. While that is debatable, mid 1990 was certainly a high stress period for Paul Denyer.

Not long after David and Julie returned to the United Kingdom in 1992, Richard Denyer approached a Frankston real estate agent to rent a flat. When he gave his surname, the agent told him that they wouldn't rent to him because his brother David had skipped owing them so much money.

Continuing his almost nightly routine of long walks, Paul struck trouble one night. Melissa and Steve were in bed asleep when they were awakened by a banging on the door. They opened it to Paul covered in blood and an ambulance in the driveway. He was as white as a ghost and was explaining that he had been stabbed. A paramedic had urged Paul to go to hospital but the young man had insisted the ambulance bring him home. Apparently he had been stabbed in the carpark of the Langwarrin Hotel restaurant and had staggered in and they had called the ambulance. Paul had instructed the ambulance to take him home rather than to the hospital because he wasn't a subscriber to the ambulance fund and was worried about the cost of the trip. He wanted Steve to drive him instead. Steve quickly dressed and rushed his brother to the hospital.

Detective Colin Clark, who would later work on the murder investigations with the homicide squad, was called in by uniformed officers to investigate the stabbing. He drove to the carpark and saw a large amount of blood and figured that this was where the stabbing occurred. Just as he was about to drive to the hospital to interview Paul Denyer, a call came over the radio informing him that the victim did not want to press charges against his attackers and wanted the investigation dropped. Colin Clark shrugged and went on with other pressing duties, figuring that the victim probably knew his attackers and that the fight may have been over something that they didn't want brought to the attention of the police.

At the hospital, Paul had a stab wound to his leg and a slash across his hand tended to. Indignant about the attack, he told Steve that he hoped the police would catch the guys responsible and charge them. Paul described walking across the carpark when a couple of guys had jumped him from behind and stabbed him. Steve vowed to try to find the people responsible for the attack on his brother. He believed Paul's story—he had no reason not to. Steve was later angry that the police had done nothing in relation to the stabbing; he had no idea that Paul had stopped the investigation before it had begun.

When Melissa Denyer fell pregnant, she remembers the family being pleased. The baby would be the first grandchild and niece or nephew in the family. Paul, however, reacted strangely. Melissa vividly remembers a fleeting but powerful look of disgust crossing his face when they told him the news. The look quickly faded, but nonetheless, it bothered her. Paul was uninterested in the pregnancy and when Melissa was hospitalised with high blood pressure a month before the baby was due, she was surprised when Paul arrived at the hospital to visit her. He carried a bunch of flowers and chatted happily with his sister-in-law.

In many respects, the whole family was pleased with the way Paul was shaping up. He lost weight and began to read self-help books in the vein of *How to Win Friends and Influence People*. For the first time, Paul was finally dressing well and seemed to be getting his life in order. Nonetheless, Paul went through a number of jobs, all ending in his being sacked for dishonesty or laziness. He eventually ended up working for Safeway at Karingal Hub but was sacked for ramming a customer with a stack of empty shopping trolleys. At Safeway, Paul had met Sharon Johnson and the two became close. Before long he moved out of home to live with her.

An obese woman with round doe eyes and a little girl voice, Sharon quickly established a control over Paul that made many who knew him uncomfortable. His brothers recall times when Paul would come around for a visit and minutes later, Sharon would be on the phone demanding to know if Paul was there, telling him to come home again. To outsiders, it seemed as if Sharon had Paul well and truly under the thumb. Paul didn't seem to mind. He loved her. The new couple mainly stayed at home watching television and Paul quickly regained all the weight he had lost.

Around the time that Paul moved in with Sharon's family, he became increasingly remote with his own. One day, Paul telephoned his mother and told her that Sharon's mother Pauline had put her hand on his heart and had a vision that he, Steve and Richard had been sexually abused by their older brother David. Maureen told him that it was nonsense. Discussing the bizarre claim, the family decided that Pauline was trying to break his ties with his family, knowing that they wouldn't believe him. Steve and Richard also thought the so-called vision was nonsense.

Little things continued to happen that drove the wedge further. Paul could be easily led and soon he began to side with Sharon. After they moved into the flat, Richard stayed with Paul and Sharon for a couple of weeks. One night, Melissa and Steve visited Richard while Sharon and Paul were out. Sitting on their old green couch, Melissa absent-mindedly put her hand between the cushions and felt something. She pulled out Sharon's watch and, having experienced Sharon's odd behaviour before, drew her husband's attention to the watch. 'It's Sharon's,' she said. 'Watch me put it back, I don't want her to accuse me of stealing it.' She replaced the watch where she had found it.

Sure enough, when Steve visited Richard a few days later Richard told him that Sharon had accused him of stealing her watch. When Steve returned home, Melissa reminded him that the watch was down the side of the couch. Steve drove back to the flat, walked over to the couch and retrieved the watch, much to Sharon's embarrassment. Meanwhile, the fact that she had accused Richard of stealing her watch rankled the family.

Then came the christening. Melissa and Steve had their baby baptised at a local church and Paul and Sharon came along. At the party back at their house, one of the visitors told Melissa that Sharon had complained loudly throughout the service that Melissa wasn't a true Christian and that the christening was a farce. Melissa was furious but not surprised. In the short time she had known Sharon, she had found her to be opinionated and often rude.

The christening was marred by ill-feeling and two days later, Paul broke into a neighbour's flat and slashed her photographs, cutting the woman's throat in all the pictures and carving what newspapers later described as 'a message designed to offend her Christian beliefs' into a bureau. He had spoken occasionally to the attractive young neighbour, and had earlier challenged her beliefs after seeing a Christian sticker on her car. Nobody connected Paul to the break-in until after his arrest for the three murders.

Sharon and her mother belonged to a church called the Christian Reform Crusade which met weekly at the Seaford Community Centre. The religion was a fundamentalist organisation; its members spoke in tongues and believed in modern miracles. Members of the church weren't happy that Sharon was living with Paul without the blessing of marriage, but Sharon defied them on that particular issue. Paul wasn't really interested in the church but he told others that he respected Sharon's beliefs.

Early in 1993 Paul applied to join the police force but was knocked back. Being around thirty kilograms overweight, he failed to pass the physical. To his family, it seemed to be no big deal to Paul. The police force had never been a life-long ambition, it was just something he talked about a few months before he applied; he didn't seem to be very disappointed when he didn't make it.

In February, Paul began his final job, with the boat building company Pro Marine in Seaford. He only lasted a couple of months, during which he found the time to make the knives that he planned to use in his attacks, and to melt the soles of his runners with the welding torch. Paul Denyer was preparing himself.

With Paul unemployed and Sharon working two jobs, she was away from the flat from early morning until around nine o'clock at night, leaving him to his own devices. Paul tinkered with cars, visited his family and Sharon's mother — and plotted to kill women. He had wanted to kill since he was fourteen and days and days of free time allowed him to stalk women and make reconnaissance missions to find locations to dump their bodies. He continued to make weapons and practised firing the glove gun he made. He would load a ball bearing into the rubber finger, pull it back tight then let it go, sending the missile shooting through the pipe towards a target.

Sometimes Richard would call in to visit. Paul would usually answer the door to him but sometimes he would be home and Richard would know he was there, but he wouldn't answer the door. Richard wondered why.

Paul also began to collect things he could use to strangle women.

When his binocular strap broke, he kept it and when the cord came out of his tracksuit pants, he kept that too. His solitary pursuits became devoted to planning the murders he would commit. Living in Langwarrin and then Frankston, Paul knew the areas well from his walks and later drives around the streets and parks. He spent a lot of time at Lloyd Park and the at Flora and Fauna Reserve, mapping out suitable locations for his crimes.

On 19 February 1993, Paul broke into the flat in Claude Street, Seaford to kill Donna Vanes, once again choosing someone he knew. When he found the flat empty, he killed Donna's cat and two kittens, and with their blood wrote 'Donna you're dead' on the wall. Paul Denyer had begun.

In April the Denyer family gathered for Paul's twenty-first birthday. Steve had had a big party for his twenty- first but because Paul had no friends, they celebrated the occasion with dinner at a local club, just the family and Sharon. As they sat toasting his coming of age, the Denyer family had no idea that the silent alarm inside him had triggered and was urging him to act out his lethal fantasies.

On the night of 11 June Paul was at Pauline Johnson's home and it was from there he left to walk through the rain to murder Elizabeth Stevens. He later described how all the blood washed off him in the rain on his walk back to Pauline's house and that she didn't notice anything odd when he returned. Sharon arrived not long after and they all sat around and ate dinner

A week later, on 17 June, Richard Denyer celebrated his birthday at Maureen's house. After the party, Maureen drove Paul and Sharon back to their flat and Richard and Natalie came along for the ride. Sharon told everyone that Paul could be a suspect in the murder of Elizabeth Stevens because he was in Langwarrin on the night. Questioned further, both Paul and Sharon laughed about it. Paul told his family that he had a couple of drinks at Pauline's house and that he had walked to his mother's to check a battery. Natalie remembered the night and said that she was home and she didn't remember him coming around. Paul said that he didn't make it known he was there.

The day Debbie Fream died, Steve and Richard visited Paul at his flat. Richard returned alone later to collect twenty dollars that Paul owed him. He intended driving on to Steve's house and Paul wanted to come along for the ride. Unsure whether Steve wanted Paul to visit because of the tension involving Sharon, Richard refused.

Steve and Melissa had moved to a house in Cannons Creek and they hadn't seen much of Paul for a couple of months. Neither of them thought much of Sharon or of the way Paul seemed to have changed since he had known her and, without knowing why, Melissa had become nervous around her brother- in-law. Somehow, she didn't trust him any more. One day Paul had telephoned Melissa at Cannon Creek and asked if Steve was there. Melissa experienced an uneasy feeling and she lied and told Paul that Steve was in the shower. Paul rang twice more until Melissa finally said that Steve had just left to visit Richard. Not long afterwards, Melissa glanced out the front window and saw Paul's yellow car turn into their street. He cruised past searching for their car so he could find their house. She was nervous. Why was Paul coming around if he knew Steve wasn't home? He didn't know their exact address and, while Sharon was being so difficult, Melissa didn't want him to. Once a happy-go-lucky sort of person, Paul had changed and Melissa was disturbed. She remembered Natalie telling her how Paul had recently hit her over the head with a broom handle when she asked him to help clean up. Melissa kept the curtains drawn and Paul eventually drove away.

When Richard told Paul that he couldn't come to Steve's, Paul was angry and asked to go to Richard's house instead. Richard dropped him there and drove on to Steve's house. After Paul's arrest, Richard recalled that, though he could not be sure of the exact day, it was around this time that Paul had brought a home-made knife to his house and asked if he had a file to sharpen it with. Richard had told him to put the knife away.

On the Sunday morning of Paul's arrest, Melissa Denyer was awakened by the telephone ringing at 9 am. Sleepily, she heard her father say, 'It's Paul,' before he quickly went on to explain that Paul had been arrested for the Frankston murders. In a split second, her uneasy feelings about Paul over the past couple of months suddenly took on a terrible meaning. She put the phone down in shock, the words, 'It's Paul,' echoing in her mind as she walked in a daze into the bedroom. Steve lay in a peaceful sleep that Sunday morning and Melissa, tears in her eyes, painfully realised that what she had to tell her husband would ruin his life forever. It would taint all his memories and it would take away the brother that he had loved and protected for over two decades. She shook him gently awake and told him that his brother was a murderer.

While Steve drove to Langwarrin trying to figure out how to break the news to his mother, Melissa went to stay with her family. As soon as she got there, she began to cry uncontrollably. She cried for the women her brother-in-law had killed and she cried out of guilt: could they have known? Were there any signs they could have picked up on? Most of all though, she cried for Garry Blair. Having seen him on television, she saw the striking resemblance between Garry and her own husband Steve. And she was the same age as Debbie Fream. She had a baby too.

The enormity of Paul's arrest began to hit Melissa Denyer within hours of her seeking refuge at her parents' home. She walked around to the local chemist to get a prescription filled for her baby and she heard people talking. 'Did you hear they caught that Frankston killer? Paul Denyer...'

Melissa and Steve Denyer stayed away from their home for three days. They couldn't face anyone and they couldn't face the media. Finally arriving home one night at 11 pm, the phone was ringing persistently. It was Sharon. Melissa gently asked how she was going but Sharon immediately burst into an angry tirade. It was all their fault, she screamed, they hadn't believed him when he told them about the sexual abuse. It was all their fault. In shock, Melissa handed the phone to Steve, and Sharon continued the outburst. She yelled into the phone that the family never loved Paul or cared about him and it was because of this that he had done what he'd done. When Steve tried to tell her that the family had always stood by Paul and taken care of him, Sharon hung up in his ear. Two days later, the restraining orders arrived. Sharon had issued orders against the family.

The news hit the Denyer family like a nuclear bomb: it exploded and blew them all apart. They kept away from each other and tried not to watch television as every news bulletin featured the same footage of Paul being led from the prison van. It went on for months. When he finally went to trial, every news bulletin was headed, 'The Denyer Trial' or 'The Denyer Tapes'. Paul Denyer's family felt as if they had no control over their lives.

Every one of them suffered and many people kept away. Melissa and Steve wanted to move but they found that when they left their name at real estate agents, nothing would be available. They changed their names.

Pushing people away, Melissa and Steve clung to each other and their baby. They couldn't talk to anyone, they just wanted to be alone. It would take them eighteen months to begin to emerge from the shock and open up to people again. By that time, the family slowly began to pull together again. They all agree that it would have been easier for them if Paul had died in an accident or something, anything other than what he did. He nearly destroyed them all. Their love for Paul turned to hatred and loathing for what he had done.

Because Maureen didn't want to go alone, Steve accompanied her to visit Paul in Pentridge days after his arrest. They had to ask him why. Paul shrugged and said in a soft voice, 'I don't know.' Melissa didn't go, but the burning question she would have liked to put to her brother-in-law is: was it worth it? Was it worth ruining so many lives to satisfy your sick, perverted fantasies? Was it worth ruining your own life too?

Natalie Denyer wanted to visit her brother, and Maureen took her to Pentridge. At sixteen years of age, Natalie was pretty and slightly built. She was still in shock over what her brother had done and needed to see him. At the prison, they ran into Sharon. Natalie smiled at her but Sharon didn't return the gesture. Instead, she glared at the girl and turned to Maureen and said coldly, 'It's good to see you acting like a mother for a change.' Maureen was hurt. After years of struggle looking after her six children alone, it seemed that Sharon was trying to lay the blame at her feet. Maureen said, 'One day, when you have kids, you'll know.'

Sharon told Natalie that she was only allowed to visit for twenty minutes and that she was lucky to be going in at all because she wasn't on the visitors list. Maureen had just checked at the guard station and she knew Sharon was lying. Sharon ignored Natalie after that and waited silently until Paul was brought to the visiting area. Then she rushed over to Natalie and put her arm around the girl. Natalie couldn't believe the change. Tears rolled uncontrollably down her cheeks as she saw her brother. But she hardly had time to speak to him before Sharon began telling Paul that she had been fighting with his family and that they had been making trouble. Natalie knew it was a lie; there had been no contact with Sharon.

Natalie tried to change the subject by talking about her recent debutante ball. She held out her arm to show her brother the bracelet she had received from her partner. Sharon quickly thrust out her left hand to show a ring from Paul. It had been her grandmother's but they were regarding it as an engagement ring. She had been wearing it since Paul's arrest.

Like the families of the victims, the Denyer family will never recover from the shock of what Paul did. But unlike the families of the victims, very few people offered the Denyer family sympathy. They were tainted with Paul's crimes. Angry at the people who rushed to the media with stories about the family dating back a decade and a half, the Denyer family felt they were painted as strange and the children as wild. They were no different from anybody else. This could have happened to anyone. They felt that while Paul had done some strange things in his life, he was perfectly normal most of the time. They couldn't have known.

Slowly, things have begun to make sense, but only with the wisdom of hindsight. The daydreams weren't innocent. Neither were the long walks at night. Neither was his interest in making knives. But they couldn't have known.

They have also had to rethink all their memories of Paul. Nothing was real. They never knew him. It was all a lie. Steve used to share a bedroom with his brother. They used to talk together, laugh together. It was all a lie. And it will never end.

Recently, Steve and Melissa found a Melway street directory at her mother's house. Flicking through it, they noticed strange markings and a penis sketched at the top of a page featuring the streets of Frankston. Puzzled, they flicked to the front page and saw Paul's signature. It was his. Somehow they must have picked it up, perhaps when they borrowed Maureen's car a couple of months after his arrest. Looking back at the Frankston pages, they saw Lloyd Park marked at the exact location of Elizabeth's murder. Kananook railway station was marked where Sarah McDiarmid went missing from, so too were some sand quarries behind Lloyd Park as well as the Flora and Fauna Reserve. The find brought it all back in a flood of memories. They handed the Melway to homicide detectives — just in case.

38

Why?

WHY did Paul Denyer kill three women in Frankston in 1993? By his own account, he killed because he felt his 'own life had been taken,' alleging that his brother David had sexually abused him. Yet the idea wasn't a real memory festering since childhood; it was a message given to him, according to what he told his family, by Sharon's mother, Pauline Johnson.

There is a lot of room to postulate and toss around theories to explain why Paul Denyer chose to do what he did. Many, including Denyer himself, try to use mitigating circumstances to explain the murders but millions of people world-wide suffer the same difficult experiences without becoming serial killers.

Even if Paul Denyer had experienced sexual abuse at the hands of his brother, it still doesn't explain his hatred of women and the fact that he chose women as his victims rather than men who might resemble his brother. And what about the time when Denyer was a boy, when he was charged with assault after making another boy masturbate in front of a group of kids? In this incident, Denyer was the offender not the victim in a form of sexual abuse.

An important thing to remember when studying Paul Denyer, is that he is a compulsive liar. Even Sharon in her police statement states that he lied and she often caught him out. His family say the same. Paul Denyer fooled a lot of people during his life. When he doesn't lie blatantly, he lies through omission. Who could believe him when he said that Debbie Fream said nothing during the drive to Taylors Road? Having recently given birth, it is almost certain that she begged him to let her go, told him that she had just had a baby. But Denyer never admitted to that. He told Rod Wilson that he didn't remember the post-mortem mutilation of Elizabeth Stevens or the strange pinpoint stab wounds to Debbie Fream's back. He did concede that if they were there, he must have done them; he just didn't remember, he said. Considering that he was acting out things that he had been fantasising about for years, it is unlikely that he didn't remember inflicting the wounds. More likely is the fact that he didn't want to explain the post-mortem mutilations to the detectives. Explaining the marks would give something away.

Paul Denyer had one life that other people saw and an inner life in which he fantasised about killing. For years he stalked women, waiting for the right time to begin his murder spree. Unsuccessful at most things, Paul Denyer was, for a time, a successful murderer. It made him feel special and clever — more clever than the police who couldn't catch him. And then, when they did, he basked in the glory, confessing most of the things he had done and leading police step by step through his murderous activities.

Does he feel remorse? Serial killers are typically without conscience and, while it may be comforting for the average person to hear that he is now sorry, he wasn't sorry when he murdered. He didn't telephone the police after he killed his first victim to beg forgiveness and even when he was caught, he didn't break down with the burden of what he had done. His confession came only after he realised that police could perform DNA tests on his blood and match it to Natalie Russell's crime scene. The timing of his so-called remorse is significant. He professes sorrow and repentance only when he has something to gain. He is a dangerous and manipulative individual and there is no guarantee that, if released, he won't kill again.

Another reality is that Paul Denyer is a nice man. There is a side to him that is courteous, polite, caring and funny. He manages to hide the dark side and has had over twenty-one years to practise hiding it, more or less successfully, even from those closest to him. Devoid of female victims in prison, Paul Denyer may well prove to be a model prisoner and that is the danger: will he be able to convince a future parole board that his dark side is a thing of the past?

Paul Denyer had fantasies of killing that he chose to act upon. Were they irresistible urges or urges not resisted? He could resist the urge to kill when others were around, he could resist the urge to kill when it was dangerous to him, but when the opportunities arose when he thought it was safe, he killed without pity and without remorse with no regard for his victims.

Denyer seems to have no grasp of the terror and suffering of his victims. He sounds indignant in his police interview when he says that

Elizabeth Stevens lied about her age. He sounds indignant when he says that Roszsa Toth went against her word and ran away from him — almost as if she owed him something. In his next breath he describes his intention to kill her. He expresses his disgust when he relates how Natalie Russell offered him sex or money. He cannot acknowledge that she was trying to bargain for her life. These failings to understand the plight of his victims are a recurring theme in his confessions.

Religion may have played a role in the killings. It is also a recurring theme. Roszsa Toth was abducted from the Seaford railway station, only fifty metres from the Seaford Community Hall — the place where the Christian Reform Crusade meets regularly, the church to which Sharon Johnson belongs. Debbie Fream's car was left outside a Christian centre owned by the same church. Elizabeth Stevens had a series of crosses carved into her chest. Natalie Russell was wearing a Catholic school uniform and when Denyer confesses it is to Darren O'Loughlin who is wearing a crucifix. And then there is the incident before the murder spree began, when Denyer had ransacked the flat of a neighbour who was a devout Christian. He had earlier challenged her about her religion when he realised she was a Christian. He told her then that he had seen the light and didn't need the church any more. Two days before the attack on the flat was the church christening of his nephew at which Sharon Johnson accused Melissa of not being a proper Christian.

There is also a pattern of his hatred towards young mothers. Denyer's murder attempt on Donna Vanes was thwarted because she wasn't home when he broke in but he admits his intent to kill her. He knew that if he killed her, a tiny baby would be left without a mother. He shows no mercy to Debbie Fream even though he noticed the baby seat in the back of the car, and then there was the contempt he held for Melissa when she told him she was pregnant.

While the connections could be tenuous, or mere conjecture, it seems nonetheless important to look more deeply into the psyche of the killer. Only Paul Denyer knows why he began to kill and where the urges came from. And only he knows whether there were other victims.

There was a knife attack against a couple crossing a walk bridge over the Kananook Creek before the murders began. The walk bridge is at the end of McCulloch Avenue from where Debbie Fream was taken. As they were walking across the bridge in the evening, a man approached the couple and lunged at the woman, stabbing her in the chest and the face. When her companion came to her aid, the attacker savagely cut his throat. Both survived — just. While the attacker was never caught, investigating officers were surprised that he went for the woman first rather than the man who might pose a greater threat.

And then there is the mysterious disappearance and probable murder of Sarah McDiarmid. Serial killings are mostly precipitated by stress and the most stressful period of Paul Denyer's life occurred with the family problems with his brother David, coming to a head around July 1990 — the time that Sarah vanished. Paul was eighteen at the time with access to a car. While he told detectives that he wasn't responsible for her death, it certainly fits his pattern; she vanished from a railway station in the evening, possibly suffering a wound to her throat. There is a significant point near the end of Paul Denyer's confession when Rod Wilson points to the Kananook railway station on the map. After nearly ten hours of gruelling interviewing, Wilson has momentarily forgotten Sarah McDiarmid's name: 'So you are aware that there was a woman who was taken from the Kananook railway station in 1990?' Paul Denyer replies quickly, 'I didn't do that, not Sarah McDiarmid.' It was Wilson's job to be thinking of Sarah McDiarmid at that moment. Denyer had no reason to remember the name of a woman who disappeared three years previously; his stress level should have been much higher than Rod Wilson's yet it is Denyer who immediately came up with her name. If he had no intimate knowledge of her disappearance, why should she be in his mind at this moment when he would presumably be concerned only with the predicament he was in? By his own admission, Denyer had been stalking women for four years. Because Sarah McDiarmid had never been found, it would be difficult to pin her murder on anyone. While Denyer freely confessed to the other murders, it was after the detectives asked for his blood samples. He knew the game was up. If Denyer was found to be responsible for any other murders, he would know it would severely limit his chances of ever being released. That he killed others is not impossible, but only Paul Denyer knows for sure.

39

Living with the Loss

RITA Webster doesn't answer the telephone at home any more. She used to before Elizabeth was murdered but the onslaught of media people ringing for interviews was so disturbing that she invested in an answering machine to take the calls for her. Rita believes that it is the small things that affect people after such a tragedy.

After Liz died, a relative told Rita she had said she wanted to stay with her aunt and uncle forever. Apparently, she told everyone that she would never leave them. Rita was deeply affected by the way they had touched Liz's life in the short time she had been with them — and the way she had touched theirs. Going through Liz's things after she died, Rita realised how much they still had to learn about their niece. She was such a lovely girl. Six months just wasn't long enough.

Paul and Rita Webster have no children of their own and Liz was their chance to leave their mark on the future generation. Liz had been in foster care since she was fourteen and there were many things she had never experienced or done. Everything the Websters did for her was appreciated; when they took her to see the penguins at Phillip Island she laughed and jumped around like a child in pure joy. Rita remembers that Liz was touched not only because they took her, but because they cared enough to take her. But she was like that with everything.

When Liz first moved into their home, Paul and Rita gave her a bedroom at the back of the house and told her that the adjoining bathroom was hers. Liz could hardly believe it. Rita suggested they paint the bedroom and that Liz choose the colour. After shopping for the paint and a matching bedspread, Liz said, 'What happens now?' Rita told her, 'We paint it.'

Both women donned old clothes and set about the painting. When the job was done, Rita decided that the shocking chocolate-brown carpet had to go, so she bought a carpet square and laid it herself. Liz told her that she was amazing and Rita responded, 'I'll try anything.' Liz looked thoughtful and said, 'That's a good motto. I think I'll use it.'

Paul Webster remembers how Liz used to help him around the house. They had fun in the garden and together got into a scrape trying to clear some huge trees that were causing problems. Paul would be up the tree sawing off branches while Liz would grab ropes and pull the branches down. One day when her uncle was out, Liz decided to continue the dangerous work alone and used the hand saw to work on the Tasmanian blue gum in the front yard. Unfortunately, she cut away all the branches that her uncle had been using as foot holds. But he couldn't be angry. She was trying so hard, and was so willing to learn.

Liz also gained the dubious reputation of being the person who dared push her uncle into the family pool. On one warm day, Paul changed into his bathers and approached the water in his typical unhurried way; he always entered slowly, adjusting to the temperature. His time-honoured tradition was respected by all — except Liz. She waited as he dipped his toes into the cold pool and then with one well-timed shove sent him flying. By the time Paul surfaced, Liz was nowhere to be seen.

She loved the pool and would go flying down the slide into the water like a child. Rita would tell her that the slide was for children but Liz didn't care.

She loved the dog, Blaze, and played with her all the time. One of her favourite tricks was to run down the passage to the front of the house and hide, then knock and call Blaze who would run searching for her. Then she would run back to her own room and repeat the knocking. Blaze would turn and come running through the kitchen where the tiles were too slippery for her to stop in time for the turn into Liz's room. Every time, Blaze would slide across the kitchen floor and end up crashing into the wall. Liz would giggle with delight and call, 'Where's the little doggie?'

After Rita and Liz had painted her bedroom, the decorating bug bit and they started on Liz's bathroom. On Good Friday morning, Liz was putting the finishing touches to the wall above the bath. She was trying to balance herself with a foot on either side of the bath when she suddenly let out a yell and went crashing though the bathroom window. Rita and Paul raced to where she lay. Liz was moaning that her back hurt but Rita said, 'Forget your back, you're bleeding!' Liz had cut her arm badly and the three of them spent the day in Frankston

Hospital where Liz was initially told she might need thirty stitches. 'I'm going to beat Grandma!' she had cried with childish glee — her grandmother had had a great number of stitches after an accident. Liz was disappointed when eventually there were only eleven stitches.

Another thing Rita Webster doesn't do any more is forward plan. She, Liz and Paul had made so many plans, all of which came to nought with Liz's death. They had been talking about Christmas in the weeks before Liz died. It was six months away, but Liz wanted a Christmas party like one Paul and Rita had given when she was young. All the relatives had been there and Liz had a wonderful memory of it. This year had to be the same and the two women had already begun planning. But Christmas 1993 held nothing to celebrate. Paul and Rita spent the time just before the festive season attending the trial of Liz's murderer. To Rita, it seemed that any more plans for the future were futile — tempting fate.

Paul Webster stopped doing the garden. He had spent so many hours there with Liz that after she died, it just didn't seem the same. Everything seemed to have her mark on it and it didn't feel right to do it without her. The couple considered moving but they finally realised that there was nowhere to run. They are only now beginning to confront their memories and their grief, to begin again without Liz.

Liz shared her uncle's love of motorbikes. When he got himself a bigger bike, Liz convinced him to keep his old bike for her. Two months before she was murdered, she went with Rita and Paul to an annual motorbike rally. Rita remembers Liz taking in everything with wide-eyed curiosity. Rita wouldn't go to the 1994 rally. The memories were too painful. Paul went. He had faced the media and appeared regularly on news bulletins and he wondered what the reaction would be. When he arrived one of the bikies, Spider, came up and put a big arm around his shoulder and said, 'Sorry about that mate.' The simple, honest gesture moved him.

Public reaction after Liz's murder affected the couple greatly. Sometimes people would drive up to their house in Paterson Avenue and stop and point. Paul remembers a woman with a car load of children stopping and staring and he still doesn't understand the curiosity. Another time, he was on the roof of the carport when an old lady stopped in front of his house. He quickly jumped down and waved at her and she drove away shocked.

One of Rita Webster's greatest sorrows is that no-one will ever know Liz's potential. When she had come to live with them, Liz had been shy and rather distant. When Rita hugged her, the girl would freeze up, unresponsive and afraid of gestures of affection. After six months, she was finally starting to melt and to respond to the unconditional love of her aunt and uncle. Rita says Liz was a blossom emerging from a bud and wonders what the years would have brought. Liz had made so much progress in everything. 'No-one will ever know what she would have become,' Rita says, 'Denyer took that.'

Trying to capture the essence of Debbie Fream is like trying to catch and bottle a wisp of smoke. A free spirit since she was a child, Debbie developed into a young woman who rejected ties and whose life objective was to be happy. Being unhappy made no sense to her and with any hint of it she would simply remove herself from the situation whether it be a job, the place she lived or a group of friends. Debbie would say, 'I'm not happy, I'm going,' and would leave. Her family were used to her and loved her free spirit. Once, she went to go grape picking in Mildura. She never picked a grape but had a great time.

Torn between the security of Casterton and the freedom of the city, Debbie tried both, regularly returning to her home town and then living again in the city. It was not unusual for her to live on the lounge room floor of any of a number of friends for a couple of months and then move on. When she finally returned to Melbourne for good, she told her cousin Sara Smith that she was sick of being broke and she wanted to get a job and settle down. She admired the fact that Sara had settled and she wanted to emulate her cousin.

Debbie got a job and began to buy the simple things that had so far eluded her. Her first major purchase was a black wooden bedroom suite which her friends realised was something that she couldn't throw in a suitcase and move on. In a subtle way, the bedroom setting represented a change in direction for Debbie Fream.

Debbie loved people and could talk to anyone; most of her conversations ended up being about the world, the universe, and most of all, dreams. She read voraciously all she could lay her hands on about dreams and dream analysis and it gave her great pleasure to interpret other people's dreams. She also loved fantasy; a favourite pastime was to scour bookshops for yet another fantasy novel. She covered every book in plastic before she read it — she read all her books over and over and they wouldn't last the distance if she didn't cover them.

Debbie was someone who people could turn to with their problems.

She knew how to listen and then help people work out the best course of action. It was just her way. She also loved matchmaking. The day her cousin Sara married her husband Steve — after Debbie died — it was a special pleasure to Sara that Debbie had introduced them. Her matchmaking efforts had finally borne fruit.

She worked hard and spent many nights at clubs. She loved going out but a few months into her new job, intense feelings of nausea overcame her and persisted. She was two and a half months pregnant. Finally it was time to settle down. She and Garry moved to the tiny rented house in Kananook Avenue and Debbie began to plan for the baby. Used to living on very little money for so much of her adult life, she never gave up her frugal cooking habits, her cooking bible was *101 Meals to Have With Mince*. If it couldn't be cooked with mince, according to Debbie, it wasn't worth cooking.

Pregnancy didn't slow her down. Debbie was determined to do as much as she could to make a home for the baby and took great delight as the baby grew and her stomach extended. At 9.30 one morning, she turned up at Sara's door saying excitedly, 'I've got a gap!' The night before, she had felt the baby dropping. Unable to wake Garry, she had stood alone in front of a mirror and watched enthralled as the baby's movement created waves in her stomach. Finally, the baby settled lower in her abdomen, creating the gap between her stomach and chest about which she was so excited. The baby was getting closer to being born! She had to share the news. So excited was Debbie, that Sara led her out to the backyard, camera in hand, and took photographs of her smiling and heavily pregnant cousin posing in a maternity smock.

Reality touched Debbie Fream for probably the first time in her life with the birth of her son Jake. He was permanent, something that she couldn't run away from and she took her commitment as a mother seriously, so seriously in fact, that within a week of his birth she was talking about having another baby. Her labour had been short and Jake had arrived a few days early, coinciding with a visit from her mother. Ann feels so lucky to have been with her daughter and held her tiny grandson just half an hour after he was born. The moment became even more precious less than two weeks later when the young mother's life was so cruelly and tragically taken.

Only a few days after he was born, Jake looked alert and intelligent and was moving his head around to look at things. Debbie was delighted. It pleased her no end to think of reading him stories and teaching him things when he got older. She had been very bright at school and she hoped Jake would take after her in that respect.

In the short time she had Jake, Debbie was finally and totally happy and settled. Garry was a doting father and she happily embraced her new role in life: all she wanted was to look after both of them.

And then she was murdered.

The saddest aspect for Debbie Fream's family is that Jake will never know his mother. He will never hear her laugh, will never learn from her. He will never know how happy he made her. She wasn't there for his first words or his first steps and she won't be there for his first day at school or when he falls over and scrapes his knee. She will never be there. They want him to know about her free spirit and they want him to know that she was a fine person who touched everyone around her.

Last Christmas, Debbie's grandfather brought out a tiny piece of plastic mistletoe from a hamper that Debbie had given him the Christmas before she died. He carefully placed it in the centre of the Christmas cake and said, 'This is from Debbie.'

Natalie Russell's sister Janine recently married. On an unseasonably cold day in early October, dressed in a beautiful off the shoulder wedding gown, Janine's day was clouded by her missing sister. Natalie wasn't there. Janine is not only angry that Paul Denyer deprived her sister of her life, but that he deprived the whole family of her life. Her absence is keenly felt. The Russell house is quiet since she died. Her laughter no longer echoes through the family room, the kitchen.

Ten years older than Natalie, Janine, as older sisters often do, took on part of the parenting of her little sister, giving her an evening bottle or a bath and taking care of her. Natalie's mother worked in a family business when Natalie was young and the whole family pitched in to help. They were all very close.

Natalie had cried when Janine moved to Sydney. Carmel Russell recalls that Natalie only cried when something really sad happened — when her dog had to be put down or a sister moved away. Tears, as far as Natalie was concerned, were reserved for important things.

In the Easter break before she died, Natalie and her brother Damien visited Janine in Sydney. The beginning of that visit put Janine in a panic. She was waiting at Central Station to meet the bus but it didn't arrive; people in the office couldn't tell her anything. Finally telephoning the head office, she learnt that the bus didn't stop at Central Station — it stopped at Oxford Street. Janine raced there knowing that it was a favoured gay hangout — people that her little brother and sister may never have come into contact with before. Relief replaced panic when she met Natalie and Damien waiting patiently in Oxford Street. They'd had a great time watching the colourful population arriving at the clubs, and weren't a bit disconcerted.

Natalie and Damien looked alike and had similar personalities. Janine laughed when her house guests took off the Simpsons characters word for word. It was a great holiday for all of them. Janine took them to Darling Harbour and Bondi Beach and they all laughed at the antics of Reckless Kelly in a dark movie house.

One night, Janine's fiance Martin went to a party. Janine figured that it would be too late a night for her little brother so she, Natalie and Damien stayed home. Martin was going to stay overnight at the party so Natalie curled up in her sister's bed with her and slept there. Changing his mind about staying, Martin arrived home in the small hours of the morning. Seeing his bed occupied, he went to asleep in the lounge room. Natalie awoke early the next morning, went into the lounge and turned on the television, keeping the sound low so as not to disturb Martin who was snoring loudly in an armchair. When he woke up, he looked over at Natalie. 'Was I snoring?' he asked, embarrassed. 'Yep,' Natalie told him simply. 'Why didn't you wake me up?' Natalie shrugged. It didn't bother her. To Martin, that moment epitomised Natalie. She accepted, she didn't judge, it didn't bother her.

At the party, Martin had been given a pair of small round John Lennon sunglasses which he in turn gave to Natalie. She was delighted and wore them everywhere.

A week later, Natalie and Damien boarded the bus for home. It was the last time Janine saw her little sister alive.

In late October 1994 — days before what would have been Natalie's nineteenth birthday, the Russell family moved from the house their daughter never came home to. Her things were lovingly packed into boxes and moved with the rest of their belongings to a new house; not too far away, but far away enough to make a new start. In the boxes, the Russells took with them the legacy of a bright young life cut short by a serial killer. Natalie was a prolific writer. Diaries dating back to primary school show an articulate writing style of a girl who wanted to be a journalist. Ironically, in one of her year twelve essays, she writes about murder and retribution: 'Retribution is considered necessary to avenge a crime, the law cannot be taken into the family or the injured party's hands. Retribution is the duty of the state and is necessary to maintain non-violence and order.' So much of what Natalie wrote before she died took on new meaning after her murder.

Carmel Russell found a story Natalie had written called 'The Letdown'. In the piece of fiction, Natalie writes about winning tickets to see her pop idol in concert. Included in the prize is a backstage pass to meet him. She writes that the star was a strong anti-drugs campaigner and was considered a good role model for teenagers. However, when she goes backstage, the police arrive to arrest the pop idol for drug abuse and he suddenly grabs her. *'The next minute, I felt myself tightly grabbed from behind with a knife to my throat. I had never felt so much fear, not knowing what was going to happen...'* Carmel Russell was stunned. It was unnerving that Natalie had written such a story only months before she herself was grabbed with a knife at her throat.

When Natalie was born, Carmel Russell had wanted a son after her two daughters. Disappointed as she lay on the delivery table at the news of yet another daughter, she heard the doctor say, 'It is a beautiful baby.' Carmel looked at her new daughter and her heart immediately melted. Before her lay a tiny infant with dark curly hair. She was beautiful.

Natalie's father Brian had a special affinity with his youngest daughter. Carmel says it is because she took after him, bright and clever. Brian helped her with her school work and taught her to swim. She loved her father. Natalie was rather a shy child, having little confidence with people she didn't know, and she gravitated towards younger children; she looked after them and they loved her.

When Natalie was fourteen, Carmel was concerned about her. Teachers at her schools would ask Carmel whether there was a problem at home; Natalie never smiled at school. They were worried and Carmel was at a loss. When they met people they knew in the street, Natalie would merely greet them with a solemn hello. 'Why can't you smile, Nat?' her mother would ask her afterwards. But Natalie didn't feel like it; it wasn't genuine. Did her mother want her to gush over people when they met?

When Natalie turned sixteen, Carmel saw a big change in her daughter. It was as if she had discovered life. Her attractiveness bloomed and she was filled with a confidence that had so far alluded her. Now it was as if she wanted to cram as much living into her teenage years as she possibly could. Her sense of humour, ever witty, became dry and she had a remarkable knack of imitating people with a sharp accuracy. Everyone was drawn to the dark-haired young woman with large green-brown eyes. Natalie became the girl that friends turned to. She had an aura about her that people trusted and her friends were many.

Visiting the Russell family, one is left with the strong feeling that while her life may have been short, her death will last forever. Photographs, videos, her writings and memories are all that are left of a beautiful young woman. Many of her friends seemed to give up hope when Natalie died; some began university only to drop out, others left school to take low-paying jobs. Natalie's brother-in-law Martin says that if Natalie had lived, many of her friends would have achieved more of their potential — such was her influence. She was the shoulder to cry on, the friend they trusted. It all adds to the hidden costs of Paul Denyer's killing spree.

It took Carmel Russell many months to stop putting out four plates for dinner. When people ask her how many children she has, she has to think for a moment before answering, 'Four, but now I only have three.' Something is missing all the time and Carmel's burning question is: 'Why her? The one who was wanted and needed so much?' It is easy for her family to discuss her death one minute, and be laughing about some of the funny things she did the next. Such is the nature of the loss. The reality for the Russell family is that she is never coming back and nothing will change that.

Natalie Russell's aunt, Bernadette Naughton, took great comfort from Bev McNamara, a woman she met through the Crime Victims Support Association. Bev's daughter Tracey was murdered and she knew how the Russell family was feeling. The two women would speak often on the telephone and conversations would invariably begin with the question, 'What sort of day did you have?' Bev understood why Carmel Russell kept all Natalie's things when others would tell her to put it all behind her and start over. Bev had been through it all before. Everyone grieves in different ways. She understood.

Bernadette often visits Natalie's grave at the new Cheltenham cemetery to weed around it and lay fresh flowers. Natalie was buried with her grandparents and Bernadette talks to her niece, joking that she is buried with the oldies. But the bereaved aunt takes comfort in the fact that on one side of Natalie, a sixteen-year-old girl is buried and on the other side, a girl of seventeen. She thinks it is nice that her niece has some young girls for company. Nearby is the grave of a policeman, Albert Haag, who died in 1961 at the age of thirty-five. Bernadette often says, 'Nat, you have a nice policeman to protect you now.' She weeds his grave too.

40

Epilogue

ON St Patrick's Day, 17 March 1995, the Director of Public
Prosecutions Geoffrey Flatman, instructed by Crown Instructing
Solicitor Ken Rivett, took the Denyer appeal to the High Court. The
point of the DPP's appeal was that the Full Court judges had imported
the issue of age into section 11 of the *Sentencing Act* which should have
dealt exclusively with the nature of the crime and the past history of
the offender. When Justice Crockett said that a life sentence with no
minimum would be unfair to Denyer because of his age, the DPP was
prepared to argue that his age was irrelevant.

Prior to the 17 March hearing, both the defence and the
prosecution had presented written submissions to the three High
Court judges. At the hearing, they were each allowed twenty minutes to
speak and five minutes to reply – an orange light in the court room
changed to red signalling a barrister's time was up.

Natalie Russell's mother Carmel, aunt Bernadette and sister Janine
formed part of the gallery. The three women sat watching as the first
three cases for the day were dismissed. Bernadette had been praying to
St Patrick ever since she had been given the date for the hearing. For
the staunch Catholic family, it seemed like a good omen. However,
when the other cases were dismissed, their own hopes faded.

The three judges sat slightly raised in the modern courtroom in front
of Dyson Hore-Lacy and Geoffrey Flatman. Hore-Lacy appeared for
Denyer and was confident that the non-parole period would stand up
under appeal. Under the *Sentencing Act 1991*, and legal precedents that
a sentence could not be allowed to act as one of preventative detention,
the judges would be left with little choice. Hore-Lacy argued that the
Full Court was clearly correct in its handing down of the non-parole
period, but stressed that a thirty year non-parole period did not
necessarily mean that Denyer would be released after thirty years. His

life sentence still stood.

After a tense period of complete silence, the family listened while the three judges dismissed the appeal. Carmel, Bernadette and Janine sat in the court room shattered. They had pinned so much hope on the leave to appeal. Now it was all over. People rose to leave, bowing towards the bench on the way out. Carmel rose to leave too, but she didn't bow.

After a brief statement to the media, Bernadette steered her sister and her niece to a nearby coffee shop and the women sat down to take stock of the decision.

'They didn't even mention the girls' names,' Janine said, tears rolling slowly down her cheeks.

Bernadette nodded in agreement. 'It was as if we were on the side of justice and the judges were on the side of the law.' The irony of the chasm between the two was obvious.

Neil Mitchell once again took up the cause, devoting part of his Monday radio program to the issue. 'Just what do you have to do to be sentenced to life imprisonment in Victoria?' he asked with frustration clearly evident in his voice. He told the listening audience that Paul Denyer had killed three young women in cold blood and asked, 'What's wrong with our system?'

'The Denyer case is lost,' Mitchell said before calling upon judges to acknowledge a new type of violent crime — like those committed by Paul Denyer — and to accommodate community feeling.

Speaking with Carmel Russell on air, Mitchell gently asked her reaction to the decision. 'The judges aren't in this world,' Carmel told him. 'It was all about the law and the girls weren't even mentioned. There is something wrong with the law.'

After Carmel, Neil Mitchell spoke to Dyson Hore-Lacy who stated once again that if Denyer's prognosis was correct and unchanged, then he would never be released. The barrister stressed that despite the non-parole period, Denyer still had a life sentence and could be kept in prison for life unless a future parole board was satisfied that he was no longer a danger to the community.

Mitchell then interviewed Attorney General Jan Wade who lost no time assuring listeners that Denyer was sentenced under an act made by the previous government and that her own government had tightened the rules and legislation now made provision for the community's right for protection as a consideration in sentencing.

She said that if Denyer had committed the murders weeks later than he did, the judges would have had the option of an indefinite sentence.

Mitchell asked her if it was fair that the judge couldn't give Denyer an indefinite sentence merely by a 'trick of the calendar'. The Attorney General replied that it was inappropriate to interfere with a sentence once it had been through the entire appeal system.

A few days after the High Court denied leave to appeal, Bernadette Naughton drove to the New Cheltenham Cemetery. Walking the familiar paths towards her niece's grave, Bernadette clutched a bunch of delicate purple flowers — purple was Natalie's favourite colour. She bent down and placed the flowers on the grave. Bowing her head, Bernadette said in a quiet voice, 'Nat, we didn't win — but you know we tried.'